DATE DUE

MR 16 00			

DEMCO 38-296

CONTEMPORARY HISTORY SERIES

General Editor: JAMES F. MCMILLAN
Professor of History, University of Strathclyde

FRANCO'S SPAIN

Franco's Spain

JEAN GRUGEL
Lecturer in Politics, University of Sheffield

and

TIM REES
Lecturer in History, University of Exeter

ARNOLD

A member of the Hodder Headline Group
LONDON • NEW YORK • SYDNEY • AUCKLAND

First published in Great Britain in 1997 by
Arnold, a member of the Hodder Headline Group
338 Euston Road, London NW1 3BH
175 Fifth Avenue, New York, NY 10010
http://www.arnoldpublishers.com

Distributed exclusively in the USA by St Martin's Press, Inc.
175 Fifth Avenue, New York, NY 10010

British Cataloguing in Publication Data
A catalogue entry for this book is available from the British Library

Library of Congress Cataloging-in-Publication Data
Grugel, Jean,
  Franco's Spain/Jean Grugel and Tim Rees.
      p.   cm. — (Contemporary history series)
  Includes bibliographical references and index.
  ISBN 0–340–66323–5 (hb). — ISBN 0–340–56169–6 (pb)
  1. Spain — Politics and government — 1939–1975. 2. Francoism.
I. Rees, Tim, 1960– II. Title. III. Series.
DP270.G78 1997
946.082—dc21
                                                              97–8760
                                                              CIP

ISBN 0 340 56169 6 (pb)
ISBN 0 340 66323 5 (hb)

Production Editor: Liz Gooster
Production Controller: Sarah Kett
Cover design: Terry Griffiths

Composition by York House Typographic
Printed and bound in Great Britain by J. W. Arrowsmith Ltd, Bristol

In loving memory of William Kelly (1901–1997)
and for Russell, Georgina and Jenny

Contents

Preface

This book covers a broad spread of time in the history of any country. In Europe, the years from the mid 1930s to the mid 1970s were a time of dramatic changes in almost all spheres of life – cultural, social and economic. The international relations of western Europe altered beyond recognition. Yet while these changes were taking place, a dictatorship, with its roots in the political conflicts and social unrest of the 1930s, remained in power in Spain. The Franco regime lasted for almost 40 years. The challenge to the historian is not merely how to represent and explain such a long period of rule; it is how to analyse a regime which lived through so many internal transformations and witnessed such fundamental international restructuring. Franco came to power in the 1930s, coinciding with the rise of fascism in Europe. The regime lasted through the Second World War and the Cold War. It survived into the 1960s with the rise of consumerism and the explosion of social movements and of student protest which characterised those years. And it lingered into the 1970s, as European prosperity slowed down and *détente* with the Soviet Union entered the vocabulary of western politicians for the first time. The regime started life as a variant of European fascism; it ended as an exhausted dictatorship relying on contingent support from social and political elites, without any justifying ideology left beyond that of survival.

This book is an introduction to the history of Spain under the Franco regime, aimed at the undergraduate student and at that mythical creature of publishers' dreams: the interested general reader. It is designed for an English-language audience, and draws upon the expanding literature on the subject in Spanish as well as original research by the authors. We have kept the scholarly apparatus of footnotes to a minimum, citing key works or those that offer a particularly good account or draw attention to a debate. Likewise, the select bibliography focuses on readily available works in English and some good Spanish introductions. In undertaking the task of producing a relatively short book about a big subject we have naturally had to make some harsh choices as to approach and content of which the reader should be aware. We have chosen to make our main focus the regime itself: hopefully, not uncritically and not without losing sight of the broader context in which it existed. What changes it brought about, as well as how it worked and why it lasted so long, have been our chief concerns.

Within this remit we have also tried to avoid reproducing other generally available material – such as details about the life of Franco, which are now well covered in a magnificent biography by Paul Preston. At one point we jokingly referred to the book as *Spain without Franco*, but the extent to which his name was linked to that of the regime, unlike the case of Nazi Germany or fascist Italy, makes the present title much more sensible. Readers might feel that certain topics could have received greater attention: the opposition or the local and grassroots histories of the regime, for instance. We would agree, but it has not been possible to cover everything in the depth we might have liked.

Having presented our plea in mitigation, we should now mention something about the structure of the book. We have tried to design it in such a way as to allow it to be read in a number of different ways according to the interests of the reader.

The first section provides an overview, focusing on the politics of the dictatorship and tracing the changes the regime underwent over time. Chapter 1 looks at the first stage of the regime as it emerged from a bloody uprising against a democratic government and a three-year civil war. This experience was to shape the policies of the regime until the very end. In a very profound sense, while the dictatorship lasted, the war could never be forgotten. Chapter 2 examines the state created by the dictatorship after the civil war. It looks at the institutions and the social base of the regime and discusses the last-gasp attempts by the left to try and restore the Republic. This is the 'high period' of Francoism, with politics in command, although for many – perhaps even most – Spaniards, it was the worst period of the dictatorship, with poverty, hunger and fear a daily reality. Chapter 3 looks at the complex period of change in the 1950s and 1960s. The regime had survived international hostility and was now an ally of the US; economic growth was transforming the face of the country. In some ways, therefore, it was a successful time, yet, paradoxically, the divisions which had always been present inside the dictatorship began to surface and an opposition to Franco began to emerge. Chapter 4 examines the demise of the regime, amid open opposition and internal defections.

The second part of the book looks in greater depth at the economy and culture, as well as international relations. Chapters 5 and 6 develop in detail one of the main themes of the first section of the book: state–society relations. They explain the policy shifts inside the regime as it moved from autarky (nationalist development) to the opening up of the economy to foreign investment and examine the changing role of the state. Chapter 5 also assesses whether Francoism could be said to have developed Spain economically, a claim made at the time by Francoists. Chapter 6 considers the cultural and social changes pursued by the regime. Chapter 7 is rather different in its focus: its concern is Spain and the world beyond national frontiers. The Franco regime was always acutely aware of international developments and it consciously tried to play a role in the wider world. The dictatorship did not aim to close Spain off from the world, as some dictatorships have done; rather it wished to spread the ideas behind the crusade of 1936, anti-communism and Catholic integralism, to an international audience. In this it was to be doomed to disappointment. Attempts at promoting Francoist ideas outside of Spain were a failure and Chapter 7 examines why that was so. But international relations were also important in a different and rather unexpected way; foreign policy became a tool of survival for the regime. It is therefore important to pay some attention to this vital theme. Finally, in Chapter 8, we briefly examine the transition to democracy which followed shortly after Franco's death and assess the legacy he left behind.

The book has proved a challenge to us in a number of ways. First, it presented an academic challenge. Not only did we have to cover a considerable period of history, but the Franco regime is a particularly complex dictatorship. It is also a controversial one. Strong emotions are still aroused by the civil war, in Spain and beyond, and by the ensuing dictatorship. Ken Loach's powerful cinematic account of the civil war in Aragón, *Land and Freedom*, made in 1995, is a telling reminder of this. In Spain, the film reopened the polemic about which factions of the centre or the left were 'responsible' for the defeat of the Republic and, therefore, for 40 years of dictatorship. Not surprisingly, it is difficult to write a dispassionate analysis of the regime. Anyone who carries out research on this period will meet and interview survivors and victims of Francoism. Inevitably, one becomes involved. Additionally, researchers have normative views about what constitutes 'good' and 'bad' government. We certainly do. This does not mean that our research is 'biased' but that it required an effort to consider aspects of the dictatorship from perspectives which were not always congenial. We have tried to do this without losing sight of the fact that we have no ideological sympathy with dictatorship, in Spain or elsewhere.

Second, the changes the regime went through make it enormously difficult to 'label'. Yet labelling, as a means to understanding, is an indispensable tool of all historians and social scientists. It is the way in which we understand ideology and interpret policy. It is the essence of the comparative method. So labelling is necessary, though it is always a shorthand. We have chosen to use the terms 'dictatorship' and 'authoritarian regime' as our labels for the Franco regime and to avoid debate about just how far it was 'fascist'. For while it clearly *was* fascist in the early years, it is difficult to sustain fascism as an analytical category after the 1940s. We would not wish, however, to suggest that the regime is any more acceptable to us because we do not term it fascist.

Third, the book has been a challenge because it has forced us to look outside our areas of expertise and learn about aspects of policy and state–society relations with which we were not familiar. We hope that our learning process in these areas, which was important in making us rethink our own original ideas about the book, has made for a better end product for the reader.

Writing this book has also proved a personal challenge. Although we both lived in York when we first talked about this project, we have since lived in different cities and even, for much of the time, different countries. It is perhaps a tribute to how interesting the theme of the book is that we continued to work together. But in the process of writing we have had to overcome obstacles imposed by physical distance. Telephones, faxes and e-mails have been a substitute for long personal discussions. Although they have worked as well as one could reasonably expect, inevitably this slowed us down. So we would both like to thank James McMillan of Strathclyde University (who invited us to write the book), and Christopher Wheeler and Elena Seymenliyska at Arnold for their patience and support throughout the delays to which the book was subject. Never has the maxim, 'better late than never' been tested to such limits!

Jean Grugel would like to thank her colleagues in the Department of Politics at the University of Sheffield. In particular, she would like to thank Martin Smith who was forced to listen to interminable accounts of the progress of the book and did so with patience; the democracy and democratisation cluster with whom she discussed some of the chapters; Tony Payne, Ian Kearns and Anthony Arblaster for encouragement; Steve Ludlum, Rob Collins and Chris Whittaker for resolving many problems, especially with computers; and Sarah Cooke, Sue Kelk and Lindsey Mark for patience and consideration. She would also like to thank her friends and colleagues from the Instituto Universitario Ortega y Gasset in Madrid, especially Olga Fernández, Magdalena Mora and Violeta del Monte, and Monica Quijada and Jesus Bustamente from the Consejo Superior de Investigaciones Científicas. They helped more than they probably realised.

Tim Rees would like to acknowledge the financial support of the British Academy and Exeter University Central Research Fund in the preparation of this book. He is particularly grateful for the constant support of Alison Kelly who, along with Sam, has borne the real burdens of research and writing. He would also like to thank the staffs of the Biblioteca Nacional in Madrid and Archivo General del Estado at Alcalá de Henares for their great help. At the latter institution it was an instructive pleasure to talk to Mike Richards about the Franco regime. Tim's long-suffering colleagues at the University of Exeter, as well as members of the Department of History, University of Bristol, heard papers around the themes of this book and they are to be thanked for their attentiveness and comments. Martin Blinkhorn and Jeremy Noakes kindly offered their support in grant applications. In Spain, Monica Quijada, Jesus Bustamente and Maria-Jesús and James Simpson offered encouragement and friendship. Finally he remains indebted to Paul Preston and Frances Lannon.

Jean Grugel
Tim Rees
1997

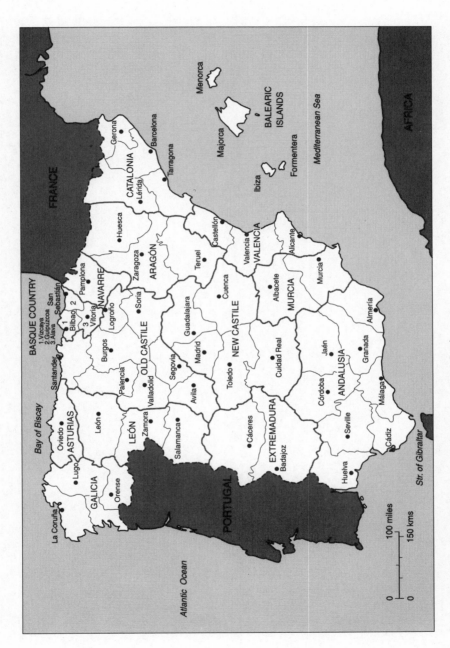

The main towns, provinces and regions of mainland Spain

I

THE POLITICS OF FRANCOISM

1

Forging the Francoist State, 1936–1939

Without the bloody catastrophe of the civil war there would have been no Franco regime. This brutal, three-year struggle, between the defenders of the existing democratic Republic and Nationalist insurgents, provided the circumstances in which a dictatorial state could be created. From the outbreak of the war in July 1936, dictatorial rule became established in all those areas which came under the control of Nationalist forces. The political structures which were to be established throughout the country after 1939 were erected during the conflict itself. For its entire existence the politics, and frequently the policies, of the regime were conditioned by this struggle to control the destiny of Spain, and the relationship between the state and its citizens for nearly 40 years was largely created between 1936 and 1939. Although the regime was to undergo many changes in the years it was in power, it always drew its legitimacy from the military defeat of the Republic, and its mission remained that of preventing the reassertion of democracy. Therefore it is important to analyse how the regime grew out of this tragic conflict and how the embryonic authoritarian state evolved before 1939 in the territories under Nationalist rule.

THE EMERGENCE OF FRANCOIST RULE

Like most dictatorships, the Franco regime needed powerful propaganda to justify its existence and it succeeded in creating a compelling mythology around its origins. In the simplistic official version, endlessly repeated in modified forms as an attempt at self-justification, Francoist rule was explained as necessary to save the nation from internal chaos and the threat of bloody revolution. General Francisco Franco was portrayed as an all-powerful and far-sighted leader, the personal embodiment of both victory in a Manichaean struggle against dark subversive forces and of the New State that emerged from it. What was misleading in the official mythology – even leaving aside the partisan interpretation of the war it contained – was the impression that calculation and clear direction had brought the regime into being. The reality was rather different.[1]

The immediate background to the regime lies in the military rising against the Republic. A gamble with unpredictable consequences, it began in Morocco on 17 July 1936 and spread to the Spanish mainland the following day. The main architects, a small group of senior officers, aimed for a coup that would swiftly remove the government and bring the entire country under army control. All the group's energies were absorbed by the complex and secret organisation needed to achieve this immediate objective. The form of a future state or the government policies to be pursued were largely neglected. Such vague plans as existed supposed that these decisions would be taken after the coup by a military directorate, to be composed of the plotters and leading figures from the right-wing political parties with whom they were in contact. None of those who answered the call to arms in July, either military or civilian, anticipated that they were beginning a bloody and destructive three-year civil war. Nor did they know that from their victory would emerge one of the longest dictatorships of European history, headed moreover by the most apparently reluctant, though highly ambitious, of the military conspirators.[2]

Spain had a long tradition of military intervention in politics, including a period of dictatorship during the 1920s under General Miguel Primo de Rivera. But the real cause of dissatisfaction amongst the military before the civil war came with the overthrow of the monarchy and the establishment of a democratic Republic in 1931. During the first two years of this regime liberal-left governments pursued modernising policies for agrarian reform, the clear separation of church and state, secular education and increased rights and benefits for workers and women. In the view of the military and their allies on the right, these reforms were dangerous attacks on property, the established social order and traditional morality. Even more outrageous in their eyes was the granting of greater self-government to the culturally and linguistically distinct region of Catalonia, which was seen as a direct assault on the integrity of the unified nation state. Similarly, they were horrified at attempts to reform the structures of the military itself. Problems between the army and the Republican government surfaced as early as September 1932, when the commander of the paramilitary civil guard, General José Sanjurjo, attempted an abortive rising along with a small group of military personnel. Its failure and the election of a right-wing government just over a year later led to the suspension of further military plots. But despite the reversal of earlier reforms by a centre-right government elected in 1933, conservative army officers remained alarmed at continuing social and political unrest which culminated in a rising led by militant miners in Asturias in October 1934 and which was crushed only by a brutal military campaign. When a new centre-left government committed to change was elected under the banner of a Popular Front alliance in February 1936, disaffected army leaders began to plan in earnest. Amidst rising class conflicts in agriculture and industry, renewed tensions over regional rights and the church, and a sharp increase in political violence, important factions of the military prepared to intervene.[3]

By 1936 the military plotters were not alone in wanting to overthrow the

Republic. They were joined by virtually the whole of the organised political right and their supporters after they had failed to win the elections of February 1936. The chief strategist of the army conspirators, General Emilio Mola (dubbed 'the Director') persuaded the different factions that only the military possessed the means to effect a successful coup.[4] By the summer, conventional political activity was suspended by supporters of all sections of the right in anticipation of army action. In the event, after much delay and prevarication, the rising was only a partial success. Fierce resistance from the organised left, particularly the working-class movements, often supported by army and police units that remained loyal to the Republic, led to the defeat of the rebels in most of the major cities and large parts of the countryside. Only in those areas, mainly in northern and central Spain, where the political geography favoured the right and the military acted with unity, did the rising gain a foothold. In these circumstances the coup leaders had either to admit total defeat or to press ahead to fight a prolonged civil war in order to gain control of the country – a dauntingly difficult venture. Nationalist forces (as they quickly became known) were physically fragmented and lacking in central direction. Real power resided with local army commanders and political leaders who were busy consolidating control of their own regions in myriad small actions. Initially, it looked as though the Republican government, once it had recovered its own authority, might mop up the insurgents piecemeal.

The question of leadership was therefore thrust into the centre of political debate inside the Nationalist camp. There was no clear leader on the Nationalist side because a number of the leading military and political figures on the right had been killed or captured. Even before the rising began, Calvo Sotelo (leader of the monarchist party, Renovación Española) had been assassinated by Republican police. General Sanjurjo, once again the initial leader of the uprising, was killed in a plane crash in Portugal, while José Antonio Primo de Rivera (head of the fascist Falange) was captured and later executed.[5] At the start of the rising, Mola created a military junta of seven members, quickly expanded to eleven, but this was incapable of taking a decisive lead. The cautious Mola felt no inclination to take control, and the temporary figurehead-president of the junta was the ineffectual and ageing General Miguel Cabanellas.[6]

Franco emerged as leader out of this power vacuum. He had taken a very tentative part in the plans for a military rising. Only days before it actually began, Mola was unsure whether Franco was prepared to act against the Republican government. Apparently it was the assassination of Calvo Sotelo that finally persuaded him to risk joining the conspiracy. Though not the senior figure in the plot, Franco's support was considered to be important. He was one of the army's most prominent officers, having risen rapidly to become the youngest general in Europe. This had been achieved through military service in Spain's colonial campaigns in North Africa. Here he had become enormously respected as a professional soldier, if not liked as a personality. Ambitious, careful and cunning, Franco enigmatically guarded his opinions but was known as a conservative and as fiercely loyal to the authoritarian traditions of the Spanish officer corps.[7]

Franco's main role at the start of the rising was to take command of the Army of Africa in Morocco. This placed under his control the best organised, most experienced units of the army. As the rising faltered, African troops were transported to the mainland at the end of July by German and Italian transport planes. In addition to making Franco the chief conduit for early aid from the Axis powers, this put his soldiers in a position to swing the course of the war decisively in favour of the Nationalists. In August they drove rapidly north from Seville to link up with insurgent forces in Extremadura, creating a unified Nationalist zone, and then pressed on towards Madrid. From the prospect of defeat, the rebels had seized the military initiative and thereafter, though a long Republican resistance was mounted, they were never to lose it.[8]

With this success behind him, Franco was recognised as having the strongest claim to the leadership when the temporary junta met in Salamanca, at his request, on 21 September 1936 to decide the issue of command. He emerged as commander-in-chief, with supreme authority for military affairs until the conclusion of the war. Initially, political affairs did not come under his command, but a week later he was given responsibility for all areas of public policy for the duration of the conflict, when it was argued that there was no sense in dividing the military and political command during war.[9] In addition to his military victories, Franco's vague conservatism was also part of his appeal. It rendered him less politically threatening than a more stridently ideological figure might have appeared. This was, in fact, an early example of Franco's role as a figurehead: like many of the European dictators of the 1930s a certain lack of political definition allowed others to see what they wanted to see in him. This was perhaps one of the greatest strengths he brought to the role of leader at this stage.

Underlying his move to a position of authority was a curious mixture of ambition and reticence. Franco had been eager to take full military control but he had only taken the step towards assuming full powers of government at the prodding of a small group of supporters. Led by his brother Nicolás, they included the airforce general, Alfredo Kindelán; his mentor from Africa, Millán Astray; and one of the commanders of the troops in the south, Colonel Juan Yagüe. The first hint that Franco had embraced a longer term view of his position came when the decision to appoint him to political power was published. Suddenly, there was no mention of a temporary appointment and Franco described himself not just as chief of government but as head of the Spanish state.[10]

The appointment of a supreme leader satisfied the desire of the small group of officers for a firm chain of command. Franco was Caudillo (warlord) in name and instantly became the chief symbol of the Nationalist cause. However, there was little further substance to his position at this time. There was no time for abstract theorising and debate about government and a future political system in the midst of a civil war, when the immediate priority was to ensure the military and political defeat of the Republic. Consequently, the immediate solutions to this problem were entirely *ad hoc*. By decree Franco replaced the Junta de Defensa with a new administrative body, the Junta Técnica del Estado (State Technical Committee). This was directly under his command through a president who oversaw the workings of seven commissions dealing with different areas of policy.[11] These were headed by a mixture of military and civilian figures, only one of whom, General Fidel Dávila, had been part of the previous Junta de Defensa. In addition a General Secretariat of the Chief of State was created as a private office directed by Nicolás Franco, as well as a Secretariat for Foreign Relations and a Ministry of the Interior. This formed the bare bones of an administration, but one which initially possessed little sense of political direction or, indeed, power.[12]

Pursuing an effective war effort meant, above all, grappling with the social and political realities of the Nationalist zone as they had emerged in the confused aftermath of the rising and early insurgent campaigns. Looked at from this perspective, extending the power of the state was something of a daunting prospect. Within the Nationalist zone was a complex mosaic of different social and political groups which, though they supported the insurgency, had very different programmes. Their continued support was vital to the military struggle against the Republic and in building an alternative regime. In fact this had been true from the very beginning of the civil war, in that the rising had only succeeded in those regions with a strong right-wing political presence and with the active participation of militias linked to the parties of the right. This put the central and northern countryside largely in Nationalist hands, but left the remainder of the country, including the main cities and industrialised regions, with the Republic. At this stage, real power outside the battlefield lay with local military commanders and rightist political leaders, not with the self-appointed central authorities.

The outbreak of the war was accompanied by a shift within the political right towards the authoritarian and radical end of the spectrum.[13] The only mass political force on the right, the Catholic conservative Confederación Española de Derechas Autónomas (CEDA), had sought to defend the status quo largely from within the Republic. Although many of its adherents had been supporters of the Alfonsine monarchy replaced by the Republic or were drawn to fascist ideas (particularly in the youth movement), the party had attracted a broad sweep of conservative opinion. Backed by the powerful agrarian elites and their industrial allies, the conservative landed peasantry, middle classes, and practising Catholics, CEDA was successful as long as it was capable of resisting the reforming ambitions of the Republicans. But after the right failed to win the

decisive elections of February 1936 its strategy of working within the Republic
was discredited. By the summer of 1936 its leader, José Maria Gil Robles, was
marginalised and the party was beginning to dissolve. The outbreak of war
simply accelerated this process, leaving the field clear for the smaller parties of
the ultra-right.[14]

In the north of the country, the Carlist Comunión Tradicionalista was in a
strong position, particularly in its heartland of Navarre. Here the Carlist
militia, the Requeté, played a key part in consolidating the rising and in
supplying forces to subjugate surrounding regions. Ideologically Carlists were
deeply reactionary, fiercely religious and hostile to liberal, Marxist and separatist ideas. Above all, they favoured a decentralised corporatist system of
government under the Carlist monarchist succession — an aim that had led to
three civil wars in the nineteenth century. Self-consciously archaic, the party
attracted the support of the most backward sections of northern peasant society
and upper-class reactionaries.[15]

Monarchism constituted an important, if divided, force inside the Nationalist camp. It was also at the heart of Renovación Española, the party of the
assassinated Calvo Sotelo. Formed around the journal *Acción Española*, the
party supported the Alfonsine branch which had presided over the monarchist
system of government from 1875 until its collapse in 1931. Otherwise the party
shared the approach of the Carlists in most respects – strongly defending the
socio-economic and religious status quo, and deeply distrustful of political
alternatives, regional nationalism and democracy. Though initially a small
party with no clear regional base, many of its members had served in the failed
dictatorship of General Primo de Rivera during the 1920s. As it grew, it tended
to recruit from the ranks of the rural upper classes in central and southern
Spain, with the nobility particularly prominent members. Significantly, as a
recognition of its prestigious clientele and perhaps as an indication of his own
views, when Franco appointed three civilian heads of commissions within the
Junta Técnica, all came from Renovación Española.[16]

The two monarchist parties represented the most traditional forms of the
ultra-right. Both benefited to a degree from the collapse of CEDA, but the real
beneficiary was Spain's fascist party, the Falange. An alliance of two movements, the JONS (Juntas de la Ofensiva Nacional Sindicalista) and the Falange
Española – hence the full acronym of FE y de las JONS – the party was led by
José Antonio Primo de Rivera, the son of the former dictator. It professed a
radical if rather contradictory version of fascism, similar to that in Italy. The
Falange remained insignificant, with only a few thousand members among the
middle classes, until the eve of the civil war when the youth movement of the
CEDA joined *en masse*. In the spring of 1936, Falangists took the offensive in
street battles with the left. As a result, the party leadership was arrested and the
organisation suppressed by the Republican government. From the start of the
war there was a rush to join the ranks of the Falange and to enlist in its militias,

most noticeably in central Castile and the southern areas of Andalusia and Extremadura where the CEDA had been strong. Both the urban and rural lower middle classes were particularly prominent in seeking membership, though the party attracted a broad swath of supporters. Joining the Falange was a statement of identification with the Nationalist cause – as it was in the case of the other parties of the right – but it was also an identification with a radical and modernising movement, rather than with the traditional and establishment views of the monarchists.

Many accounts have stressed the ways in which the Falange was to be transformed by an influx of new members who had little close identification with the original aims of the party. The division between the old guard and recent converts (old and new shirts in the language of the time) was an important one, particularly as new members did not come to the Falange with exclusively fascist motives, but brought their own agendas. However, they chose to enter a movement that was unmistakably fascist in its rhetoric and symbolism (blue-shirted uniform, straight-armed salute, anthems and mystic nationalism), adopting its language and style in the process. Though most of the original leaders of the party, most prominently José Antonio, were captured or killed at the start of the war, the seven man collective leadership that took over remained committed to the existing Falangist programme. In the uncontrolled environment at the start of the war, the party rapidly became by far the largest and most influential political force in the Nationalist zone.[17]

THE NATIONALIST CRUSADE

Each of the Nationalist political groups naturally saw the civil war as an opportunity to put their ideas into practice. The lack of ideological certainty within the embryonic central administration meant that there was no immediate antagonism amongst any of the political forces, and anything seemed possible. The proclamations and pronouncements that flowed from Franco's headquarters also carefully nurtured different ambitions by following suitably uncontentious themes that could appeal to all who opposed the Republic. Denouncing the spread of social and political unrest as the products of a dangerous democracy, attacking regional rights as a threat to national unity, and promising an authoritarian alternative played to the common prejudices of the political right. However, promoting effective unity for the Nationalist war effort out of such diversity was no easy matter. Finding some form of ideological and social legitimacy for the new regime which had to be created at the same time was even more difficult. Fortunately for the leadership, it was able to draw upon the support of the two institutions whose authority was recognised by the overwhelming majority of conservative Spaniards: the army and the church.

The army was automatically placed in a position of primary importance.

Although disrupted by the rising and its aftermath, it remained largely intact as an institution, with its own disciplined organisation and methods. It was through command of the army above all else that the Franco regime was able to establish itself in power. This was the origin of its legitimacy. In particular, most of the middle-ranking officers and non-commissioned officers supported the insurgents, providing them with a core of experienced leaders who took a vital role in organising the war effort. Within the Nationalist zone a process of militarisation began that subordinated all other organisations to the army. Superior training and access to weaponry – particularly modern arms from Germany and Italy – meant that the army was bound to dominate despite the important contribution made by the rightist militias. From the start of the war, the army hierarchy and local officers began to take the volunteers into the orthodox structure of the military, a scheme for training new officers (*alféreces provisionales*) was established and the existing conscription system was used to call up successive drafts from within Nationalist territory. In December 1936 Franco issued a decree that gradually incorporated all the civilian militias into new units within the command structure of the army and a monopoly of military force at the disposal of the Nationalist leadership was created. This was not entirely unequivocal, in that regional commanders were often able, in the confusion of the war, to exercise considerable independence. A good example of this was the case of Queipo de Llano who effectively ran his own regime in the south during the first part of the war, while paying lip service to the high command. In short, the military became both an instrument for winning the war itself – far superior to the ramshackle forces of the Republic – and an important means of extending the reach of the Francoist leadership and administration.[18]

The Nationalist cause also received crucial institutional support from the Catholic church. Although no mention of religion had been made in the initial phase of the rising, Spanish Catholicism had long been widely identified with the social and political status quo. Catholic antipathy to the Republic was intensifed by its anti-clerical measures. Not surprisingly, then, the church hierarchy made its sympathies clear when the fighting broke out, further prompted by the obvious support amongst many, probably most, ordinary practising Catholics for the uprising and by the attacks on church property and the clergy in the Republican-controlled areas of the country. With the exception of Basque Catholics who supported the Republic in the cause of regional rights, and a few dissident figures within its ranks, the church threw its weight behind the insurgency, declaring it to be a defence of Christian civilisation against barbarism. In the earliest months of the war, Bishop Enrique Pla y Deniel supported the Nationalists both by lending his palace in Salamanca, which served as Franco's headquarters, and by his pen. The pastoral letter he wrote, to be read out in churches in praise of the Nationalist cause, was an important symbolic support for the rising. His lead was followed by Cardinal

Isidro Gomá, Primate of All Spain, who lavishly praised the insurgents as defenders of religious values and of the true church. The climax of church support came in July 1937 when the Spanish bishops, with three exceptions, issued a collective pastoral letter, wholeheartedly underwriting the Nationalist side in the war and condemning absolutely the Republic. This public endorsement officially brought the church, with its extensive network of organisations and personnel, behind the emerging regime. Perhaps even more importantly, it provided a powerful religious justification for the Nationalists.[19]

Borrowing military and religious language, the Francoist leadership articulated a high moral purpose for the war that played on the existing fears and anxieties among its supporters. Far from being a sordid plot against the elected government, the rising was transformed into a Crusade: a military campaign with a spiritual purpose. 'Crusade' was a term that evoked strong images of the Spanish past, drawn from the long wars waged by the medieval Christian monarchs to 'reconquer' the country from Arab rule, eventually leading to the creation of a unified kingdom in 1492 under King Ferdinand and Queen Isabel. Some mental gymnastics, though, were needed to make the historical metaphor fit. This time it was a war to 'save' Spain from other Spaniards, and the Arabs were fighting on the Nationalist side in the form of Moorish troops from the African Army – an irony that Republicans were quick to point out. But by speaking of good and bad Spaniards, of true Spain and anti-Spain, the analogy with the past was made and readily understood. In this case, the enemy was not Islam but a hydra of social and political revolution that had flourished with the Republic. It comprised above all the organised working classes, both rural and urban, seen as a major threat through their support for leftist ideologies (anarchism, communism and socialism), trade union activity and attacks on property rights. Also culpable were middle-class Republican liberals, the architects of Spanish democracy and enthusiastic reformers of the 'sacred' institutions of army and church. Finally, there were the Basque and Catalan regionalists, pilloried as the destroyers of national unity.

The pre-emptive counter-revolutionary Crusade proved to be an ideal umbrella under which all anti-Republicans could gather. It had the great advantage of defining the Nationalist cause in terms of what it was against. Its supporters could comfort themselves with the thought that they were not simply defending their own selfish interests but were saviours engaged in a holy war. Insurgent propaganda also claimed the nation, and the national will, as the private preserve of their supporters. 'Arise Spain', 'Spain: one, great and free' screamed the popular slogans, normally linked in the same breath with a hearty 'and long live Franco'. In this way the Crusade could transcend partisan political programmes, in part by simply ignoring them, and appeal to all those who for a variety of reasons feared the reforms attempted under the Republic. They included property-owners ranging from the agrarian and industrial elites to masses of peasant farmers, small businessmen and shopkeepers. Others who were also likely to respond included managers and white-collar employees – factory and estate foremen, for instance. Finally, there were practising Catholics of all classes, at least in the Castilian-speaking regions. What was striking about the 'natural' supporters of the Nationalist cause was the prominence of those with privilege and power, even if it was often only aspired to or possessed in a modest degree. Above all, the Crusade ensured that the war became a struggle waged in defence of their interests.[20]

The rhetoric of the Crusade helped to place the Francoist leadership at the head of a powerful social and political coalition. Even though a majority of Spaniards probably backed the Republic, there was a relatively diverse mass base of support for the new dictatorial regime. What cemented it solidly in place was the harsh reality of counter-revolutionary activity. Repression was not forced on reluctant Nationalist supporters, but had spread spontaneously with the army rising when local insurgents – both military and civilian – attacked anyone seen as an actual or potential opponent. Known members of trades unions or the political parties of the left (republicans, socialists, anarchists and communists) were the immediate victims. But anyone considered dangerous or subversive was vulnerable. News of similar atrocities in Republican-held areas – particularly against priests and nuns – spurred on the violence. However, while the authorities tried to prevent attacks in Republican regions, repression became increasingly institutionalised in the Nationalist zone. It became a natural counterpart to the promise of salvation in the Crusade: first, the evil which was undermining national greatness was identified, then it had to be expurgated. 'Cleaning up' and 'purging' were the euphemisms deployed to mask a grassroots terror of execution, imprisonment and persecution that was intended to destroy all possibility of the Republic being recreated by its supporters. Even Franco's military strategy was shaped as a war of political annihilation: wearing down the Republic through attrition, steadily taking territory and always securing the rearguard before pressing on.

Martial law was declared throughout Nationalist-controlled territory and, in a stunning reversal of legal realities, all opponents of the rising were declared to be in rebellion. Random atrocities and mass executions of captured prisoners in bullrings and cemeteries were complemented by the hasty decisions taken by military tribunals, which offered summary justice, usually leading to a death sentence and the firing squad. Almost anyone could become suspect: a climate of fear and recrimination spread, as old scores, both personal and political, were settled. Existing prisons were augmented by makeshift jails and by a system of concentration camps, into which captured Republican soldiers and civilians were herded. Gradually, the repression became more formalised. A series of decrees established a set of penalties for opposing the Crusade, from death to imprisonment with hard labour. Death sentences passed by tribunals were referred upwards for approval, to Franco amongst others. This gave official sanction to arbitrary decisions made at the local level. Estimates for the number of deaths are a matter of great dispute, and range from 35 500 to 200 000.[21] Because all the different social, political and institutional supporters of the Nationalist cause were involved, none dared break ranks for fear of Republican vengeance. Not surprisingly, the legend of the Crusade erected by Francoism glossed over the darker side of the ties that bound together its participants. Their nature was perhaps better rendered in an alternative graphic description of the real substance holding together the Nationalist camp: the pact of blood.

POLITICAL ORGANISATION: THE MAKING OF THE SINGLE PARTY

The Crusade provided a necessary and immediate rallying cry for the insurgent war effort but it was an insufficient basis for defining a new regime. What was needed was a set of institutions, albeit temporary ones, to administer the embryonic state. However, although all shades of Nationalist opinion could readily agree that the destruction of the Republic and the suppression of its supporters were vital, the problem of what was to replace it was potentially far more divisive. For the Francoist leadership, the military dictatorship of General Primo de Rivera during the 1920s was a precedent of recent memory. Its collapse in a welter of internal dissension and growing external opposition had paved the way for the Republic.[22] In this way, its fortunes served as an important lesson for Franco and his advisors. One of the earlier dictatorship's main difficulties had been that it had never managed to create an independent political base for itself, a problem that the Franco regime also potentially faced in 1936.

Initially, ideological uncertainty had been an advantage for the Nationalists. But in the longer run the administration risked becoming prey to the ambitions of any of the various political forces within the Nationalist coalition. Consequently, attempts to form a united political front began almost immediately after Franco was appointed to the supreme command, directed in the first instance by his brother Nicolás. His initial proposal for the creation of a Citizens Action Party (Acción Ciudadana) was dropped as too close to Primo's failed Patriotic Union (Unión Patriótica), which had never succeeded in developing either a mass following or an independent base of ideas.[23] In early 1937 Nicolás was displaced as Franco's main political advisor by his wily brother-in-law, Ramón Serrano Suñer, who had been a CEDA parliamentary deputy but who was politically and ideologically close to the Falange. It was his advice that led to the creation of political structures to support the dictatorship. This began in earnest in the first half of 1937. The strategy was to unify the existing right-wing parties from above and create one single organisation. This would bring the right under central control and would serve as a means to fashion an ideology that would draw upon the range of ideals they represented.

It was a bold move, and proved to be a decisive step towards making the right the prisoner of the authoritarian state and not its master.

There was no effective resistance when Franco and Serrano Suñer announced a Decree of Unification in April 1937 creating the Falange Española Tradicionalista y de las JONS, usually shortened to FET and later dubbed the National Movement (Movimiento Nacional). The small size of Renovación Española and the final dissolution in February 1937 of an already prostrate CEDA precluded any response from them to the decree other than mute acquiescence. Carlism constituted far more of a potential problem, however. Luckily for Franco, an internal struggle over wartime political strategy within Carlism ended with the victory of moderates grouped around the Conde de Rodezno, who favoured co-operation with the army and the Nationalists, over purists backing the leadership of Manuel Fal Conde. Attempts by the latter to ensure a separate Carlist political programme and military forces were thwarted by this internal dissent and the objections of the army. This had allowed Franco to exile Fal Conde to Portugal in December 1936, leaving Rodezno in place to agree to unification four months later. The Falange proved equally vulnerable to political take-over, despite a greater willingness among its leadership to oppose the creation of the FET. Their chief handicap was that the leadership had never really recovered from the loss of José Antonio at the start of the war. As a stop-gap measure, a seven-man committee had temporarily taken charge, headed by the ineffectual Manuel Hedilla. Unimaginative and plodding, his leadership was contested by a faction around Sancho Dávila and undermined by the powerful position of the provincial party bosses whose hands were strengthened by the flood of local recruits to the party. On the eve of unification, Hedilla survived an internal coup by Dávila's supporters but his leadership was weakened in the process. When he tried to reject the decree by refusing to join the Political Committee (Junta Política) of the new organisation, Franco ordered the arrest of all his faction and their trial by a military tribunal. A death sentence on Hedilla, later commuted to life imprisonment, decisively silenced all open dissent.[24]

Dragooning political heads into a union did not mean that all hearts automatically followed – a limitation that had to be accepted. In practice the FET was from the first an uneasy compromise between a desire to impose some outward political conformity on the Nationalist camp and the necessity of recognising a degree of practical political diversity. To have expected more might have undermined the whole unification project. As it was, the representatives of the different factions, now joined in the Junta Política of the new single party, maintained a wary eye on their influence and privileges. Each was still backed by supporters who remained essentially faithful to their original ideology after unity was proclaimed. Although there was no open unrest from any quarter, the limits of unity were often symbolically and rhetorically defined. Most common was a refusal to wear the new uniform of the FET, itself an amalgam of the Falangist blue shirt and red Carlist beret, or to display the party symbol of a yoke and arrows. Local party leaders and militants still marched under their own banners and still preached their own particular programmes and political obsessions. Also there were often considerable tensions between the supporters of different political groups that now found themselves forced together in the FET. In some regions, such as the rural south, this took on something of a class divide, with the traditional elites linked to monarchism at odds with Falangists drawn from the lower social orders. All this left Serrano Suñer, as guiding hand of the new party under the formal leadership of Franco holding the title National Chief (*Jefe Nacional*), with a delicate task when it came to framing the ideological and organisational position of the movement.

The official doctrine created for the FET generally drew on the pool of ideas on the Nationalist side, although it mostly reproduced the fascist language of the Falange. The strident atmosphere of the counter-revolutionary Crusade ensured that the resulting ideological mixture was far from anodyne. It was agreed across the whole of the Nationalist political spectrum that the future lay in a hierarchical, authoritarian state, the function of which was to bury Republican and democratic forms of government. At the same time, the term 'totalitarian' – meant in the sense of 'all-embracing' – was freely used to describe the relationship the new state would enjoy with society. However, this broad agreement on the desirability of a dictatorship marked the end of the consensus. Thereafter the radical Falangist end of the political spectrum was favoured, at least in theoretical terms, over the more traditionally conservative groups. The 26-point pre-war programme of the Falange was incorporated almost completely into the statutes of the new party, including its attacks on the excesses of unrestrained capitalism and calls for a corporatist regime modelled on the lines of fascist Italy. National syndicalism, as this was dubbed, was decreed to be the revolutionary guiding principle of a new order. Much of the political imagery of the Falange was also taken on board: the straight-armed fascist salute, the use of 'comrade' as a term of address, the red and black banner, and the anthem 'Face to the Sun'. Above all, the radical and charismatic figure of José Antonio was turned into a kind of secular saint, and his name, writings and speeches were used almost as political theology. At the same time, the importance of religion was mentioned, which drew together most of the Nationalists. Significantly, no commitment to a revival of the monarchy in either of its possible forms was made.[25]

This radical party policy, endorsed by the Nationalist leadership, was acceptable to a broader audience beyond the Falangist faithful for a number of reasons. In particular, it was evident that the civil war had made a direct return to the pre-Republican status quo impossible. Even conservatives who had campaigned for a return to the order before 1931 realised that this ideal was discredited because it would only have the effect of recreating the circumstances in which the Republic had been born in the first place. Instead, the Falangist programme represented a break with the past and offered the prospect of creating a social and political order that would be permanently immune to the influence of the liberal left. Falangism also had the appeal of utopianism and youthfulness and symbolised dynamic action, all of which fitted well into the context of the military–political struggle being waged. As in Germany and Italy in the inter-war years, reactionary conservatives effectively threw in their lot with a radical right with which they shared some common ground when there seemed little realistic alternative. In a war to save themselves from oblivion in the face of a revolutionary threat – for this was how they perceived the Republic – they had to accept that a measure of change was unavoidable, and this included sacrificing some important political ideals of their own. But at the same time they hoped that the political principles of the new FET were just that: principles which might be tempered in practice by working from within the movement. For the conventional conservatives some reassurance that this was to be the case was provided by Franco at the end of 1937 when he secured the public support of the heir to the throne, Don Juan, then exiled in Portugal, for the Nationalist cause in return for a promise to consider the future of the monarchy once the conflict was concluded.

An additional, if not the principal, incentive to widespread participation in the FET was the prominent position it was assigned as part of the new order by the Nationalist leadership. Again it was the model offered by the pre-war Falange which was officially adopted, closely following that of institutionalised fascist parties in other countries, particularly Italy. The FET's political organisation was strictly hierarchical. At the top level, the head of state was also chief of the party, aided by a secretary general, with an appointed national council and advisory political committee. Below this every province had its own party machine, with appointed leaders down to the level of local chiefs and secretaries. In addition twelve party bodies, known as national delegations, with their own bureaucracies were created to cover every aspect of public life: education, foreign affairs, press and propaganda, youth, justice and law, women's section, social works, unions, communication and transport, treasury and administration, information and investigation, and initiatives and orientations of the work of the state.[26]

This sprawl of organisations linked to the FET created remarkable opportunities for individuals to gain power and prestige at all levels of Spanish society. Accordingly, membership was seen not only as a sure way of showing attachment to the Nationalist cause but also as a means of entering the political and administrative apparatus of the new regime. As such, there was a strong incentive for the right-wing supporters of all political factions seeking to preserve their particular positions, as well as for the individually ambitious who sought advancement, to become militants or adherents if they could. The rapid growth of FET to around 650 000 members by the end of the war confirmed both its appeal and the degree to which it was in practice a coalition.[27] Certainly old guard Falangists were much in evidence throughout the new organisation. They included the pre-war secretary Fernández Cuesta who was returned to his post in December 1937, allowing Serrano Suñer to slip into the background, having completed the task of fashioning the single party. However, the appointments to the national council were such that, in fact, committed Falangists were only a substantial minority, along with Carlists, conventional monarchists and military officers, who also had representation. Moreover, in the provinces the leaderships of the new organisations were based upon the existing cadres from all the right-wing political groups. This, too, effectively diluted the dominance of Falangism within the National Movement.

From the viewpoint of the Nationalist leadership, the FET was a masterly if rather delicate creation, giving it a political base that was theoretically a rigid single party but which in practice was a flexible instrument. Outward political unity was achieved but not at the price of completely alienating any particular group. The FET represented a truly national political organisation that was the vital underpinning for the consolidation of Francoist rule. It presented a strong and coherent ideological rationale for the new regime in the fashionable fascist mode of the 1930s, but disguised within it was the continuation of a number of different currents of rightist thinking. In its administrative roles it tied Nationalist supporters into the state through the strong bonds of self-interest and career advancement. Its limitation was that, as a result of these compromises, almost nobody was wholly satisfied with it. For Falangists it was not the radical vanguard of the fascist revolution they had envisaged, nor was it the more conventionally conservative and reactionary body that Carlists and monarchists would have preferred. Yet none dared ignore the party, after some initial objections, for fear of handing it over to their political rivals, and all could continue to hope that it could become the vehicle for their ambitions once the war was won.

WARTIME GOVERNMENT AND EARLY POLICIES

The construction of the FET was the first decisive move in establishing the formal structures of the regime. It also illustrated one of the most important guiding rules for the dictatorship – that of carefully harnessing together all forces in order to maintain both support and stability. This principle fostered a spirit of competition, the price of which could be a tendency towards immobility and administrative confusion, but it also strengthened central control. It was extended further when the Nationalist leadership took the next steps towards the construction of a full state apparatus in January 1938 with a decree which named Franco as prime minister (*presidente del gobierno*) as well as head of state; replaced the Junta Técnica with a permanent cabinet of ministers; and announced the creation of government ministries. All the usual areas of government activity were to be covered. No specific mention was made of the FET, making it clear that there was to be no fusion of party and state as national syndicalism demanded: instead the party apparatus would work either in parallel with other government bodies or with overlapping control. Unsurprisingly radical Falangists saw this as a severe blow to their hopes while conservatives and monarchists were again placated. This was a highly significant decision that shaped the evolution of the state apparatus. As in fascist Italy and Nazi Germany, despite the assertions of party ideology, there was to be no monopoly of formal political power for the FET.

Appointments to the first cabinet of Francoism reflected a similar attempt to maintain a balance of forces. Six posts went to leading figures within the FET, of whom three were Falangists, two were monarchists and one a Carlist. The Carlist and one monarchist were also closely linked to the Catholic church and supported an important role for religion in the new regime. Of the Falangists, one was Serrano Suñer, another was a recent convert, leaving only Fernández Cuesta as a representative of the old guard. Likewise, of the three military officers appointed, two were authoritarian monarchists who had played prominent roles during the Primo de Rivera dictatorship of the 1920s and one was a relatively apolitical childhood friend of Franco. The final two members of the cabinet had professional/technical backgrounds, one of whom was a monarchist.[28] So although the FET was apparently strongly represented, only the more minor post of Minister of Agriculture went to a radical Falangist. Overall, in one guise or another, it was the military and monarchists who held the lion's share of posts, as well as dominating the most important ministerial appointments.

However, when it came to defining the exact form and content of the New State (as it was quickly dubbed) that was to be created, radical national-syndicalist rhetoric still dominated over the language of reactionary conservatism and Catholicism. Even so, there was clearly still a lot of common gound, and indeed most of the promises made for after the war maintained the approach of the Crusade. All threatening ideologies of the liberal left – including Franco's own bizarre obsession with freemasonry – along with the democracy that was seen as allowing them to flourish unchecked, were to be permanently suppressed. Regional rights were to be most vigorously opposed as a challenge to the unity of Spain. The 'moral pollution' of secularism and anti-clericalism was to be rooted out and the country re-evangelised in the Catholic faith. The family, traditional relations between the sexes and the social hierarchy were to be reinforced. Property rights were to be respected, though at the same time security and justice were promised to workers. Above all, Spain was to be made, as the regime slogan had it, 'great and free' once again. Economic and social renewal were promised as national goals. The ultimate prize was the restoration of a Spanish empire to replace that lost in the disastrous wars of 1898.

These ideas were rather general – and deliberately so. Avoiding too much discussion of the shape that the new Spain was to take was a pragmatic measure on the part of the Francoist leadership. Unlike their Republican opponents who were fatally divided over the means and ends of the war, the Nationalists never lost sight of the need to achieve victory on the battlefield above all else. In the meantime, the military campaign absorbed most of the attention and energy of the Nationalist leadership. Yet, despite the sense that the New State was on hold until the war was terminated, important measures did emerge. The common thread that united them was a commitment to the principle of intervention. State control was accepted by all the different forces within the insurgent camp as a necessity: indeed, the whole thrust of the idea of the New State led in that direction. In fact, initiatives in the rear were sometimes responses to particular crises by individual ministers, though their real power was limited by the lack of a proper bureaucracy. But mainly they were the result of individual institutions or powerful groups within the Nationalist camp seeking to entrench their interests. In some cases this involved barely muted conflict for control: as in social and cultural affairs where the FET and church vied for influence.

The scope of intervention was very wide indeed. Perhaps the best example of this approach produced during the war itself was the so-called Labour Charter (*Fuero del Trabajo*), inaugurated in 1938. This conformed, in its ideals at least, to Falangist ideas on the corporate state. Indeed, it was the closest thing to fully-fledged national syndicalism that was ever to appear under the Franco regime. It dealt with one of the chief obsessions in the Nationalist camp – the fear of an independent organised working class. In theory it proposed to create unity between employers and employees by bringing them together into a system of official unions, known as the Organización Sindical Española (OSE), under state direction. Together they would work for the national good, in the fascist ideal of a 'third way' between communism and capitalism. In practice, it became a means of further disciplining labour, as Nationalist employers rejected any control over their interests. Intervention was inaugurated in every other area of life as well. In the economy a policy of national self-sufficiency, or autarky, and state direction was announced as the ideal. All aspects of society and culture, from the position of women to the role of poets, were to be similarly regulated. The implications of a Nationalist victory were made clear: the country was to be shaped only by the guiding principles found in the Nationalist camp and no other.[29]

CONCLUSION

The civil war marked a decisive break in the modern history of Spain. Unable to accommodate themselves to a reforming democracy, a wide range of conservative interests sought to eradicate all traces of the Republican regime, which they had come to fear as a fundamental threat to their position and privileges. Conservative salvation came through a bloody social, political and military struggle, the legacy of which was a fundamentally divided Spain. The Nationalist uprising involved a collaboration between the army and rightist civilian leaders and their supporters. Only in a series of uncertain steps did Franco establish his own leadership and the creation of a Francoist regime take place. By the end of the war, however, the skeletal structures of the dictatorship were in existence.

The chief success of the Francoist leadership at this time was to lay the building blocks of a new regime while maintaining a fragile unity amongst its supporters. This was no slight achievement, given the considerable social and political differences among Nationalists. Here the central roles of the army and church were of vital importance, both for their institutional support and in the elaboration of the rhetoric of the Crusade. Also important, of course, was the repression of opponents, in which all sections of the Nationalist coalition were implicated. Within this context, political resistance to the centralising intentions of the Franco leadership proved impossible, even when it was attempted. The creation of a single party, amalgamating all the different forces of the right, ensured that no particular political group would dominate, despite the adoption of a radical Falangist programme as official doctrine. The driving force that allowed all these developments to take place was the overwhelming desire within the Nationalist camp to eliminate the Republic and all its works. In its place there was to be a new Spain, framed in the image of the Crusade and committed, in principle, to national syndicalism. Not surprisingly, as it became clear that victory would go to the insurgents, Republican supporters were gripped by an even greater fear of the coming order.

NOTES

1 For a commentary on this official version see Paul Preston, 'Resisting Modernity: Fascism and the Military in Twentieth Century Spain' in P. Preston, ed., *The Politics of Revenge: Fascism and the Military in Twentieth Century Spain* (London, 1990), esp. p. 3. Official histories portrayed this view with unrelenting enthusiasm. For a typical example see Joaquín Arraras, *Historia de la Cruzada española* (Madrid, 1940–44).

2 For accounts of the conspiracy, see Stanley Payne, *The Franco Regime* (Madison, 1987), pp. 78–100 and *Politics and the Military in Modern Spain* (Stanford, 1967), pp. 314–40; Gabriel Cardona, *El poder militar en la España contemporánea* (Madrid, 1983), pp. 197–247.

3 The best general accounts of the Republic are to be found in Julio Gil Pecharromán, *La Segunda República* (Madrid, 1989); Paul Preston, *The Coming of the Spanish Civil War. Reform, Reaction and Revolution in the Second Republic*, 2nd edn (London, 1994); Stanley Payne, *Spain's First Democracy. The Second Republic, 1931–1936* (Madison, 1993). Accounts of the praetorian traditions of the army are to be found in Cardona, *El poder militar*; Payne, *Politics and the Military*; Carolyn P. Boyd, *Praetorian Politics in Liberal Spain* (Chapel Hill, 1979).

4 These negotiations are outlined in the biography of Mola by Jorge Vigón, *Mola (El conspirador)* (Barcelona, 1957). The abandonment of the Republic by the right is detailed in Preston, *The Coming*, pp. 239–75.

5 Federico Bravo Morata, *Franco y los muertos providenciales* (Madrid, 1979) gives a rather sensationalist account of these deaths, and also that of Franco's Republican brother, Ramón.

6 Payne, *Franco Regime*, pp. 108–9.

7 The essential study for all aspects of Franco's life is Paul Preston, *Franco* (London, 1993); see pp. 120–43 for his part in the conspiracy.

8 See Preston, *Franco*, pp. 144–70.

9 Preston, *Franco*, pp. 177–83.

10 See Preston, *Franco*, pp. 183–4 on this episode.

11 The seven commissions were Exchequer, Justice, Industry, Commerce, Agriculture and Labour, Culture and Education and Public Works and Communications.

12 On these changes, see Javier Tusell, *Franco en la Guerra Civil. Una biografía política* (Madrid, 1992), pp. 57–67.

13 For an excellent overview of trends within the Spanish right as a whole, see Martin Blinkhorn, 'Conservatism, Traditionalism and Fascism in Spain, 1890–1937' in M. Blinkhorn, ed., *Fascists and Conservatives* (London, 1990), pp. 118–37.

14 For CEDA, see J. R. Montero, *La CEDA. El catolicismo social y política en la II República*, 2 vols. (Madrid, 1977).

15 On Carlism, see Martin Blinkhorn, *Carlism and Crisis in Spain, 1931–1939* (Cambridge, 1975).

16 For excellent analyses of the Alphonsine right, see Julio Gil Pecharromán, *Conservadores subversivos: la derecha autoritaria alfonsina (1913–1936)* (Madrid, 1994) and Raul Morodo, *Los orígenes ideológicos del franquismo: Acción Española* (Madrid, 1985).

17 On Falangism, see Javier Jiménez Campo, *El fascismo en la crisis de la II República* (Madrid, 1979) esp. pp. 221–62 on the limits of pre-war support; Stanley Payne, *A History of Spanish Fascism* (Stanford, 1962); Sheelagh Ellwood, *Prietas las filas. Historia de Falange Española, 1933–1983* (Barcelona, 1984) and 'Falange Española, 1933–39: from fascism to francoism', in M. Blinkhorn, ed., *Spain in Conflict 1931–39. Democracy and its Enemies* (London, 1986), pp. 206–11.

18 Payne, *Politics and the Military*, pp. 383–408 remains a good account of the military during the war.

19 On the attitudes of the church see Frances Lannon, *Privilege, Persecution and Prophecy. The Catholic Church in Spain, 1875–1975* (Oxford, 1987), chapter 8. See also J. M. Sánchez, *The Spanish Civil War as a Religious Tragedy* (Notre Dame, 1987).

20 Herbert Southworth, *El mito de la Cruzada de Franco* (Paris, 1963) remains a trenchant dissection of the Crusade rhetoric.

21 Figures from R. Salas Larrazábal, *Pérdidas de la guerra* (Barcelona, 1977), pp. 428–9 and Gabriel Jackson, *The Spanish Republic and the Civil War in Spain, 1931–39* (Princeton, 1965), p. 539. These two authors give estimates of Nationalist deaths at Republican hands of 72 500 and 20 000 respectively. The number of religious killed was over 6000 according to the reliable A. Montero Montero, *Historia de la persecución religiosa en España, 1936–39* (Madrid, 1961). The numbers of deaths due to the terror in both zones of the war remain the subject of considerable controversy. For a general discussion of the repression see Alberto Reig Tapia, *Ideología e historia: Sobre la represión franquista y la Guerra Civil* (Madrid, 1984) and Josep Fontana, 'Introducción: Reflexiones sobre la

naturaleza y las consequencias del franquismo', in J. Fontana, ed., *España bajo el franquismo* (Barcelona, 1986), pp. 17–24. For examples of the local origins of the early repression, see the studies by Julián Casanova *et al.*, *El pasado oculto. Fascismo y violencia en Aragón (1936–1939)* (Madrid, 1992); Francisco Cobo Romero, *La Guerra Civil y la represión franquista en la provincia de Jaén, 1936–1950* (Jaén, 1993), pp. 491–510; Ian Gibson, *Granada en 1936 y el asesinato de Federico García Lorca* (Barcelona, 1979); Justo Vila Izquierdo, *Extremadura: la Guerra Civil* (Badajoz, 1983); Josep M. Solé i Sabaté, *La repressió franquista a Catalunya, 1938–1953* (Barcelona, 1985); F. Gómez Moreno, *La Guerra Civil en Córdoba, 1936–39* (Madrid, 1985).

22 See Shlomo Ben-Ami, *Fascism from Above. The Dictatorship of Primo de Rivera in Spain, 1923–1930* (Oxford, 1983).

23 Payne, *Franco Regime*, pp. 167–8.

24 For the process of unification, see M. García Venero, *Historia de la Unificación. Falange y Requeté en 1937* (Madrid, 1970); M. Hedilla Larrey, *Manuel Hedilla. Testimonio* (Barcelona, 1972); Ellwood, *Prietas las filas*, pp. 99–100; Herbert Southworth, *Antifalange* (Paris, 1967).

25 The best guides to the development of the FET during this period are Ricardo Chueca, *El fascismo en los comienzos del régimen de Franco* (Madrid, 1983) and Ellwood, *Prietas las filas*.

26 Chueca, *El fascismo*, pp. 233–64 gives details of party organisation and responsibilities.

27 Cited in Payne, *Franco Regime*, p. 238.

28 The list of cabinet members and their affiliations was Pedro Sainz Rodríguez (Education) FET, monarchist and Catholic; Fernández Cuesta (Agriculture) FET, Falangist old guard; Pedro González Bueno (Syndical Action and Organisation) FET, Falangist; Ramón Serrano Suñer (Interior) FET, Falangist; Conde de Rodezno (Justice), FET, Carlist and Catholic; Francisco Gómez Jordana (vice-president of cabinet and Foreign Minister) military, monarchist; Fidel Dávila (Defence), military, monarchist; Severiano Martínez Anido (Public Order) military, monarchist; Juan Antonio Suanzes (Industry) military, friend of Franco; Alfonso Peña Boeuf (Public Works) civil engineer; Andrés Amado (Finance) monarchist. See Tusell, *Franco en la Guerra Civil*, pp. 223–37; Payne, *Franco Regime*, pp. 180–2.

29 On the syndicates, see Miguel Aparicio, *El sindicalismo vertical y la formación del Estado franquista* (Barcelona, 1980). On the trend towards regulation in the Nationalist zone, see Rafael Abella, *La vida cotidiana durante la Guerra Civil: la España nacional* (Barcelona, 1978).

2

Francoism Triumphant, 1939–1950

On 1 April 1939, Franco's headquarters announced that, 'Today, with the red army captured and disarmed, our victorious troops have achieved their final objectives.' With Franco refusing any outcome except unconditional surrender, the end had come with the collapse of the Republic into a final internal conflict. Nationalist soldiers had only to walk into the area of territory that remained in Republican hands, roughly one quarter of the country including the city of Madrid. The policy of war by attrition had taken nearly three years to subdue the more than half of Spain's population that had opposed the insurgency. But superior military effectiveness allied to greater unity of organisation and purpose had won through. With triumphal celebrations and religious services of thanks, final victory was trumpeted as validation of Francoist rule.

To the victors in the war went the spoils. With all of Spain under its control, the dictatorship now had the opportunity to exercise virtually unqualified power. Not surprisingly, it did so in the interests of its coalition of social, political and institutional supporters. Despite the diversity of forces represented, there was sufficient agreement over basic priorities for the regime to preside over a form of collective project. Much of it arose directly out of the experience of civil war, and regime policies became a kind of continuation in peace of the wartime struggle. The permanent subjugation of the regime's enemies, economic and social reconstruction and control, and the renewal of Spain's international position were the agreed aims. There was also a large degree of common ground on the approach to be taken. In particular, the war had validated the idea of a strong state as both the protector of the regime and its supporters and as a tool to reshape Spain. Accordingly, the 1940s saw an attempt at massive state intervention and control in the name of national renewal and a return to greatness. The results, however, were far from a spectacular success, even in their own terms, and they were a disaster for the losers in the war.

Consensus did not extend, however, to the basic organisational and administrative structures of the regime that were formalised after 1939. Observers began to see the dictatorship as composed of a number of different institutionalised 'families', of which the FET, military and church were the most important. Power and responsibilities within the New State were distributed unevenly amongst them, and strong rivalries for influence meant that no permanently accepted settlement was possible. Conflicts were contained within the regime by a policy of balance, or divide and rule, presided over by Franco himself. Fear of the consequences of deserting the dictatorship also played an important role. But serious internal tension was the inevitable result, leading to a series of running disputes within the regime throughout the 1940s.

RESHAPING SPAIN

Though the 'Year of Victory' (as 1939 was now described in official communiqués) marked the end of the Republic, it did not mean the end of the struggle. Although open warfare had finished in 1939, politically the civil war was never to come to an end. Its simplistic 'lessons' – that democracy led to subversion and revolution, that 'true Spaniards' had to stand permanently vigilant against 'anti-Spain' – were to be repeated for decades to come. The counter-revolutionary Crusade was a permanent struggle, not just a temporary necessity. There was no room for leniency or reconciliation towards the defeated. They remained enemies in peace as much as in war and were to be treated accordingly. All the liberal and leftist political parties, independent trade unions and regionalist movements that had flourished under the Republic needed to be suppressed lest they threaten the social order, religion and integrity of the nation.

Thus, far from relaxing with the end of the war, repression of opponents both intensified and became even more institutionalised. With all of Spain now controlled by Nationalist forces, the number of potential victims expanded enormously. Even if the Francoist authorities had wished to contain the post-war terror, it is doubtful whether their supporters could have been restrained from settling old social and political scores. As it was, the leadership acted to make the suppression of opponents even more systematic and to throw a legal cloak over it. This had begun in the final months of the war, when the Francoist leadership had signalled its intention to institutionalise further the persecution of opponents by the enactment of legislation to deal specifically with political offences. The Law of Political Responsibilities, published on 9 February 1939, was a blanket retrospective measure that criminalised anyone who had belonged to a Republican political party or trade union, or had supported the Republican war effort or, even, who had not actively aided the Nationalist side. By making passivity illegal almost anyone was suspect. This law signified the complete rejection of post-war reconciliation. It caused some disquiet within the Nationalist camp, as is evident from the cabinet discussion of the draft legislation. In the end, however, only the education minister, Rodríguez, objected to the law, and even then his objection was not on any humanitarian grounds. His reservation was that the new law would serve to harden Republican resistance and therefore it would be better to wait until the war was actually over before implementing it. The law defined different levels of culpability and a range of punishments including terms of imprisonment with or without hard labour, internal exile, loss of citizenship, dismissal from work, and the confiscation of estates and fines. The regional courts and central tribunal established to try cases under the law allowed no opportunity for the accused to appear in person and there could be no appeals against the sentence handed down. It was applied not only to particular individuals, but often also to their families.[1]

In March 1940, additional legislation against political enemies was introduced. The bizarrely named Law for the Suppression of Freemasonry and Communism was aimed at the two greatest supposed enemies of the new regime. Freemasonry was a catch-all term applied to liberalism and also an obsession – particularly on the part of Franco – with the idea that a masonic plot was at work in Spain.[2] Communism was applied to any ideology of the revolutionary left, including anarchists and socialists as well as true communists. Special tribunals were established to operate the law and procedures and penalties similar to those of the Law of Political Responsibilities were outlined. Although the death penalty was not included as one of the punishments for political crimes', the system of military tribunals which did have the power to pass the death sentence also remained in operation. With 'military rebellion' and 'offences of political violence' under their jurisdiction, the military courts had plenty of scope for action. The result was an overlapping set of agencies charged with eradicating all possible opposition to the new order. In this way, a framework for continuing persecution was laid down by the Francoists.

This terror formed the harshest part of a post-war punishment directed by the Nationalist victors at those social forces which had resisted them. Often, longstanding conflicts lay behind the application of this extreme violence. There was a strong class aspect to the repression, which consequently fell most heavily on the rural and urban lower orders. It was perhaps at its most rampant and naked in the countryside, which still contained the largest part of the population. This was particularly the case in the south, where the landed elites ruthlessly reimposed control over their great estates (*latifundios*) – many of which had been collectivised in the war – and of society in general by crushing the labouring poor, whose anarchist and socialist unions had opposed them. Considerable violence was also meted out in other areas which had a history of agrarian conflicts. In Catalonia, for instance, tenant farmers who had protested at the terms of their leases were the focus of a repression directed by their landlords. Even amongst the overwhelmingly conservative peasant regions of central and northern Spain, rural labourers and sharecroppers who had joined unions during the Republic were hunted down and dealt with. The repression was also strongly felt amongst the urban working class. Employers seized the opportunity to reinstate firmly their hold over factories, workshops and mines, many of which had been expropriated during the war by their workers. In industrial areas such as Asturias, Catalonia and the Basque country, with traditions of union and leftist political activity, special commissions were sometimes arranged to deal with the large numbers of individuals awaiting processing by the tribunals and courts. The latter two regions also witnessed the persecution of separatists, mainly middle-class, who had campaigned for regional rights. Although anathema to all of Nationalist opinion, they were the particular hate-objects of the military, which was obsessed with the concept of national unity. Elsewhere, intellectuals, teachers and university professors, the bastions of liberal republicanism, were targeted for repression.[3]

While the social categories of the chief victims of the repression have always been clear, the numbers affected by it are not easy to define exactly. Even though greater organisation was involved compared to wartime, records of deaths, imprisonments and fines were not systematically kept. In particular, almost all of the continuing extra-judicial killings went unrecorded, and in any case the regime did not seek to advertise the scale of its activities. It is clear, however, that these acts of vengeance were at their height in the immediate aftermath of the war and only really began to abate seriously by the mid-1940s. Estimates of the total number of executions (the most debated aspect of the repression) vary wildly from an unlikely high of 200 000 to a totally improbable low of some 23 000.[4] Any figure in between gives a suggestion of the grim realities. To an extent, an obsession with figures underplays the wider effects of the terror. When families and friends of victims are considered, the numbers affected by the repression are even higher than the figures indicate, high though they are. Everyone was aware of the daily round of killings, generating a widespread climate of fear. Many more individuals were imprisoned, sent to labour camps or suffered fines and the seizure of their belongings. The regime's own figures suggest that some 400 000 persons passed through the prisons between 1939 and 1945 (not including some half a million prisoners of war). Even after this period, the imprisoned population was steady at around 40 000. In another example, it was reported at the end of 1941 that in the eighteen months the tribunals administering the Law of Political Responsibilities had been active they had processed over 100 000 cases.[5] Thus in many ways a constant fear of retribution, as well as its reality, cowed the population as a whole.

The eventual reduction in executions was due partly to Francoist concern that they would provoke Allied action against Spain after the Second World War, but mainly it was because outright repression had largely served its main purposes and was threatening to become counter-productive. There were simply far fewer readily identifiable enemies to deal with and the vengeful passions that had driven the persecution along were becoming spent. More-over, denunciations to the various courts and tribunals were clearly often a means to pursue personal, non-political, vendettas or were part of the disputes between rival regime supporters. Faced with the danger that the repression would begin to undermine the regime itself, the authorities began to make serious efforts to tame it. Legislation was altered to reduce the severity of punishments and existing sentences were frequently reviewed and reduced. By 1945 the numbers of executions had dwindled, though they were not completely ended, and a series of amnesties reduced the prison and concentration camp populations. But the easing of repression did not mean that the vigilance of the regime against its perceived enemies diminished. A police state was now in place, along with a network of informers, controlled by the army, the paramilitary civil guards and the secret police. There were severe punishments for a wide range of offences. Any kind of independent organisation outside the regime was banned, and strikes and demonstrations were illegal.

The fear of a Republican revival was not, in fact, entirely groundless, though the direct threat did not mainly come from within the country. Remnants of the Republican political parties had survived abroad, mostly scattered between Mexico, France and the USSR. In the immediate aftermath of the civil war they spent most of their time engaged in bitter internecine quarrels about who bore responsibility for defeat. However, in 1944 a Republican government in exile, excluding the communists, was formed in Mexico (later moving to Paris) to take advantage of impending Allied victory in the World War. A communist-dominated front was also formed in southern France amongst the 300 000 Spanish refugees. In the final months of 1944, guerrilla bands representing both groupings began to infiltrate across the border, with the expectation that they would rouse the population to renew an armed struggle against the regime. This was based upon the common opinion amongst the exiles that the regime merely represented a small clique of army officers, church leaders and Falangists lacking any significant social support. Thus, with a determined push, they could be overthrown in a popular uprising.[6]

It was a naive analysis of the nature of authoritarianism in Spain and the hopes of the guerrillas were to be cruelly dashed. Firstly, the exiles grossly underestimated the degree of active support the regime continued to mobilise not only amongst the agrarian and urban upper and middle classes, but also among large sections of the smallholding peasantry. Secondly, they overestimated the capacity, or even will, amongst former supporters of the Republic to respond to the call to arms. The last thing in most people's mind by 1945 was a desire to see the civil war restart; for most of the remnants of Republican Spain simple survival was much more important. Even so, some particularly brave individuals did respond, including scattered remnants of the Republican army who had maintained guerrilla resistance within Spain.

The thousands of guerrillas who infiltrated across the border were met by a well-prepared counter-insurgency campaign spearheaded by the civil guard and backed by troops. In numerous brutal clashes, usually in the remote countryside, often with no prisoners taken, the guerrillas suffered defeat after defeat. Lacking popular support they had no real chance. Desperation often led to raids for food and funds that only succeeded in alienating the civilian population further. There was consequently a certain accuracy to the description of their activities in the special Law for the Repression of Banditry and Terrorism passed by the regime in early 1947. Harsh penalties were laid down for anyone suspected of aiding or harbouring the fighters. By 1948 the campaign was in serious decline, enough for martial law to be lifted. The communists did not officially abandon the armed struggle until 1952 (after Stalin had withdrawn Soviet support), but any threat the guerrillas represented had long since been wiped out.[7] And with the Republican government-in-exile in a state of collapse due to internal dissension, any immediate hopes of overthrowing Francoism also effectively died at this time. The real lesson of the guerrilla struggle was that the regime during the 1940s was impregnable, and the main effect of the campaign was to provide the regime with convincing proof to place before its own supporters that they must stick with the dictatorship.

Protection and the need to root out all alternatives also informed the regime's relationship to society in general. In the post-war period a moral crusade, to match that of the civil war, was declared. Supposedly deviant ideas and ways of living were to be rigorously suppressed and Francoist notions of decency enforced and promoted. By and large, it was Catholic thinking – shared by virtually all the forces of the Nationalist coalition – that was the model followed. Indeed, the church itself exalted at the possibilities for the 'rechristianisation of Spain'. National renewal required a wide range of preventative measures: divorce, abortion, and non-religious marriage were banned; censorship of words and pictures was enforced. Meanwhile, almost all aspects of social life were organised and controlled through the regime or its supporters in one form or another. Cultural production, education and intellectual life were all regulated. Organisations for youth, women, sport and recreation were introduced. Notions of an eternal 'Spanish national character' (a movement known as *hispanidad*) were promoted. Public spectacles, monumental architecture and invented celebrations to laud the regime were also the order of the day. The result was tight control of the public sphere in the interests of rigid conformity. Life during the 1940s was very grey indeed. Only by entering or compromising with the regime were many forms of normal social activity possible. For those active supporters of Francoism it was a time of comfortable security. But for the rest of the population the only possible response was to retreat into private life.[8]

The use of unchallenged state power to entrench the position of the regime and its supporters was also evident in the post-war approach to economic reconstruction. And once again malign influences on Spanish life had to be contained. The property rights of the agrarian and industrial elites were sacrosanct and heavily protected. This was most clearly seen in the expansion of the regime's corporatist approach to controlling labour relations, first enshrined in the Labour Charter of 1938. During the 1940s the Syndical

Organisation, Organización Sindical Española (OSE) grew to encompass most areas of economic activity.[9] Theoretically a means to unite the interests of workers and employers, in practice the official unions served to discipline labour in the interests of capital. On their estates and in their factories, owners relished their unquestioned dominance. Regime supporters received the right to impose lower wages and were also rewarded with guaranteed prices and subsidies, as well as a reduction in direct taxation, all of which benefited producers at the expense of workers and consumers.

Such measures were part of a whole battery of interventionist measures introduced to direct the economy. Economic intervention was seen by a wide range of Francoist opinion as a means to reverse Spain's perceived economic decline. A policy of self-sufficiency or autarky was the second main plank to restore national economic greatness. With the exception of links to Nazi Germany until 1945, this cut Spain off from the rest of the world throughout the 1940s. Although a degree of economic isolation would have occurred anyway, due to the Second World War and the ostracism of the Franco regime in its aftermath, autarky was positively embraced in order to protect the country from malevolent foreign influences – in effect the counterparts of the liberal-left at home, which were seen as responsible for the decline of Spain. Autarky was part of the policy of a fortress Spain, and was reinforced by the strong military justifications produced for it. Franco and the army were among its strongest advocates. However, in production terms it proved to be a disastrous ideological experiment.[10] The economy stagnated throughout the 1940s, producing widespread hunger and distress. In the latter part of the decade it even resulted in outbreaks of wildcat strikes by desperate workers in some industrial regions – though these protests were easily dealt with by the authorities.[11] However, regime supporters were mostly protected from its worst effects, while their enemies suffered, and no serious proposals were made to alter course.

The nationalist principles behind autarky were also to the forefront in foreign relations. The obsession with a return to greatness amongst Francoists was at its most acute in this area. The loss of most of the last remnants of the empire in the Spanish-American war of 1898 – leaving only Spain's Moroccan possessions – remained an open sore for all sections of the right and the military. A return to an imperial status was strongly desired and demanded, particularly by Falangists. Racist notions of a timeless Spanish destiny to dominate and rule, linked to *hispanidad*, were raised as justifications.[12] In the period after the civil war, joining the regime's Axis allies in their conquests appeared the shortest route to achieving these ends. The Second World War was also seen as a continuation of the Nationalist struggle in the civil war, with the enemies of Germany and Italy identified as the same as those of Francoism in Spain. After the outbreak of the world conflict the regime considered entering the war, something that was strenuously denied later. Only by chance did the dictatorship avoid complete involvement in the war, though Spanish troops did fight on the Russian front.[13] When it became clear that an Allied victory was going to occur, the regime rapidly backtracked and managed to survive international opprobrium after 1945. International survival rather than dreams of empire dominated for the remainder of the decade.[14]

INTERNAL STRUCTURES AND ORGANISATION

At the end of the war it became common practice to refer to Francoism as resting on three institutional pillars: the army, the FET or National Movement, and the Catholic church. These were the forces which had provided the physical, the political/organisational and the moral/cultural elements to the Nationalist victory. Their representation within the post-war state was, therefore, crucial. More generally, the set of wider political and social interests in the wartime Nationalist coalition underpinned Francoism. Participants in the FET included the Falangists, Catholic conservatives and monarchists. Meanwhile, the main base of social support was constituted by the powerful landed class, industrialists, and to a lesser extent conservative peasants and the urban middle classes. All the most powerful groups were represented in government. For the alliance to continue to hold it was important that they felt that they participated in managing the state.[15]

The idea of the families is a useful shorthand to describe the bases of the post-war regime, but it conceals the degree to which they were not distinct, well-defined political and social interests. Francoists often fitted into a number of different categories of family simultaneously. Individuals crossed the boundaries separating one family from another and alliances between groups changed according to issue. For some in the army, for example, waging the civil war and fighting the long Crusade of the dictatorship can only be explained through their commitment to a Catholic Spain and their view of the *patria* as threatened by the godless forces of communism. Others, such as General Kindelán, Head of the Nationalist airforce, appeared to have been motivated by a desire for order, a belief in the role of the army as the ultimate guarantor of the nation and a commitment to the monarchy.[16] At the same time, the families were also sometimes riven with rivalries which were both personal and political. So to talk of 'the families' of Francoism is in reality a heuristic device useful for understanding the relationship between the political elites and the state. It is an analytical tool for understanding the Francoist state, and it gained currency partly because it appears to have been Franco's own way of thinking about the social base of the regime. He seems to have been concerned to balance out government in such a way that all the 'pillars' and most of the rightist groups would enjoy some of the spoils of victory. The means by which this was achieved was through appointment to ministerial positions and the allocation of areas of particular influence to different 'families'.

One urgent problem facing the new regime in the immediate post-war period was how to regularise the organisation, running and staffing of the state bureaucracy. Much of its structure was either rough and ready, the product of wartime pragmatism and stop-gap measures, contradictory, or simply absent. Turf wars between different ministries, party bodies, the military and the church went on unchecked by any clear delineation of authority – with the benefit that divide and rule was still possible, but also with the problem of administrative inefficiency and the danger that the conflicts could get out of hand. During the war, corruption and graft had become ingrained within the party and administration at all levels, making for unreliability in decision-making. There was no official constitutional or legal framework. Everything existed as the result of decrees or *ad hoc* measures sanctioned by Franco as head of state and prime minister. The sense was of a state that was temporary rather than permanent.

Improving this situation became a further means to reward the regime's supporters and allow the 'families' to extend their influence. At the start of the war, the insurgent military command had decreed that all public employees, including civil servants, who had served under the Republic were automatically dismissed. Therefore, for the most part the Nationalist leadership began with a clean slate, creating a new job market within the state at both the national and local levels. It was perhaps inevitable, therefore, that the public sector would be divided up between different factions, though the results of this, in terms of efficiency, were mixed. Many jobs were given straightforwardly to place-fillers of little proven ability, as a perk. In other cases, however, pre-war minor civil servants were rehired after they had run the gauntlet of purge committees (*comités de depuración*) to which they had to prove their loyalty. The real prizes were appointments to the more important positions. Here proven adherence not just to the Nationalist cause but also to a particular 'family' was the chief qualification necessary for appointment to a public post. In the confusion of wartime and with no fixed seat of central government prior to the fall of Madrid, the process of recruitment had been haphazard and unsystematic until the end of the war. But a pattern developed in which jobs were allocated mostly on the basis of personal contacts and recommendations. Inevitably this led to favouritism, often corresponding to the personal opinions of the appropriate minister involved. This resulted in individual ministries becoming the preserve of particular groups, as each minister recruited like-minded supporters. Dividing up the posts between the families, however, could not conceal the fact that the new bureaucratic and political class shared remarkably uniform social and political origins. The majority of top posts in most ministries were filled from the traditional administrative class of the Spanish state – men (women were not represented at all) with professional academic qualifications in law, engineering and finance. Youth was very evident, and many were still in party or military uniforms.[17]

The free hand given in recruitment also applied in the day-to-day running of the departments of state and in policy-making, and appointees to ministerial positions were able to act with considerable independence in their fiefdoms. Although Franco could intervene with absolute authority in any area he chose, in practice he did so very selectively. In the 1940s and 1950s particularly, his direct intervention was felt most strongly in the areas of defence and foreign policy, where he had a personal interest. Otherwise, only when an issue seemed especially vital was he likely to direct a minister's actions. Left largely to their own devices, ministers and their staffs could elaborate their own projects, cultivate their own empires and pursue rivalries. The rhetorical justification for any action had to be that it fitted in with the supposed wishes of Franco or met the requirements of official doctrines. However, these criteria were open to a wide range of interpretation and argument.

The main fora for presenting major initiatives were the cabinet meetings over which Franco presided. Their pattern, and the form of policy-making that resulted, was to persist throughout the life of the regime. From the start they were interminably long and dull affairs. All ministers had the right to speak and many did so at length. The meetings were also occasionally intimidating with Franco suddenly deciding to interrogate a minister over policy. In view of this, and the independence with which ministers usually made day-to-day policy, meetings did not function as an instrument for collective decision-making. Tensions between ministers representing different political and institutional interests were often barely concealed at these rituals. Not surprisingly, intrigues and backstairs deals abounded. Lacking communal solidarity, the cabinet often functioned in a reactive manner. Sudden crises would lead to a frantic search for immediate solutions. Otherwise, it was largely a matter of waiting to see what individual ministers, or groups of ministers, came up with as preferred policies in their particular areas of competence. Such leeway also meant that any failures or unpopular policies could be blamed on individuals, rather than on the government as a whole or Franco personally.

Franco's theoretical powers as head of state were extended even further in August 1939, enhancing the impression of a personal dictatorship, and he continued to lead government in a markedly military style, issuing orders and decrees. Regime propaganda constantly stressed his central role, and pictures and portraits of him were widely distributed. Although hardly a charismatic personality, he successfully embodied the different faces of the regime, appearing in the uniforms of the party and army, posing as the perfect Catholic gentleman and family man. Yet decisive personal political leadership did not really result. The regime was constrained by the continued need to maintain the balance within the varied political and institutional coalition that supported it and which made Franco's rule possible. In many respects Franco was forced to follow rather than lead developments, and he waited to see which way the wind was blowing before acting. By standing as final arbiter and court of last appeal he remained of central importance, and could act to forestall any one group becoming too powerful a threat to his influence. His real power was that of appointment. In reality, as long as individual ministers and party leaders could show themselves to be working within bounds acceptable to Franco, a great deal of administrative power remained devolved to them. And while others plotted and planned, Franco retained an aloof distance, a position symbolised by his post-war occupancy of the Pardo Palace, just outside Madrid, as an official residence until his death.

It was perhaps inevitable that the end of hostilities would allow differences and contradictions within the Nationalist camp to flourish more openly than during the war. What was tolerable in wartime was not so easily accepted in peace. Even before the war had ended, there had been signs that the different groups of Falangists, monarchists, Catholics, Carlists and various military factions were looking to ensure the triumph of their ideals and interests. The clearest ideological divide was between radical Falangists in the FET who wished to see the national syndicalist revolution pushed forward, and the conservatives, military and Catholics who wanted a more conventional approach to dictatorship. Certainly, when the conflict ended each of the major forces within the regime pressed their own claims to power with an equal determination to have them recognised.[18]

In the major cabinet reshuffle initiated by Franco just after the war was over the early winners in the struggle for position appeared to be the Falangist section of the FET. Of the only two members of the wartime group who were left in office, one was Serrano Suñer. At the same time five other Falangists received posts. Yet this apparent sign that the regime was becoming more Falangist and more civilian in orientation, bringing it closer to fashionable fascism, looked less convincing on closer inspection. In fact the military element was also reinforced by the creation of cabinet posts for each branch of the armed services, an arrangement which was to persist throughout the life of the regime. Even the dissident army general, Yagüe, was brought into the government as Minister of Aviation. Overlapping interests meant that some of the Falangists were also from the armed forces. Perhaps the most significant appointment of this kind was of General Muñoz Grandes, a wartime convert to Falangism who was surprisingly given the post of Secretary General of the FET. Carlists and monarchists also had their representatives, both as civilian members of the FET and as military officers. In fact this was an early post-war indication that Franco aimed to maintain some balance between regime forces.[19]

This gesture towards Falangism reflected the fact that immediately after the war the calls from within the ranks of the party for a truly national syndicalist state increased dramatically. They had to be taken seriously because the party represented the only political base the regime possessed, and Falangism was a force within it that seemed too strong to ignore. Moreover, these demands coincided with the rise of the Axis powers during the Second World War.

Fascism in Spain won more adherents as Axis successes at the beginning of the conflict multiplied. As the outside world became more fascist, the desire to emulate the example of Italy and Germany – the Nationalist's vital supporters in the civil war – grew. As a result, old guard radicals and even figures like Serrano Suñer who had a power-base in the party, pressed for a greater role for the FET in directing the regime. Most vociferous of all the pro-fascist groups was the university student group (SEU) which became the main focus of radical Falangism. In the middle of 1940, Serrano, as Minister of the Interior, even sponsored a party proposal for a new Law of Organisation of the State which would regularise the structures of the regime. This proposed a strong head of state, a corporate parliament (Cortes) representing different institutional and social groups and an important role for the Junta Política of the FET. At the same time, fringe plots to overthrow Franco and seize power in a Falangist revolution were hatched, further increasing the pressure.[20]

The main gain for the Falangists within the FET from the cabinet reorganisation was the securing of control over some areas of policy and administration within the regime. These were enshrined initially in the so-called 'permanent statutes' of the FET produced in 1939 which maintained the system of national delegations, covering just about every area of administration and policy. The FET assumed sole responsibility for the Syndical Organisation, the basis for the corporate system of labour promised by the regime in its first major policy decree issued during 1938, the Spanish Labour Charter. Salvador Merino – a radical old guard Falangist – was given the task of overseeing the creation of syndicates. In 1940 membership was made compulsory for virtually all employers and workers. At the same time, the Youth Front, the Women's Section and propaganda organisations of the FET became more prominent – all of them strongholds of Falangist influence. All of this addressed to a degree Falangist demands for a national syndicalist regime, but it still fell far short of the compete monopoly of power they claimed. Falangist influence, and that of the FET in general, was extended only in areas where it seemed safe to do so or where it was countered by other forces.

The 'family' most directly involved in balancing the party at this time was the military.[21] The army's claim to a share of power was strong in many respects. After all, Franco came from their ranks and whatever else the dictatorship represented it relied upon military force for its existence. The senior officers who had led the rising and directed the war effort, including Franco, were also steeped in an authoritarian tradition that jealously guarded military privileges, saw the army as embodying Spanish nationhood and resented civilian political interference. Furthermore, they had defeated the Republican military and political forces, and the security of the regime was ultimately their responsibility. Additionally, they exercised huge discretionary powers under martial law. Military influence permeated every corner of the new regime, including the FET. Officers were automatically party members and most were monarchists. Not surprisingly, for all these reasons the army was also rewarded materially after the war. Soldiers – both professionals and those in wartime service – were appointed to a whole variety of positions, including the main economic ministries. Indeed, in some cases, veteran status became almost a prerequisite for public employment.[22]

Like the FET, the army was also allocated particular tasks at this time, which it was to continue to fulfil throughout the life of the dictatorship. Senior officers were called upon to fill sensitive posts and served as members of the cabinet, particularly as Ministers of Defence and Foreign Affairs. However, the main role of the military was in preserving the regime against internal enemies. The country was divided into military districts, each headed by a captain general with strong powers under martial law to use troops as an army of occupation. Even everyday policing was dominated by the paramilitary police force, the civil guard, whose members, in their distinctive patent-leather tricorn hats, had been a byword for a brutal defence of the established order since the 1840s. In addition, during the 1940s the army operated its own investigation branch and separate courts, and ran a prison and concentration camp system.

However, although the regime owed its existence to the military and it was the ultimate line of defence – the big stick that was always to be there if needed – relations with the army were not always smooth, even at the beginning. Politicised senior officers in particular were aware that they had made Franco Caudillo. He, in turn, was acutely conscious that the army could also represent a danger to the new state. But Franco was very much on home ground with the military; he was at ease with his fellow officers and understood military institutions and the mindset of the officer corps. He always retained a sharp eye for military intrigues. By taking a personal interest, particularly in the composition of the officer corps, he was able effectively to mould the armed forces into an institution loyal to the regime. The military was never given too much institutional power and was always placed firmly under the control of the regime. Senior officers were kept in careful competition for influence both amongst themselves and with the civilian political leaders of the party. Talented officers were rewarded with advancement and the incompetent but important were sidelined. But Franco was also prepared for confrontation. This had occurred even during the war, with the clearest threat coming from Mola, who clashed with Franco over military strategy and on political matters. In particular, Mola favoured the retention of many of the rights and reforms granted under the Republic and was critical of the moves towards a full dictatorship. The two men clashed on a number of occasions. An open rift was only avoided by Mola's death in an aircrash in June 1937: another potential rival to Franco fortuitously removed by a timely accident. Challenges also came from Queipo de Llano who increasingly resented the erection of a Franco regime, and from Juan Yagüe who was the only senior figure closely associated with radical Falangism. Criticism from these two figures became so great that

Franco acted in 1938 to curb Queipo's power in his fiefdom and dismissed Yagüe from his command – only to reinstate him later on.[23]

The second main institutional 'family' that checked the influence of the FET was the church.[24] While the military became an integral part of the new regime, the church was accorded a slightly different status. Spanish Catholics (with the notable exception of the Basques) had been overwhelmingly supportive of the Nationalists and had been horrified by the violence against priests and nuns in the Republican zone at the beginning of the war. Religious practice certainly grew in Nationalist territory, for reasons of conviction but also because it became another badge of loyalty to the cause. Accordingly, the church had quickly lent strong moral and material support and acquiesced in the Crusade rhetoric used to characterise the Nationalist cause. The personnel of the church had been active in the war effort: every unit in the army had its priest, military and political banners were usually blessed, and the church's charitable and medical institutions were put into service. In return, the hierarchy, led by the primate Cardinal Isidro Gomá and the Vatican, looked to the new regime to defend religious rights and to restore the privileges of the church after the secular reforms which had been carried out during the Republic. This had effectively been promised in December 1936, in an informal agreement signed between Cardinal Gomá and Franco which guaranteed religious freedom and offered protection for the church's cultural and social activities. Significantly, the collective letter signed by the Spanish bishops six months later did not specifically endorse any particular form of future government.

It was understandable, however, that both the church and the formative new state should seek to retain a certain distance. Though a practising Catholic, Franco had no wish to see the regime become a confessional state, submerged by the influence of the church. Nor did the church hierarchy or the Vatican want to find themselves endorsing a regime they were not completely sure of, particularly when one section of Catholics in Spain was suffering at its hands. There was also tension over the position of the large network of lay Catholic organisations created under the doctrine of social Catholicism. These included student and women's groups, trade unions, rural banks and syndicates, and political parties. The last of these, particularly the CEDA, was absorbed into the FET but the unification decree also declared all other organisations to be part of the single party. This led to the eventual absorption of most of the Catholic bodies that were not strictly religious in nature into their party equivalents. Surprisingly little protest came from the church, largely because it was assumed that the regime would uphold the very Catholic doctrines that these organisations had existed to defend. Evidence for this included the presence of convinced Catholics in government, which persuaded the church that religious interests were safe and that its views would be listened to. The church also received a variety of commitments including: restoration of the state subsidy abolished by the Republic; the right to maintain its own education system; a role in censorship; and a virtual monopoly over marriage and definitions of public and private morality.

From this position the church was particularly dedicated to resisting Falangist influence in education. This had been the overwhelming concern of the wartime Minister of Education Sainz Rodríguez, for example. After the war, the church was able to retain control over education since José Ibáñez Martín, minister from 1939 until 1951, came from the influential lay group, Catholic Action, which supplied many of the representatives of the church in early cabinets and staffed appointment boards in schools and universities. Martín Artajo, Foreign Minister from 1945 until 1957, was also associated with Catholic Action. At the same time, the church was also allowed to maintain its extensive national press network, and the organisations of Catholic Action and the influential National Association of Catholic Propagandists (Acción Católica Nacional de Propagandistas, ACNP) which, though defined as 'cultural' bodies, were influential in Catholic politics. It also gained control of a new research institute, the prestigious Consejo Superior de Investigaciones Científicas (CSIC), set up in 1939, which was dominated by another principal lay Catholic group, the elitist Opus Dei.

The result of the compromise between church and state was that the Franco regime was by no means a theocracy but was to have a strong clerical influence and made extensive use of religious symbolism. The lines of demarcation between the church and the New State remained blurred, neither completely separated nor totally integrated. While in religious affairs the church was guaranteed total freedom, underwriting its mission to re-evangelise Spain, it was unclear how far its influence extended into more secular affairs. Its rights in some areas were effectively reduced, as the regime would permit no challenge to its monopoly of public organisations, but in other areas they were entrenched. In many respects there were strong similarities with the concordats that the Vatican achieved in fascist Italy and Nazi Germany. What was different was the importance placed by the Franco regime on its Catholic credentials. This was in line with the way in which rightist political ideology of all persuasions owed a great deal to Catholicism and looked to church teaching as a model. The CEDA, Carlists and monarchists all trumpeted Catholic credentials, and even the majority of Falangists, save an outspoken anti-clerical clique, endorsed the importance of the church as part of the traditions of the 'true Spain'. This allowed the regime to draw upon a tradition of Catholic authoritarianism, as well as on its pledges to defend religion, to declare itself not only national syndicalist but also national Catholic in nature – a description the church was only too happy to endorse.

THE EVOLUTION OF INTERNAL DISPUTES

With the battle lines within the regime drawn up, a struggle over Falangist influence rapidly took hold in 1940. Most military leaders and Catholics, joined by conservative voices within the FET ranging from Carlists to Alfonsine monarchists, acted to rein in any tendency towards national syndicalism. The first casualty was Muñoz Grandes, who resigned from his post in March 1940, unable to cope with the difficulties of running the party under this pressure.[25] Significantly, rather than replacing him immediately, Franco chose to leave the post open pending future developments, which left its everyday administration in the hands of the vice secretary, Gamero del Castillo. Meanwhile, protests at the proposed Law of Organisation led by the Carlist and strongly anti-Falangist generals Aranda and Vigón persuaded Franco to intervene to have the project quietly downplayed. In fact the officer corps became increasingly determined to downgrade or eliminate the whole of the FET from government and the administration. Such an aim had little chance of complete success, however, as it pitted the military against the whole of the civilian political class, not just the Falangists. The regime would have been left without any independent political base or much of its administrative organisation.

Tensions burst to the surface again during a further reallocation of cabinet posts in May 1941. Serrano Suñer had already been moved to the Foreign Ministry, maintaining his position as a prominent Falangist figure in a very important post in the midst of the Second World War. He continued to suggest the need for greater party control over the regime, turning him in the process into the *bête noire* of non-Falangists who resented both his influence as 'brother-in-law-in-chief' (*el cuñadísimo*) and his arrogance. Meanwhile FET newspapers editorialised on the need for a party-dominated government that would diminish the role of non-Falangists, in line with the world of fascist powers that seemed to have dawned in the rest of Europe. Franco appeared to agree with this when he gave the Ministry of Labour to an old guard Falangist, Antonio Girón. However, the next appointment as Minister of the Interior – considered by the Falangists to be their terrain – was allocated to a military monarchist, Colonel Valentín Galarza, for the sake of balance. Other posts went to representatives from the armed forces, to Carlists and to monarchists. A furore of Falangist protests was followed by an equally vociferous reaction from within the military. Franco stepped in to placate both sides by keeping Galarza but rewarding the FET with further cabinet posts, including a new secretary general of the party, José Luis de Arrese.[26]

On the surface, the result of these balancing acts seemed to be stalemate. But in fact the tide was turning against the Falangists. In part this was due to internal developments within the FET as a whole. Membership had continued to mushroom, reaching just under one million members in 1942, with jobs in the numerous parallel state organisations a major part of the attraction. Corruption was rife and graft prevailed. There were also continuing complaints from within the party that ideologically unreliable elements, including former Republicans, had infiltrated its ranks. Though there had been minor purges of the party during the war to weed out undesirables, pressure to take more drastic action mounted in peacetime. As secretary general, Arrese initiated a campaign to clean up the FET and regulate membership at the end of 1941, but this quickly fuelled a struggle within the FET. Political and personal rivalries were fought out at every level of organisation as purge committees looked over the backgrounds of party members. Although only 6000 were eventually expelled over a number of years, the investigations helped bring the party under the closer control of its leadership. Despite being an old guard Falangist himself, Arrese put in his own supporters with the connivance of the Carlists and monarchists and largely broke Serrano's influence in the FET.[27] Franco also seized the opportunity to order an internal reorganisation, abolishing the national delegations in favour of four vice-secretariats with a whole range of responsibilities.[28] The effect of this was to streamline the FET but also to emphasise the limits to its administrative authority.

Though increasingly isolated and weakened by Arrese, radical Falangists continued to press for greater party control and a national syndicalist state. Some, such as the poet Dionisio Ridruejo, even quit the FET and plotted against Franco from outside its ranks. In turn other parties in the FET and the military continued to demand decisive action to bring the Falangist element under control. Various clashes and incidents occurred, but in August 1942 a full internal political crisis erupted after a hand grenade was thrown by a group of Falangist students into a Carlist crowd at a religious procession in Begoña (near Bilbao), wounding many and killing two people. The army arrested and tried by court martial six Falangists, one of whom was executed. Senior officers, led by Varela and Galarza, demanded immediate action to control the Falangists and pressed for the dismissal of Serrano Suñer. Franco responded in September with a reshuffle that finally eliminated Serrano from government but merely swapped the fractious army officers for new military blood.[29]

Once again, balance was apparently maintained. Yet this struggle marked a decisive shift in the orientation of the upper reaches of the regime as a whole. There was no question of disbanding the FET, as the military would have liked; it was too important a part of the regime and thus remained a powerful interest that continued to compete for its share of the administrative and political spoils. In particular, labour relations, control of propaganda and the press, housing and social security remained special preserves of the party. Nor did radical Falangism die out – though many Falangists did just that in service with the Blue Division that fought with the Germans on the eastern front. However, from 1942 onwards the concept of a party regime, to say nothing of a state-backed Falangist revolution, declined in importance. Much of the rhetoric of the FET remained the same, including the veneration of José Antonio – much to the disgust of the old guard who felt he must be turning in his grave at the misrepresentation of his ideas. Official doctrine even played up some of the features of Falangist thinking, most especially in its version of the leader principle, dubbed the *teoría de caudillaje*, which stressed the centrality of

Franco to the regime. An additional spur to this reinterpretation of the official line was provided by the clear signs that the Axis powers were losing the war, making it a good moment to distance the regime from overt fascism. Accordingly, much of FET symbolism was quietly dropped for official occasions, though it continued in many of the provinces – the straight-armed salute being the first thing to go.

The marginalisation of radical Falangism resolved the first major political tension within the Francoist coalition. It confirmed the limits of the national syndicalist revolution and showed that ultimately the party was the creature of the regime, albeit of vital importance to it. Conservatives and reactionaries could breath a small sigh of relief, but the main burden of elaborating some plausible ideological alternative for the regime now fell to them. This task was made even more difficult by the hostility of the victorious Allied powers to former friends of the Axis. The pressure to live down the past and find some means to survive in a western Europe dominated by reconstructed liberal-democratic states became intense. The regime was now faced with the task of legitimising itself, not just internally but also externally.

One set of developments that could be exploited in pursuit of this goal was the creation of a 'legal' framework to govern the operation of the new state. In a country where law was the most popular university discipline, the idea of a codified administrative system had a powerful appeal in and of itself. It was a sign of the permanence of the regime as well as an opportunity to present Francoist rule as something other than a naked dictatorship which carved up power amongst its supporters. The first attempt at such 'constitutional cosmetics', as they have been called, was the opening of a parliament (Cortes) in 1943.[30] Unelected and made up of state appointees and representatives of different administrative and party organisations, it had no real power, played no active part in the government and could only debate laws introduced to it. The formula was applied again in July 1945 with the issuing of the *Fuero de los Españoles*, putatively a bill of citizen's rights based in part on the monarchist constitution of 1876. Most of these rights were bogus and in no way even hinted at basic democratic norms of freedom of speech, assembly and organisation. The charter was clearly for foreign consumption, an attempt to further distance the regime from the defeated fascist powers.

To this liberal facade was added the curious notion, repeated by Franco *ad nauseam* after it was invented in 1944, that Spain was now an 'organic popular democracy' rather than a dictatorial state – the distinction with 'inorganic' democracy being that the divisiveness of unconstrained political competition, with the attendant threat of communist subversion, was removed. At the high-point of international pressure in 1945–6, the regime promised a variety of pseudo-elections. These were not, of course, to involve independent political parties – or even the FET too directly – but were based on corporatist notions of representation. Accordingly, elections to reformed municipal councils were promised in October 1945, on a franchise consisting of household heads and the leaders of economic syndicates. In March 1946 elections on a similar basis to some of the Cortes seats were announced. Few within Spain took this spurious legalism seriously. Debate was only possible within the narrow terms defined by the regime, and political power clearly remained exclusively in the hands of the Francoist coalition.

To accompany these attempts at constitutionalism, Arrese, backed by the Carlists and Alfonsine monarchists in the party, refashioned official doctrine to stress the Catholic roots of the FET and the importance of traditional Spanish institutions to the regime. As national syndicalism was downplayed so national Catholicism was boosted. The main source of ideas and personnel was Catholic Action and in particular the Acción Católica Nacional de Propagandistas (ACNP), which endorsed a Catholic version of the dictatorial state complete with its own notions of corporatism. Personalities associated with the ACNP were also increasingly drawn into the government. The most significant of these was Martín Atajo, the head of Catholic Action, who was appointed Foreign Minister in July 1945. During the same cabinet reshuffle, the faithful Arrese was himself dismissed as Secretary General of the FET; the post was left vacant, further emphasising the decline of Falangist influence. By these means the regime sought to draw once again upon the imagery of the Crusade, to present itself as the defender of religious values and the institutions of the church.

Although the Vatican remained wary of moving too quickly into an official concordat – after having its fingers burned by its close relationships with the Nazi and fascist dictatorships – the church remained strongly identified with the regime. While some members of the hierarchy had become disillusioned, including Cardinal Gomá, most remained enthusiastic adherents of Franco-ism.[31] Religion had become a prominent part of public life, with few events not including the participation of priests. The walls of churches throughout Spain were inscribed with the names of José Antonio and Franco, and lists of the clergy and local Nationalists 'murdered by the reds' in the civil war were displayed next to altars. Religious observance remained in part a means of showing allegiance to the regime. The church exhorted its followers to play a part in the regime, but only as long as they did so in order to support religious values. In return the church had its privileged position confirmed with the restoration of state subsidies, gaining a monopoly over primary education and an important role in censorship and the framing of social legislation. In 1945, the Catholic press was given greater liberty to publish and the following year the creation of a new organisation aimed at promoting Catholic concerns amongst workers, the HOAC (Hermandades Obreras de Acción Católica), was officially sanctioned.

Moves to modify the image of the regime had the effect of emboldening the ill-defined (non-Carlist) monarchist faction to press their claims even harder, to the extent that they began to be perceived almost as an internal opposition. For

former members of Renovación Española, many military officers and Catholics
– including ministers like Martín Atajo – the restoration of the Alfonsine
monarchy continued to be an important political aspiration. The death of
Alfonso XIII in 1941 had left his son, Don Juan, as the heir to the throne. As the
war had turned against the Axis, some monarchists within the regime thought
that the tide of events was turning in their favour, and that Franco would
shortly be forced to resign. Consequently, in 1943 a small group of *procuradores*
(parliamentary deputies), including army officers and even prominent Falangists, petitioned the dictator to return Spain to a monarchist state. The
fortuitous conversion of Don Juan to the cause of constitutional monarchy
allowed his supporters to present him as a respectable third way between the
dictatorship and a revived Republic.[32] Exchanges of confidential letters between
Don Juan and Franco, and attempts to create a united monarchist front within
the regime, followed but to no great effect. In March 1945, on the eve of the
Allied victory, Don Juan issued an open manifesto from his Swiss residence in
exile calling for a constitutional monarchy and demanding Franco's resignation. A year later, he moved to Portugal and renewed efforts both to negotiate
with Franco and to mobilise the monarchists within the regime. Petitions and
plots flourished once again; the most serious involved a letter of support for
Don Juan signed by 458 members of the Francoist political elite, including
former ministers and high-ranking officers.

As it turned out, these efforts to remove Franco by threats and persuasion
actually strengthened the regime. Monarchism went some way towards creating
a facade of political pluralism and the 'normalisation' of the regime away from
fascism. Moreover, in view of the search for international respectability, the
monarchists represented an opportunity to show another face of the regime. And
they helped shape debate about Franco's successor, for even the Caudillo realised
that some arrangement would have to be made in this respect. Franco was not in
principle opposed to the monarchy as an institution, though he did distrust Don
Juan. He therefore played the situation very carefully, continuing to negotiate
but never giving an inch on his own position. And the monarchists could not
bring themselves to break completely with a regime which they had contributed
to establishing, even when they were urged to resign by Don Juan and his chief
advisor, Gil Robles, erstwhile leader of the CEDA. Thus, while they constituted
no real threat at all, they helped give the impression, particularly to the outside
world, that there was a kind of political debate within Francoism.

To foreign ambassadors as well as to the monarchists themselves, Franco
dangled the possibility of a non-Francoist alternative in Spain. In 1947 proposals
for a new Law of Succession were put forward. This was largely drafted by Luis
Carrero Blanco, a future admiral and the subservient close advisor to the
dictator. Carrero urged Franco to give no substantial ground to monarchism but
to use the opportunity to legitimise the regime. Accordingly, the law stated that
Franco would remain head of state until death or incapacity, and would name his

royal successor. The future king would have to swear loyalty to the regime and to the National Movement. In the meantime, Spain was declared to be a Catholic kingdom. It simply lacked a reigning monarch. Despite the protests of Don Juan, the law was ratified by the Cortes in June and put to a national referendum (another measure introduced to give a pseudo-democratic tone) in July. Relations between Franco and the pretender to the throne wavered between coolness and hostility, but contacts continued. Finally, in 1948, after a personal meeting, it was agreed that Don Juan's son should be brought up and educated within Spain. This began the process whereby Juan Carlos would be trained to become Franco's successor, bypassing the claims of Don Juan to the throne. But for the time being monarchism had proved a paper tiger and the regime emerged from this challenge as firmly entrenched as ever.

The relative ease with which Franco manipulated the monarchists was due to a number of fundamental weaknesses in their position. They were divided in their political opinions between those who favoured a more liberal monarchy and outright reactionaries who wanted Francoism but with a king as head of state. This division was to haunt the monarchists throughout the life of the dictatorship. Consequently, it was impossible for them to act with any real unity of purpose, allowing Franco to divide and rule in his accustomed fashion. Attempts to organise a monarchist opposition foundered in great part because of this division, and also as a result of the ruthlessness with which the regime responded to those individuals who were seen as having gone too far in their actions or opinions. They also lacked a solid constituency of support that could be drawn upon to put substantial pressure on Franco. The closest adherents of the monarchy tended to be part of the social and political elites, continuing a tradition dating back to Renovación Española. Hence, monarchists were well represented within the regime but they had no controlling interest in any of the main institutions and forces. Even the army – the closest thing to a bastion of monarchism – could not be said to be dominated by them. The monarchy had been rejected by all Republicans but it had also been discredited in the eyes of many on the right by its failure to prevent the creation of the Republic in the first place. Here also lay its fundamental flaw as an alternative to Francoism. At the end of the day, the regime was regarded as the saviour of the very conservative classes that monarchism sought to represent. Even the monarchy's most fervent supporters came running back to the regime when there was any chance of serious conflict that might undermine it. Most of them swallowed their resolve in the face of Franco's intransigence and accepted his limited terms for fear of opening the way to something worse – a return to the Republic.

CONCLUSION

In many respects the Franco regime was at its most stable and at the height of its power during the 1940s. The dictatorship was able to impose itself on

Spanish society and was able to resist all challenges from within and without. From its inception in the midst of the civil war it had rallied a powerful and relatively diverse base of active and tacit support. A network of mutual self-interest bound together this coalition, giving its partners strong incentives to stay within the regime. Although internal divisions and disputes were never overcome, they allowed a policy of divide and rule to operate and provided the regime with a fund of new political possibilities to draw upon. Thus it was possible for the outward character of the dictatorship to evolve, switching images between the radical fascist and Catholic and conservative. At the same time it retained its fundamental features, born in the civil war, perhaps the most important being the figure of General Franco himself.

NOTES

1 The comments of Sainz Rodríguez are to be found in the discussion documents presented before the cabinet. 'Informes de Ley de Responsibilidades Políticas', Archivo General de la Administración Central (AGAC), Presidencia de Gobierno, Caja 4022. Numerous examples of cases processed under the law are also to be found in this archive.

2 See José A. Ferrer Benimeli, 'Franco y la masonería' in Josep Fontana, ed., *España bajo el franquismo* (Barcelona, 1986). pp. 246–68.

3 For an excellent recent discussion of the objectives and victims of the repression, see Michael Richards, 'Civil War, Violence and the Construction of Francoism', in Paul Preston and Ann Edwards, eds., *The Republic Besieged. Civil War in Spain, 1936–1939* (Edinburgh, 1996), pp. 197–239. See also Francisco Moreno Gómez, 'La represión en la España campesina', in J. L. García Delgado *et al.*, eds., *El primer franquismo* (Madrid, 1989), pp. 189–207 and *Córdoba en la posguerra* (Madrid, 1990); F. Cobo Romero, *La Guerra Civil y la represión franquista en la provincia de Jáen* (Jáen, 1992); Josep Solé I Sabaté, *La repressió franquista a Catalunya* (Barcelona, 1985); Ramón García Piñeiro, *Los mineros asturianos bajo el franquismo* (Madrid, 1990).

4 Figures from Gabriel Jackson, *The Spanish Republic and the Civil War in Spain, 1931–1939* (Princeton, 1965), p. 539 and Ramón Salas Larrazábal, *Pérdidas de la guerra* (Barcelona, 1977). On the continued dispute over the numbers of deaths, and broader comments on the analysis of the repression, see also Alberto Reig Tapia, *Ideología e historia: Sobre la represión franquista y la Guerra Civil* (Madrid, 1984) and *Violencia y terror: estudios sobre la Guerra Civil* (Madrid, 1990); P. Preston, 'The Politics of Revenge: Francoism, the Civil War and Collective Memory', in P. Preston, *The Politics of Revenge* (London, 1990), pp. 33–4.

5 Figures cited in Stanley Payne, *The Franco Regime, 1936–1975* (Madison, 1987) pp. 222–7 and in 'Estadística de los Juzgados Instructores Provincials de Responsabilidades Políticas, December 1941', AGAC, Presidencia de Gobierno, Caja 4020.

6 Harmut Heine, *La oposición política al franquismo* (Barcelona, 1983), pp. 157–214.

7 On the guerrilla struggle, see Daniel Arasa, *Años 40: Los maquis y el PCE* (Barcelona, 1984); Enrique Marco Nadal, *Todos contra Franco* (Madrid, 1982); Carlos Kaiser, *La guerrilla antifranquista: historia del maquis* (Madrid, 1976). An example of resistance by Republican army stragglers is given in Justo Vila Izquierdo, *La guerrilla antifranquista en Extremadura* (Badajoz, 1986).

8 For details see Chapter 6. Also Rafael Abella, *La vida cotidiana en España bajo el régimen de Franco* (Barcelona, 1985).

9 Miguel Aparicio, *El sindicalismo vertical y la formación del estado franquista* (Barcelona, 1980).

10 For details of policy and its effects see Chapter 5.

11 The most important were in Barcelona, Madrid and the Basque country. They coincided with the high point of regime fears of Allied intervention against Spain after the Second World War. See Sebastian Balfour, *Dictatorship, Workers and the City. Labour in Greater Barcelona since 1939* (Oxford, 1989), pp. 9–12.

12 The classic example of these demands was José María de Areilza and Fernando María Castiella, *Reivindicaciones de España* (Madrid, 1941).

13 The best recent interpretation of wartime intentions is given in Paul Preston, *Franco* (London, 1993).

14 Details given in Chapter 7.

15 The concept of 'families' has been much debated. Some have seen in their existence evidence of the 'limited pluralism' of the regime while others stress the strongly dictatorial character of the Francoist state. Rival interpretations are offered by Juan Linz, 'Spain: An Authoritarian Regime', in E. Allardt and Y. Littunen, eds., *Cleavages, Ideologies and Party Systems* (Helsinki, 1964) and Eduardo Sevilla Guzmán and Salvador Giner, 'Asolutismo despotíco y dominación de clase: el caso de España', *Cuadernos de Ruedo Ibérico 43–4* (1975). Still the best overall study is Amando de Miguel, *Sociología del franquismo* (Barcelona, 1975).

16 His views can be gleaned from Alfredo Kindelán, *La verdad de mis relaciones con Franco* (Barcelona, 1981).

17 For an analysis of the recruitment, training and role of officials see Julián Alvarez Alvarez, *Burocracía y poder político en el régimen franquista: el papel de los cuerpos de funcionarios entre 1938 y 1975* (Alcalá de Henares, 1984).

18 Payne, *Franco Regime*, p. 234.

19 Payne, *Franco Regime*, pp. 235–6.

20 On the activities of the Falangists in general, see Ricardo Chueca, *El fascismo en los comienzos del régimen de Franco* (Madrid, 1983) and Sheelagh Ellwood, *Prietas las filas. Historia de Falange Española, 1933–1983* (Barcelona, 1984).

21 For a general discussion, see Stanley Payne, *Politics and the Military in Modern Spain* (Stanford, 1967), Chapter 22.

22 Carlos Viver Pi Sunyer, *El personal político de Franco* (Barcelona, 1978), pp. 70–2.

23 For the position of the military, and on these problems, see Carlos Fernández, *Tensiones militares durante el franquismo* (Barcelona, 1985). Paul Preston, 'Franco and his Generals, 1939–1945', in P. Preston, *The Politics of Revenge*, pp. 85–108 also offers a succinct analysis.

24 For most of what follows see Frances Lannon, *Privilege, Persecution and Prophecy. The Catholic Church in Spain, 1875–1975* (Oxford, 1987), Chapter 8; Guy Hermet, *Los católicos en la España franquista* (Madrid, 1985).

25 Payne, *Franco Regime*, p. 258 comments. Muñoz Grandes was later to command the Spanish Blue Division on the Russian front.

26 Payne, *Franco Regime*, pp. 285–8.

27 Chueca, *El fascismo*, pp. 196–8 and Ellwood, *Prietas las filas*, pp. 128–30, give details.

28 The four vice-secretariats were: Movement (responsible for party organisation); Social Works (syndicates and war veterans' association); Popular Education (press, propaganda

and education); Services (a huge range of activities including health, recreation and sport).

29 Preston, *Franco*, pp. 465–72 gives an analysis of the incident and Serrano's fall. Payne, *Franco Regime*, pp. 309–11 details the new cabinet.

30 The phrase is used by Raymond Carr and J. P. Fusi, *Spain: Dictatorship to Democracy* 2nd edn (London, 1981), pp. 40–8.

31 On Gomá see Lannon, *Privilege*, p. 216. He died in 1940 shortly after some mildly conciliatory pastoral letters he had produced were banned by the regime.

32 For what follows see Heine, *La oposición política*, pp. 251–95, 351–68; José María Gil Robles, *La monarquía por la que yo luché* (Madrid, 1976).

3

The Search for Continuity and Consolidation, 1950–1966

In this chapter we discuss the politics, understood broadly, of the regime. We will look at state policies and especially at how political decisions were shaped by social relationships. The chapter analyses inter-elite politics and the struggles for power within the authoritarian alliance; it draws attention to the shifting importance of the figure of Franco himself and to the political changes inside the dictatorship after the collapse of autarky; and it explains how some fragile spaces for political expression were opened up after 1960 for non-regime supporters, when politics ceased to be exclusively the preserve of Francoist elites. External relations are not discussed here, but in Chapter 7, below.

The primary political task facing the Franco regime at the beginning of the 1950s was still that of long-term consolidation. Having survived the immediate aftermath of the civil war, Francoism now faced a two-fold challenge: how to embed itself institutionally and how to maintain its support in society. Stability required that the state represent and protect the social and political groups which had made up the Nationalist camp and which now formed part of the authoritarian coalition. The civil war had been, overwhelmingly, a social struggle and the *raison d'être* of the regime was to institutionalise that victory. As George Collier argues, the Franco regime constituted, 'the uncontested reign of property'.[1] But stabilising the regime in power required much more than keeping the Nationalist supporters on board. It meant creating a set of institutions and a state which would be able to maintain an equilibrium among the regime's somewhat disparate supporters from the political right and the propertied classes. It also required the creation of a state which would prove effective at policy-making and at preventing and neutralising opposition from inside Spain and from beyond the frontiers. Finally, stability required that the regime deal effectively with the question of the succession.

As a first and important step towards consolidation, the regime had succeeded in centralising power. This was a very significant achievement in Spain. It owed much to the fact that Franco himself was at the apex of the state, thereby providing a figure and a figurehead who continued to legitimise the regime until his death in the eyes of all the social groups who were within the authoritarian alliance. But the persistence in power of Franco himself was not enough on its own to justify the dictatorship. And ultimately it also weakened the regime. The political structures of the dictatorship could not be separated from the figure of Franco, who provided a focus for opposition and a reminder that the regime had emerged out of a long and bloody civil war. This was to condemn the regime to a slow and painful withering, as Franco himself declined in health and vitality.

But the authoritarian regime was not a personal dictatorship in the traditional sense of the term. Personalism is generally taken to imply that the dictator, in conjunction with a small coterie of friends and/or family, is able to choose policy and has exclusive access to the state. In a personal dictatorship, the state is run as if it were a family enterprise and the jobs within the state, including cabinet positions, are within the gift of the dictator. Individuals within the government are loyal only to the dictator. This chapter will analyse Francoism, conceptualising it as a system based on aggregating the interests of a variety of social groups which together made up the social base of the dictatorship. It depended on support from social and economic elites from within Spanish society. This meant that there were important constraints on policies, on the one hand, but also that no one group or individual could consistently dominate policy-making. These constraints were embedded in the very structures of the dictatorship in the form of the powerful institutional state apparatus which developed.

Perhaps the biggest threat to the regime in the 1950s was the considerable economic vulnerability which resulted from a combination of the legacy of the civil war, bad policy-making since 1939, comparative economic backwardness and isolation. The survival of the regime depended on tackling at least some of the economic and social problems which beset the country. This had become evident by 1956. But tackling the economic problems was to have the effect, as we shall see, of increasing the tensions between the Francoist supporters. In particular, it meant that the regime had to choose between Falangist and technocratic policies, and between protecting the idealised rural world of Old Castile and creating a system which would favour emerging new economic groups. In policy terms, by the 1960s it was evident that the regime was making irreversible choices in favour of industrialists, foreign investors and a new bureaucratic service sector. But a peculiar skill was exercised in keeping virtually the entire authoritarian camp on board through constant reference to a state doctrine which emphasised Spain's national identity, its national Catholicism and its anti-communism.

By the mid-1960s, the regime approximated to Juan Linz's description of a stable authoritarian regime, characterised by 'limited, non-responsive, political pluralism: without an elaborate and guiding ideology (but with a distinctive mentality); without intensive or extensive political mobilisation ... and in which a leader ... exercises power within formally ill-defined limits but actually quite predictable ones'.[2] This signified a major change from early efforts to create a totalitarian state. It was achieved through relaxing the overt ideological onslaught of national Catholicism the regime had initiated in the 1940s, through promoting pro-capitalist industrialisation which forced an opening up of the country to foreign influences and through a reluctant tolerance of limited dissent. It was accompanied by an approach to economic policy-making (though not politics) which was technocratic and modernist. However, the changes which Francoism underwent in this period in economic policy and the modest, unstable liberalisation which it inaugurated were not necessarily contiguous. So the regime did not actually possess the coherence which can be imposed on it with hindsight. Indeed, in spite of the progress in moving the regime towards consolidation, it is possible to argue that the reforms actually made it less coherent.

There were, therefore, turbulent and difficult times in the 1950s. Firm commitment to autarky remained government policy. In many ways, autarky triumphed because it was not simply an economic model but signified rather a means through which the status quo among the victors of 1939 could be preserved. It had a political rationale. It complemented the belief in the superiority of the rural way of life over life in towns. The regime still proclaimed in the 1950s 'the sovereignty of the peasantry' and treated small-holders as the embodiment of true Spanish values.[3] This was accompanied until 1959 by intervention by the Francoist-created National Wheat Service to protect the smallholding cereal producer of the central plain from the vagaries of the market.

After 1959, the process of industrial development on which the government embarked meant that it was no longer able to disseminate quite so successsfully the view that the 'good life' was lived in the countryside, since industrialisation required pro-active policies on the part of the state to encourage migration to the cities. In fact, as early as 1951, the idealisation of rural life and government-proclaimed commitments to small landholders were compromised, in fact if not ideologically, on the one hand by the influence of large landowners or *lat-ifundistas* and on the other by the decision to build national industry through the Instituto Nacional de Industria (INI). Another example of how the regime effectively abandoned the small peasantry in policy terms was the fate of the Law of Manifestly Improvable Farms, which was passed in 1953. Radical in its conception, it allowed for the expropriation of under-cultivated farms to be redistributed to smallholders. In theory, therefore, it attacked the very basis of the *latifundia*. The price of implementation would have been to break the Nationalist alliance and exclude the large landowners from the Francoist camp. But like other radical measures of the early period, it was ineffectual in practice and left completely unenforced.

In 1952, as the worst of the shortages were over, rationing came to an end. This did not mean the beginning of a generalised prosperity, however.

Economic policy-making was proving so disastrous that, by the end of the decade, the government chose to put into effect the most decisive policy change of the entire dictatorship. Autarky was brought to a close and instead a strategy of encouraging industrialisation through foreign capital was adopted. As a consequence of that decision, a plan to stabilise the Spanish economy followed, along with the decision to seek multinational investment, to encourage tourism and to apply for membership of the European Economic Community (EEC). All of this was to modify the social base of the dictatorship, though it was accomplished for the most part without definitively eliminating any of the Nationalist camp. Ultimately, it was also to change the economic geography of Spain, its culture and its society, and it was to force significant adaptations to the regime's ideology. These changes were implemented between 1957 and 1962.

Meanwhile, political changes were occurring too. There were cracks in the state's control of labour and the universities. There were also struggles between competing political groups for the direction of the Francoist state. While the monarchists seemed more convinced in the belief that a monarchy would replace Franco, this was as yet by no means secure. And what kind of monarchy would it be? Would it be the 'traditional monarchy' to which Franco made repeated references? Would it owe its legitimacy to the Bourbon line of succession or to the fundamental principles laid down by the authoritarian state? Would it be the restoration of the monarchy or the establishment of a new monarchy, representing the Francoist regime? Would the future king be Don Juan, the successor to Alfonso XIII, or his son, Juan Carlos, educated in Spain according to Franco's instructions since 1948? None of these questions were clarified.

Meanwhile, the Falangists were attempting to adapt, unsuccessfully, to the changing circumstances of Spain in the 1950s. In the middle of the decade, an important clash took place between the monarchists and the Falange over the future of the dictatorship, or what would happen 'the day when Spain loses its Caudillo', as Francoists generally phrased it. By the 1960s, it was becoming evident that the Falangists had lost the fight and they were increasingly marginalised, though the National Movement – as it was now mostly called – continued to throw up ideas and policy suggestions for the regime. After 1957, the official face of the regime was increasingly the new technocratic group, Opus Dei, whose rhetoric, vocabulary and dress even, appeared more in tune with the contemporary world. They were both more homogeneous and more conservative than the Falange, and much more in tune with monarchism.

Labour protest increased in the early 1960s, especially in Madrid, Catalonia and Asturias. Until 1966, the government response was relatively moderate, and the official unions, under Falangist influence, and the Ministry of Labour, reluctantly and ambiguously attempted co-optation or even tolerance. This liberalisation even spread to other areas. There was a modicum of tolerance for Catalan as a social, though not political, language and in 1966 press censorship was lifted. This move was orchestrated by Manuel Fraga, Minister of Information and Tourism, who was committed to some opening up of the regime as a way both to change and to preserve it. The move had always been opposed by the former censor, Gabriel Arias Salgado. In retrospect, these policies can be seen to be the culmination of this period of tentative, ambiguous and reluctant opening up. It was to come to an end later in the decade as protests from workers, students and regionalists increased. In 1964, the regime launched a campaign to celebrate its 'achievements', entitled 'the Twenty-Five Years of Peace'. This was followed by the Organic Law of the State, approved by referendum in 1966 and promulgated in January 1967. Fresh, though temporary, strength flowed into the government as a result and allowed it to have the confidence to bring to a close the period of limited tolerance of dissent in the union ranks and open a new phase of repression.

INSIDE THE AUTHORITARIAN ALLIANCE

The balance of power between the 'insider' groups was changing. This was to become even more marked by the 1960s. The institutions which exercised most authority within the authoritarian alliance in the 1950s were still the army and, rather more diffusely, the church. The Falange retained a degree of structural importance and access to the cabinet but its input into policy was increasingly weakened and it gradually lost force. It made bids for power during these years which failed to do more than temporarily halt its decline. By the 1960s, the Alfonsine monarchists increased their role within the state, partly by identifying themselves with the new bureaucratic elite which was being created within the economic policy-making sphere. Meanwhile, policy changes meant that the 'popular' elements of the Nationalist coalition in the 1930s and 1940s, the small peasantry, lost out and were definitively excluded from the policy-making process.

A variety of social groups had representation within the state, therefore; but the state also developed an increased autonomy of action, especially during the 1960s. This was due to a greater professionalisation of functions within the state, making it harder for some elites to influence policy effectively. The internationalisation of the economy, which began in earnest in the 1960s, also rendered policy-making more complex than in the earlier period. It increased external constraints over policy, while making it less likely that those groups who opposed the trend of economic policy-making could change it. So the state acquired considerable latitude in terms of making policy and, as a result, the influence of the technocrats over policy decisions became greater.

By the mid-1960s, therefore, it could no longer be argued that policy was made by all groups within the authoritarian alliance. A restructuring of the

social base of Francoism had taken place. Some groups had become marginalised, while others enjoyed greater and more consistent access to
decision-making. But these changes within the state were to some degree
masked by the fact that Franco himself remained head of state. They were also
concealed by the persistence of the Nationalist ideology, forged in the 1930s,
within the formal discourse of the regime. Gilmour has written that 'General
Franco's dictatorship ... was based on a series of myths: myths about Spain,
about Spanish history, about Spanish values, even about the Spaniards themselves'.[4] What Gilmour describes as 'myths' constituted a binding ideology,
superior even to policy divisions, which brought together the followers of the
regime, and which were used to try and indoctrinate the mass of the population
through propaganda and education. To be a Spaniard was still primarily to be
Catholic. It was also to share a particular understanding of Spanish history –
the importance of the empire most notably. And it was to be committed to the
unity of the state centred on Castile, denying legitimacy to the political
expression, and indeed to most cultural manifestations, of regional identity. It
is not surprising that this was all bound together with a distrust for foreigners,
who were seen as potential sources of corruption of all that was pure.
Nationalism was widely used throughout this period and manipulated by the
government. Of course, the force of these ideas was weakening. It was difficult
to maintain an image of Spain as closed and uncontaminated by foreign ideas
after 1959 when foreign capital, foreign goods and foreign tastes – not to
mention foreign tourists – began to enter Spain with government encouragement. But, until the mid-1960s at least, a pretence was maintained. Even
thereafter, nationalism was the ultimate legitimation of the regime. It was to be
used against the emerging regionalist forces, against the trades unionists and in
order to animate foreign policy, as over the Gibraltar issue. It was not
surprising, then, that the real struggles which were taking place over policy
were concealed behind the cloak of the official Francoist ideology.

As we noted in the previous chapter, the army did not acquire institutional
authority during the war. The regime was not a military dictatorship and the
army was the instrument of the Nationalist coalition. After the war, the army
had been unable to dominate politics. The institutional strength of the armed
forces was weakened by the fact that Franco had removed generals who
opposed his personal authority or who wished to install a monarchical regime
from positions of power immediately after the war. But the army nonetheless
remained an important prop of the state and it continued to fulfil a number of
functions during this period. In particular, it played a role in the repressive
apparatus of the state. In 1958, military courts were given jurisdiction in cases
of serious political crimes. The army also had a guiding role over certain general
aspects of regime policy – commitment to the unity of the Spanish state and
anti-communism. But it was never called upon to exercise the power of veto
over government policies in defence of these principles because the Francoist

state signified their very incarnation. Rather than making policies, the army, ultimately, remained the guarantor that they would be carried out.

Although institutionally the army did not shape policies, certain individuals whose prestige depended on their belonging to the armed forces did directly influence the course of day-to-day politics. Some of Franco's most intimate collaborators came from the officer class. In particular, Admiral Carrero Blanco's star rose in this period, and he went on to become a major influence over the government. Using the office he had held since 1941 – under-secretary of the Prime Minister's Office (*Sub-Secretario de la Presidencia de Gobierno*) – he used his direct access to Franco to push the regime slowly in the direction of economic liberalisation, bureaucratic professionalisation and acceptance of a monarchical restoration after Franco's demise. He continued to play this role until his death at the hands of ETA in 1973. More generally, the regime could count on the support of most officers, whatever their political persuasions or personal relations with the Caudillo. For instance, General Muñoz Grandes entered the government in 1951 as Minister for the Army and served loyally, despite his pro-Falange, anti-monarchical sympathies. In fact, the officer class was a preferred option for cabinet: of the 120 cabinet ministers who served under Franco, 42 came from the armed forces. Many had links to other Francoist groups.[5] In this way the army participated in the dense network of contacts which bound the Francoist state together.

Of course there was always the possibility that some members of the armed forces might not agree with regime policies, though mainly the prospect of preferment for high-ranking officers, coupled with the mystique of the Nationalist victory, ensured army loyalty. Moreover, relations with the army were made easier with the signing of a deal with the US in 1953, which ensured a supply of weapons and *matériel* which the state was unable to provide due to the lack of sophisticated technological and industrial production in the country, and the fact that the military budget was spent primarily on salaries. If necessary, too, there were pressures which could be used to bring recalcitrant officers into line. Officers could be forced into retirement or even exile, if the temptation of posts in government and the administration was not sufficient to keep dissent to a minimum. For lower-ranking officers, the numbers of which had expanded significantly after the war, the situation was rather more complex. Low pay and poor promotion prospects remained a problem in the 1950s and 1960s. But it would have been 'unpatriotic' to bring these problems to the attention of a government which the army itself had brought to power. In any case, the institutional fate of the army appeared to be bound up with the regime itself, so it was much easier for the dictatorship to contain pressures from the armed forces than it would have been for any democracy.

Religion and politics were inextricably linked in the 1950s. To be a Catholic was almost certain to mean that one was Francoist too, although church and state were separate. It is true that the emergence of some Catholic opposition to

Franco in the form of the Gredos group, which included the philosopher José
Luis Aranguren, can be traced to the 1950s, but on the whole the church
remained a source of social support for the dictatorship. It constituted at this
time an essentially conservative force. This was as much a consequence of the
social profile of Catholicism in Spain at this time as it was a result of Catholic
doctrine. As Lannon has pointed out, it is quite simply wrong to imagine that
Spain was a country of churchgoers and practising Catholics until the liberalisation of the 1960s.[6] Catholicism did have an important popular presence in
the Basque provinces, especially Navarre, and in Old Castile. But in fact as
early as the beginning of the twentieth century church attendance was low and
anti-clericalism common in Extremadura, Andalusia and Catalonia. In these
provinces particularly, the Catholic church might justifiably be described as the
intellectual and moral property of the landed and the rich. With this in mind,
it is hardly surprising that until the 1960s the Catholic church, which benefited
from important concessions and was granted a significant power-base in the
educational system by the regime, constituted an important bulwark of the
regime. And while the church was an important institutional support for the
dictatorship until the 1960s, Catholicism, more diffusely, was part of the glue
binding together the Francoists. Even when the government moved towards
modernisation and technocracy, it relied on a socially conservative and Catholic
– therefore 'trustworthy' – movement to implement and oversee the process.
Opus Dei, a unique Catholic elite club, was entrusted with the task at the end
of the 1950s.[7]

In 1951, Joaquín Ruiz Giménez became Minister of Education, an appointment which was to last until the major restructuring of government in 1957. A
prominent Catholic intellectual, he oversaw the institutionalisation of the
relationship between church and state in 1953. The concordat of that year was
the symbol of the regime's doctrine of national Catholicism. It gave the state the
right of presentation of bishops, thereby ensuring a docile church hierarchy for
Franco, in return for recognition of the church's primacy in celebrating
marriage, the restoration of the clergy's legal privileges and a staunch entrench-
ment of the church within the educational system, including state funding for
religious schools. The church participated in state censorship, while increasing
the number of its own publications, particularly newspapers. In 1962, Catholic
publications were freed from the necessity of first passing through the censor's
hands, four years before press censorship was lifted.

The concordat meant that Franco was rewarded with loyalty from the
church until the 1960s. It was only at that point that sectors of the Catholic
church openly disassociated themselves from the regime. In fact, however, Ruiz
Giménez had attempted to liberalise some aspects of policy as Minister of
Education and there had been some cautious attempts to restructure the
universities to allow for greater freedom of thought and teaching. But the
impact of opposition from sections of the church in the 1960s was to be much

more substantial and sustained. Catholic groups came out in support of Basque nationalism, and were associated with the alternative trades unions, the Workers' Commissions, as well as with the opposition of the intelligentsia, expressed most noticeably though the journal *Cuadernos para el Diálogo*, founded by Ruiz Giménez himself. In fact, by the 1960s, it was no longer possible to speak of a 'church position' *vis-à-vis* the regime, with progressive sectors enthused by the teachings of the Second Vatican Council moving into open opposition and condemning authoritarianism. Conservative groups, by contrast, and perhaps particularly Opus Dei, continued to give support to the regime and uphold the necessity of dictatorial government. Opus Dei went on to expand its influence in government, the Consejo Superior de Investigaciones Científicas (CSIC) and the universities, and it became the main support for the regime from organised Catholicism.

Meanwhile, what did the policy changes of the 1950s and 1960s mean for the Falange, the basis for the official party of the regime? The Falange had expected to emerge from the civil war in a powerful ideological position within the regime. It had offered the clearest intellectual alternative to Republican politics and its ranks had been swollen after the conflict broke out by volunteers from the right. However, once the regime was established, the philosophical underpinning of the regime was increasingly provided by Catholicism. This was especially true after fascism was intellectually discredited at the end of the Second World War. In addition there were other tensions to emerge between Falangists and the rest of the Nationalist camp. Radical Falangists wished to initiate some major changes in the pattern of economic and social relations and the ways goods were produced, rather than creating a regime based on the maintenance of the rights of property. As such, implementing Falangist policies would have fractured the Nationalist alliance. Therefore, the Falange found itself at the core of the regime as the main force within the official party, but was removed from real intellectual influence. This had become clear by the 1950s. It was systematically displaced from the centres of power and blocked by other authoritarian groups. Its power was also curtailed by Franco's own project of developing an autonomous state under his leadership instead of under the authority of the party. Moreover, its role was even underplayed externally, where possible, in order to make the regime acceptable abroad.

The Falange did not accept its reduced status without a fight. Its power-base was organisational and reflected its domination of sectors of the bureaucracy. It also continued to attract a certain number of intellectuals. In the early 1940s, the Falange had enjoyed a degree of intellectual prestige as a result of the support of intellectuals such as Antonio Tovar, Pedro Laín Entralgo and most notably Dionisio Ridruejo. By the 1950s, many of these figures had moved into the opposition, alarmed by the state's acceptance of traditional conservatism and its domestication of the Falange, but they were not completely hostile to Francoism. Tovar and Laín Entralgo in fact collaborated with Ruiz Giménez's unsuccessful attempt to liberalise Spanish universities in the mid-1950s – years in which the Falange maintained some influence there. And the Instituto de Estudios Políticos of the Movement, described by Stanley Payne as something of a 'brains trust', continued to attract capable and intelligent intellectuals, though it lost much of its doctrinal purity on the way.[8]

The Falange was unable to escape its destiny, however, and it was to fade into the vaguer National Movement, a process which accelerated, especially after 1956. Under the docile leadership of José Solís Ruiz, secretary general between 1957 and 1969, the role of the Movement was to provide a semblance of mass political support to cover an authoritarian rule which depended in actuality on a powerful state and the support of a reduced number of elites. The Instituto de Estudios Políticos fell into the hands of Manuel Fraga, a man with little personal sympathy for Falangism, in the government reorganisation of 1956. He strove to retain some intellectual credibility for the Instituto, while effectively opening it up to ideas that were somewhat less pure than in the past. In the 1950s and 1960s, as a result, the Insitituto de Estudios Políticos proposed quite bold and innovative solutions to the political problems of stability and renewal within the regime and to the emerging opposition facing it, but was unable to overcome these problems due to its lack of influence. In 1961, for example, the Instituto de Estudios Políticos held a conference around the theme of *Acción Política y Cultural para Superar Conceptos Nacionalistas Disagregadores* (Political and Cultural Action to Overcome Separatist Nationalism), in which it was suggested that the state should foster strong regional identities in the north, especially among the Basques, with the aim of separating conservative elements of Basque nationalism from the emerging radicalised groups, including Basque priests.[9] The conference was impressive in the sense that it was able to accept a debate removed from the traditional concerns of Falangism, and in the detailed knowledge about Basque Nationalist groups displayed by the participants as early as 1961, before Euskadi ta Askatasuna (ETA) was active enough to put the Basque issue on to the political agenda. This stands in stark contrast to the Instituto's inability to get these issues recognised as important enough to require action by the government.

One of the problems for the Falange was of course the falling membership of the National Movement.[10] Without a dynamic role in government, the Falange could offer little to potential supporters and lost its appeal. Documents throughout the late 1950s and 1960s indicate a party in steep decline, depending on the passive affiliation of soldiers who had fought in the war and the ageing Women's Section. Most significantly, it was losing out in the universities and the trades unions, areas which were vital in any quest for building a system dependent on the principle of organic representation. The problem lay in how the Movement itself had been created. The establishment of a National Movement to which all Francoists paid allegiance had diluted the Falange and weakened it ideologically. When everyone had to be a member, what ideological validity could it retain? Its function was to provide a domesticated party for the state rather than leading the state. The Movement was ultimately a victim of the strength of the state under Franco which resisted Falangist attempts at take-over. It is perhaps ironic, therefore, that despite plans for rejuvenation, the Falange was condemned to disappear alongside Franco himself.

Despite the fact that Franco had declared the New State to be monarchist, in fact the monarchists enjoyed no more power than any other of the insider groups within the authoritarian alliance. The two rival strands of monarchism continued to differ, not only in terms of the candidates they supported for the throne, but also with reference to the kind of monarchy they envisioned. The Carlists, though Catholic and conservative, were anti-centralist and somewhat suspicious of capitalist development. The Alfonsines were divided between those who were inclined to be liberal, like Don Juan, the pretender to the throne, and a more Catholic-authoritarian faction closer to Opus Dei. Given these divisions, it is hardly surprising that the monarchists were open to manipulation by Franco. In 1956, when the young and influential member of Opus Dei, Laureano López Rodó, took up his first major political appointment as Technical Secretary to the Presidency within the Prime Minister's Office (*Secretaria Técnica de la Presidencia de Gobierno*), under Carrero Blanco, he claimed that his fundamental task was to contribute to the restoration of the monarchy.[11] Yet in 1962, he left this post to become Head of Economic Development Planning (*Jefe del Plan de Desarrollo Económico*), a decision he defended on the grounds that a solution to the succession issue was stalemated.[12]

Unlike the Falange which operated through the single party, the monarchists had only loose political associations. Instead, they depended on social interaction, since in the course of their familial and social life they would inevitably come into regular contact with each other. Apparently apolitical cultural groups were also established, with the aim of promoting monarchism through publications and discussion. The 'historic' monarchists, which included some of the traditional Catholic right and politically active members of the aristocracy, were joined by monarchists such as López Rodó and Rafael Calvo Serer, who saw the monarchy as the guarantor of a stable conservative regime, best able to conserve the Nationalist legacy. This position was therefore close enough to that of Carrero Blanco and important elements in the army, whose support for the monarchy was purely instrumental, to make them allies. This alliance was to become an important one within the authoritarian state in the 1960s.

Franco had early on proclaimed the regime to be monarchist – although it lacked a reigning monarch. He reiterated this position in 1958, following the jostling which occurred in 1957 between the monarchists and the Falangists for power, when he described the monarchy as 'traditional, Catholic, social and representative'.[13] The legitimacy of the monarchy, for Franco, derived principally from the Nationalist victory of 1939. In this sense, it hardly mattered which part of the royal family would inherit the throne since continuity with Alfonso XIII was not at issue. Fidelity to the principles of the Nationalist cause was the determining factor. In the event, Franco opted for the Alfonsine monarchy, the line which had been overthrown in 1931, but resisted the claims of Don Juan in favour of his son, Juan Carlos, who had been educated in Spain. Franco kept Juan Carlos in Spain from 1948, apparently with the intention of declaring him his successor, although this was by no means inevitable. The apparent choice of Juan Carlos over Don Juan provoked tensions among the Alfonsine monarchists, some of whom were loyal to Don Juan, who had not renounced his claim to the throne despite allowing his son to be educated by Franco. By the beginning of the 1960s, the tide had turned in favour of Juan Carlos and in 1965 the Minister of Information, Manuel Fraga, gave an interview to *The Times* in Britain, in which he claimed that it was increasingly accepted that Juan Carlos would succeed Franco. But it was not until 1969 that he was formally declared Franco's successor, having sworn fidelity first to the principles of the National Movement.

However, monarchism constituted just one strand of the right. There were other groups within or close to the authoritarian state, made up of ideologically motivated political rightists and conservative-minded elites. These could sometimes constitute important sources of support for the dictatorship in this period. Many of these were to be found in the universities or working for the media. Federico Silva Muñoz, a member of the Cortes from 1961 and Minister of Public Works from 1965 to 1970, provides an illuminating account of the intellectual development of young right-wing intellectuals around Francoism and the kind of roles they played in the universities, in the church and in the press.[14] As the dictatorship developed some of the ideological rightists who had identified with the Nationalist cause in the 1930s and 1940s became less enthusiastic about the regime, though only a few moved fully into opposition. Thereafter, the key intellectual and civilian support came from the new technocratic service elite, which was perhaps less stridently ideological, but was in practice equally authoritarian. Thus, the intellectual terms under which the regime could be justified changed considerably in this period. Intellectuals from the first period of Francoism who had a sympathy for Falangism – Antonio Tovar, Ridruejo and others – had justified authoritarianism as an efficient means for the creation of a radical Nationalist state. This now gave way to a justification of authoritarianism as a path to modernisation. Individuals without close ties to the traditional families and members of Opus Dei constituted a bulwark for the regime by the end of the 1960s, indicating the shifts within the authoritarian alliance and the disillusionment felt by the more organised and radical movements with the dictatorship.

THE STRUGGLE FOR POWER

Between 1951 and 1966 the way politics was practised changed significantly. At the beginning of the 1950s, politics was dominated by the internal struggles within the authoritarian coalition. Spanish society, understood broadly, had little sustained impact on the 'high' politics of policy-making in this period. By the middle of the 1960s, political spaces were being created by social forces beyond the state elites. Franco's own role also changed dramatically during these years. His importance as a major decision-maker declined, as policy was increasingly given over to the technocrats, though his role as figurehead and arbiter remained central to the running of the dicatorship.

Two questions in particular dominated the political agenda in the 1950s: the succession, or the institutionalisation of the authoritarian regime; and the search for economic success. The stability of the regime depended on the resolution of these issues. They were hotly debated among Francoists and there were divisions within the authoritarian alliance over what kind of state should be built, and more particularly what kind of regime should succeed Franco. There was general agreement, of course, that Spain could not adopt liberal democracy, but the question was how to preserve the 'organic democracy' which the regime claimed to stand for – through an authoritarian monarchy or through a Falangist-dominated system. While autarky lasted, no permanent victors emerged inside the dictatorship and thus the question of any final resolution of these questions was deferred. Franco himself had clearly expressed a preference for a monarchical form of government to succeed him, but he did little to resolve the issue and relations with Don Juan, the Alfonsine successor, remained poor. Don Juan's Lausanne Manifesto of 1945 had soured relations to a point from which they could not recover. Although Don Juan was never to lose support from key figures within the regime, it was only after the government changes of 1957 that the monarchical option emerged with force and relations between Franco and Don Juan recovered somewhat.

The legal framework for governing Spain during these years was provided by the Fundamental Laws. These laws, however, did not really indicate where power lay within the dictatorship. They created a set of institutions which were, for the most part, merely formal. By 1951, the laws consisted of the Falangist-inspired *Fuero de los Españoles* (Rights and Duties of Spaniards) of 1945, which set out the duties of citizens, and the Labour Charter of 1938, which regulated relations between employers and employees and conceded an important role to the state. They also included the law which constituted the Cortes or parliament of 1942. The Cortes was elected on the principles of organic democracy. It included representatives from the National Movement, syndicates, university rectors, professional associations and households, plus some representatives selected by the head of state, ministers, and municipal authorities. It could not be described as a democratic institution because, apart from the dubious nature by which the representatives were 'elected', which depended on loyalty to the state, it was powerless to control or even influence government policy. It was manipulated by government and staffed by government bureaucrats. As the Falange pointed out, the Cortes lacked confidence in itself and took little active role in politics.[15] It was a formalistic creation with no real governing function. Even as protests were emerging from other areas of the state, or state-controlled institutions, the Cortes remained loyal. A Council of the Realm was also created to give advice to Franco on important matters such as the succession and government appointments, but in practice it had very little power and was filled with people personally loyal to the Caudillo. In 1945, the Law of the Referendum was established allowing for consultation with the Spanish people, and in 1947 the Law of Succession. These laws had enabled Franco to describe the regime as emanating from the people, despite its authoritarian character. He defended the regime to a French journalist in 1958, saying that 'the head of state sometimes takes decisions which are of national importance. But the people are the final arbiter of the regime'.[16] He claimed that the law allowing for referenda meant that the 'government derives absolutely from the national will'.[17] To these was added the Law of the Principles of the National Movement in 1958, which defined the Movement as Catholic and traditional, watering down the Falangist content to a vagueness to which all Francoists could subscribe. In fact, though, the Fundamental Law notwithstanding, the centre of policy-making lay more in the cabinet, though as historians have noted, even the power of ministers over fundamental questions which affected the regime's hold on power was somewhat circumscribed.[18] Access to Franco himself was the key in the 1950s, making the Prime Minister's Office, under Carrero Blanco, the most influential body in terms of the overall political direction of the government. Ministers enjoyed greater freedom than in the 1940s, but holding ministerial office did not mean that bureaucratic resouces could be massively deployed in support of a particular policy. Power lay ultimately in the relationships which existed between the various political elites and Franco.

Cabinet composition shifted during the 1950s from relative balance between families at the beginning of the decade towards favouring Opus Dei by the end. In 1951, a new government was inaugurated which maintained a balance of power between political elites. Survivors from the earlier government included Martín Atajo as Foreign Minister and Girón as Minister of Labour. Carrero Blanco entered the cabinet. The Carlists had the Ministry of Justice under Antonio Iturmendi, while Fernández Cuesta remained in the cabinet as secretary general of the National Movement. There was some balance between hard-liners and liberalising Catholics as Joaquín Ruiz Giménez entered the cabinet but hard-liner Gabriel Arias Salgado took charge of the Ministry of Information and Tourism, which included the job of censorship. There was also some attention given to the needs of industry and a Ministry of Industry was created. The armed forces retained a Ministry for the army (Muñoz Grandes), one for the navy (Salvador Moreno Fernández) and another for the airforce (González Gallarza). This cabinet survived until 1956, when student protests brought to a close the ministerial career of Ruiz Giménez and led to the replacement of the suspect Fernández Cuesta, who was now perceived as unable to keep order in the Falangist ranks. Cabinet changes were only partial at this stage, but the crisis of 1956, ostensibly a university crisis, actually marked the close of the period of autarky during which the state balanced out power between Francoists. It brought closer the strategy of restructuring the regime's political and social base. This was to take place more fully after 1957.

Meanwhile, a political struggle was about to break out over the succession. During the crisis of 1956, amidst strikes and university protests, the Falange made an attempt to recover the political initiative. Under the secretary-generalship of Ramón Arrese, the Movement proposed tackling the crisis through the drafting of a new set of Fundamental Laws, drawn up by the Instituto de Estudios Políticos. Arrese's proposals cleverly reduced the overtly Falangist ideology of the National Movement while attempting to expand the Movement's own bureaucratic and organisational power. It defined the National Movement quite straightforwardly as 'an intermediate organisation between society and the state', dropping much of the overtly fascist language of the past. But the draft laws also tried to increase the autonomy of the Movement by proposing the creation of a set of internal statutes for elections to the National Council, which had representation in the Cortes. This would have reduced the manipulation which could be exercised by Franco himself. The new Fundamental Laws would also have increased the powers of the Movement over the post-Francoist state, and the secretary general would automatically have become vice-president in the event of Franco's death. Effectively, the proposal would have left the Movement, not the monarchy, as heir to the dicatorship. The proposed legislation, in fact, made no reference to the monarchy at all. Carrero Blanco strongly opposed the proposals, and was supported by Iturmendi, Minister of Justice; the Count of Valellano, Minister of Public Works; Gómez de Llano in the Treasury; Jesús Rubio, the Minister of Education; and Esteban Bilbao, President of the Cortes. The proposals were also severely criticised by the Catholic hierarchy. Needless to say, in view of this massive rejection on the part of other authoritarian elites, they were not adopted. The attempted internal coup had failed. Henceforth, Carrero's influence over the direction of government policy grew stronger and he tried to push the Movement towards accepting the monarchy, which in effect meant watering down Falangism. As a result, the Falange lost out further in terms of influence after the government reorganisation of 1957. Indeed, it would be possible to argue that the collapse of Arrese's proposed bill signified the beginning of a general acceptance within Francoism that the monarchy would have to occupy a key role within the state, after the death of Franco. This position was reflected in the Law of the Principles of the National Movement which was passed in 1958.[19]

The Falange did not give up completely, however, and fought a rearguard action thereafter. In the syndicalist apparatus, for example, it attempted to keep control. It also tried, unsuccessfully, to adapt to the new political circumstances. As a result, the Movement was reluctantly forced to conclude after the defeat outlined above in 1958:

> The ideological war should not go on. The basic ideas of the National Movement have had an impact on the public consciousness and even on the minority of people who do not accept them. The discussion should no longer centre on ideas themselves but rather on how to put them into practice.[20]

Instead, it was proposed that the Movement should work to activate and strengthen the official unions and the Cortes, 'with the government abstaining from direct intervention more often, so that parliament becomes more confident and more efficient'.[21] In both of these areas, however, the Falangists were doomed to further defeats.

Debates about succession and the ideological direction of the regime were played out inside Francoism in an apparently depoliticised Spain. The regime functioned within a climate of widespread apathy in the 1950s after the exhaustion of the civil war and the repression in its aftermath. This was supplemented by the maintenance of the repressive apparatus and a willingness on the part of the state to use violence. There was always an irrational element to state violence which could occasionally be turned even against its own supporters as well as against opponents. This happened in 1954 when the Student Union, Sindicato de Estudiantes Universitarios (SEU) was demonstrating against British control of Gibraltar and was confronted by the police.[22] Thus it was a combination of self-censorship, exhaustion and fear which effectively kept most Spaniards acquiescent. It is impossible to 'know' empirically how much active support the regime commanded and how much its survival in this period was rather the result of passive acceptance. While substantial popular opposition was to emerge in the 1960s and especially the 1970s, the 1950s witnessed only partial, sporadic and limited dissent.

The most important signs of social unrest came from sudden labour demonstrations and student protest. There had in fact been some strikes and labour protests as early as 1945 and 1946. But they were not on the scale of the major general strike which affected Barcelona in 1951, and which appeared to materialise almost out of nowhere. Originating in a wave of popular protest at the rise in transport costs, an official meeting of union delegates called for a general strike in the city. 300 000 Catalan workers went on strike in March, even after the cancellation of the transport increases was announced. The strike led to the removal from office of the leaders of the official union and of the civil governor of the city, who was responsible to Franco himself for public order. It constituted the boldest strike action taken until 1956, and was a city-wide protest against the costs of autarky which kept urban wages low by government fiat. Interestingly, when the strike was over, wages were allowed to rise by 25 per cent.[23]

There are a number of issues which arise out of the 1951 strike which indicate the complexity of state–society relations in the 1950s. First of all, the strike action was called by the official unions. Second, it was called against a background of steady decline in living standards and resentment in Barcelona that transport costs were much higher there than in Madrid. The strike thus had a regionalist anti-centralist element to it, uniting Catalans in their rejection of Madrid-based government. These factors indicate that it is misleading to assume a simple dichotomy between the state and society under Francoism, even in the period of autarky. Conflicts between the state and social groups, even in 1951, were mediated by regional identity and regional conflicts, and also by disputes between Francoist elites over how to deal with society and social protest. Factions of the Falangists and the official unions, mindful of the need to win and retain some popular legitimacy, were prepared to support strike action against the state. This was further complicated by the fact that the 'old-guard' unionists, who had been mainly anarchists and communists, had begun a policy of entryism and collaboration with the official unions which made it difficult to draw clear dividing lines between regime and opposition positions in the field of labour relations as early as 1951.

Further student and labour protests emerged in the 1950s. Similarly, it is difficult to see them as reflecting a straightforward division between the state and civil society. In the case of the students, demands for the free election of union representatives to the official union, the SEU, culminated in violent clashes in the Faculty of Law in Madrid and the arrest of students who proposed opening the list for election to unofficial candidates. The army moved to suppress the student meetings while the Movement, which was formally in charge of running the union, came under suspicion for inciting the students in order to increase its own power within the regime. The university problems led to the removal of the Minister of Education and a change in the leadership of the Movement. But these changes were insufficient to stem the general climate of protest and crisis, which by now was affecting even disaffected elements within the Francoist camp. Strikes broke out in Navarre, the Basque country and Catalonia shortly after. These were fuelled by the appearance of protests elsewhere and by the demands for increased industrial efficiency. Unfortunately, for most industries the only way to achieve this was through increased exploitation of the labour force with longer hours, tighter discipline and lower pay. There had hardly been any infrastructural investment taking place in industry during the post-war period, making it difficult to increase output any other way. But when the government conceded wage increases, ministers and government officials protested that it would fuel the inflationary spiral which was beginning to get a grip on the country. The worsening economic situation, coupled with the refusal of society to accept it quietly, was behind the important cabinet reorganisation in 1957 which heralded a completely new phase of the dictatorship. In this way, therefore, the important changes introduced after 1957 were a consequence of a gradual erosion in the state's capacity to control society, as well as the economic failures of autarky itself.

A combination of economic problems and social protests was, therefore, the background to the major cabinet reorganisation of 1957. The outcome was a ministerial team dominated intellectually by a new technocratic elite belonging to Opus Dei, a group without deep roots in the civil war alliance, though it was profoundly conservative. The Falangists, such as Girón in the Ministry of Labour, were regarded by Opus Dei as unable to deal with the complexities of governing an industrialising economy. Girón had approved wage rises after the 1956 strikes, a sign for the conservative technocrats that he did not understand the relationship between production, salaries, inflation and economic development. So the Falange found itself further removed from the centres of power. The new team was conservative with much fewer populist tendencies, and it enjoyed the support of Carrero Blanco, Franco's close friend and collaborator. As a result, the new cabinet also looked distinctly more monarchical in tone. Altogether, the ministerial team was more in tune with traditional European rightist authoritarianism – conservative, monarchical, anxious to establish more market-based policies and reduce the overt role of the state – than ever before. Although it was not obvious at the time, Franco had accepted the changes with a certain reluctance. So the rise of Opus Dei in policy-making also coincided with his own increasing marginalisation from economic policy-making.

However, the degree of change the new team represented should not be exaggerated. On the one hand, other Francoist elites retained representation within the state, thereby creating arenas where other kinds of policies could be implemented. And on the other hand, while the new economic team encouraged foreign investment and industrial efficiency, the state planned and directed expansion. The Opus Dei team was internationalist and modernising in its view of the economy but had a traditionally conservative vision of society. It also subscribed to a vision of the regime which was authoritarian, directive and distinctly illiberal. The design of development plans, the first in 1963, is evidence of the important role ascribed to the state in the economy. The Instituto Nacional de Industria (INI), the state holding company with considerable industrial assets, remained active and even expanded in the 1960s. This can be attributed in part to the pressure from traditionally nationalist Francoists. But INI also functioned to find jobs and employ regime supporters, including members from Opus Dei.

The Opus Dei cabinet team was composed of Alberto Ullastres, Minister of Commerce, Mariano Navarro Rubio in the Ministry of Finance and Laureano López Rodó as the top official in the Presidency of the Government. They were joined by Gregorio López Bravo in 1962, as Minister of Industry and in 1965 López Rodó moved into the cabinet. These technocrats stimulated some moves towards professionalising and modernising the civil service and the administration, though they were never able to rationalise the civil service completely. In fact, López Rodó had initiated a series of reforms to the civil service and the public administration in 1957, but many aspects of the civil service remained untouched. Entry to public sector employment was still determined by the nationally administered and impersonal system of oposiciones, though membership of the National Movement was also required. In practice, clientelism was rife and the middle and lower ranks of the civil service were often staffed by poorly trained individuals who were on the whole also poorly paid. But López Rodó did succeed in separating some major areas of responsibility within central government. In particular, the office of head of state was administratively separated from the Prime Minister's Office (*Presidencia de Gobierno*), making it possible, theoretically, for many aspects of government to be carried out without direct reference to the head of state. This laid the groundwork for the trend throughout the 1960s for government decisions to depend less and less on direct access to Franco himself. López Rodó claims that he was nervous in case Franco vetoed this aspect of the reorganisation, but relates that the measure had the dictator's direct approval.[24]

Between 1957 and 1959 the groundwork was laid for the establishment of new, more economically liberal policies, and in 1959 the Spanish economy was prepared for opening up with the Stabilisation Plan.[25] Between 1959 and 1962, the economy suffered a series of shocks as Spain adjusted to the rigours of (partial) international competition. Around a third of the economically active population found themselves out of work between 1959 and 1960 and the real value of wages declined sharply. Thereafter, the economy experienced a period of unprecedented growth, fuelled in part by the new policies but also by the expansion of the global economy and by growth in other European countries. These changes, occurring over a number of years, profoundly affected the politics of the regime. They affected the relationship between the Francoist elites, changing the balance of power between them. They altered the terms of Francoist discourse, incorporating a language of consumerism, capitalism and progress into government publicity, which was somewhat at odds with earlier Francoist visions of an idealised rural Spain, marked by difference from rather than similarity to the rest of Europe. And, by stimulating a series of social transformations across the country, they affected the relationship between the state and society and the nature of state responses to social change.

Franco himself had been dubious about the Stabilisation Plan. Nonetheless international integration and modernisation became the key to government policies in the 1960s. Spain even went so far as to approach the EEC about membership. That this policy direction could first be taken, and then maintained, is indicative of the fact that Franco's personal direction of the government was diminishing in the 1960s. Struggles for power between the Francoist elites went on, therefore, while Franco's own legitimacy by now lay more in the symbolic importance of having established the regime and steered the dictatorship through the 1940s and 1950s than in the management of new policies.

The new discourse of capitalist expansion, foreign investment and productivity, though perhaps dominant in Francoist cabinets throughout the 1960s did not mean the elimination of more traditional authoritarian groups from the state. Franco's own reluctance to embrace the new policy orientation was mirrored by other groups who retained representation within the regime. The new Foreign Minister, Fernando María Castiella, close to the church and with a flirtation with fascism in his past, proposed the modernisation of the bureaucracy and efficiency in government, but allied to a traditional defence of Spanish nationalism. His vision remained to a large extent that of Spain against the world. There was also continuity in the repressive apparatus of the state, as Iturmendi continued in Justice and Arias Salgado in Information (including censorship). The new Minister of the Interior, General Camilo Alonso Vega, was a traditional hard-liner. The Falange did not lose representation altogether either, as José Ruiz Solís took over the direction of the National Movement and was in charge of the syndicates.

The changes in economic policy were conducive to a softer, though ambiguous, government line on union activity. The Law of Collective Bargaining, introduced in 1959, allowing for free collective bargaining, in place of industry-wide agreements through the Ministry of Labour, was increasingly used and unions became more confident in their dealings with factory owners. Strikes in 1962 did not meet with such fierce repression as in the past and rises in the minimum wage followed. Changes to the cabinet in 1962 also indicated some degree of liberalisation. Most significantly, Arias Salgado was removed after 20 years in the cabinet. He was replaced by Manuel Fraga Iribarne, who worked hard to distance himself from the hard-liners and to present himself as a reformer. Fraga was to be responsible for the removal of press censorship which opened up the media and created the basis for the new cultural and intellectual climate which appeared at the end of the 1960s.

It would be a mistake, however, to assume that economic opening up was directly responsible for greater political freedom. The groups favouring economic liberalisation were not the same ones as those pushing for political reform. The Opus Dei team, in charge of the economy, was socially conservative, while Fraga and Ruiz Solís, who were identified as reformers, were suspicious of liberal economics and foreign investment and preferred to defend the role of the state. The reformers' intention, in any case, was reform of the dictatorship with the intention of preserving it; their aim was not to promote democratic change. It would also be a mistake to exaggerate the degree of liberalisation which occurred during this period. The pace of change was forced by social transformation rather than by any government disposition to reform and the repressive apparatus remained intact. As a clear demonstration of this fact, Franco resisted international pleas for clemency and allowed the execution of Julián Grimau, a clandestine communist leader arrested in Madrid, to go ahead in 1963. The universities and intellectuals also felt the weight of repression, as the unions were to do, especially after 1966.

In 1964, the regime ran a self-congratulatory campaign entitled 'Twenty-Five Years of Peace'. At the same time, the fight for the succession continued. Finally, in 1966, Franco was persuaded of the need to deal with the succession issue by means of a new Organic Law of the State. The new law altered aspects of the Fundamental Laws, including some changes in the labour legislation which reduced the role of the Ministry of Labour, formally ended the vertical syndicates, and broadened the way the representatives in the Cortes were chosen. One hundred and eight of them were now to be elected by 'family representatives', thus preserving the notion that Spain had an 'organic democracy'. The most important addition to the constitution through the new Organic Law was the separation of the head of state from the president of the government. Although Franco was not prepared to step down, it created a mechanism through which he could retire from active politics. The new law failed, however, to clarify the question of the succession. The stability of the regime therefore remained compromised and its future unresolved.

THE EMERGENCE OF SOCIAL OPPOSITION

Politics after 1960 broadened slowly in a *de facto* fashion, as social groups struggled with the state. It now consisted of more than simply the internal struggles between 'insider' groups within the authoritarian alliance and other groups could affect political outcomes through opposition. These political spaces were still precarious and recovering them had taken more than 20 years. They were the result of a combination of factors: the internal process of reform within the state; and, more importantly, the modernisation of the Spanish economy, which had led to social changes with inevitable consequences for state–society relations. A more urban society meant a more informed public, and by the mid 1960s the number of towns with more than 100 000 people had mushroomed. The industrial axis of Spain no longer comprised simply Madrid, Barcelona and Bilbao. It included towns such as Pamplona, Zaragoza and Vigo. Once quiet, small Catalan towns, most notably Sabadell, spread out in an uncontrolled urban sprawl in the 1960s as a result of foreign investment.[26] This transition generated a greater self-consciousness on the part of the Spanish of themselves as citizens, though the political impact of this was diffuse. Organisation and protest was often focused around social issues and working conditions in the cities, rather than being directed straightforwardly against the regime.

But opportunities also opened up because of the struggles in which marginalised social groups engaged with the state. The sense of unrest which pervaded Spain in the mid 1960s cannot simply be attributed to the impact of economic modernisation. It was due also to the weakening of the bonds of fear and the passing of the exhaustion which had kept Spaniards acquiescent in the 1950s. There were new generations of workers' leaders, student activists and Spanish citizens for whom the civil war was history. And a general upswing in militancy in the 1960s was taking place throughout Europe, which inevitably affected Spain too. Hence the politics of the early 1960s were immensely complicated. The government operated with a vision of the nation state which was increasingly out of touch not only with the material reality of the country but also with the mindset, concerns and motivations of many Spaniards, who were once again prepared to struggle in order to create a democratic future.

The new politics of protest in the 1960s took at least four distinct forms. First there were labour protests against employers and against the state. There was also the beginning of regional unrest. Then there were student protests which erupted periodically. Like the labour protests, these tended to be directed against the state management of social relations. There was no repeat of the crisis of 1956 in the universities until the late 1960s, but the official union, the SEU, was in decline to the point when it had to be officially dissolved in 1965. Finally, there was increasing activity from sections of the Catholic church who opposed the philosophical bases of authoritarianism, especially after the modifications to Catholic policy and practice made by the Second Vatican Council of 1962. These protests, coupled with the sense of decrepitude which began to surround Franco himself, slowly brought the stability of the regime into question. This increased as the decade progressed and the regime's response shifted from one of ignoring the protests or an attitude of ambiguous tolerance to active repression after 1966.

The early 1960s witnessed a resurgence of both Catalan and Basque identity which, given the centralism of the Francoist state, the motto of which was 'España, una, grande y libre' ('Spain: one, great and free'), was to have inevitable consequences. The expressions of Catalan and Basque regionalism were very different.[27] Catalan nationalism was expressed in music, literature and through popular culture as well as politically. It criss-crossed occasionally with religion, as Catalan priests, for example, began to promote all that was Catalan and defend the right to Catalan self-expression. In one infamous incident the abbot of the Catalan monastery of Montserrat was expelled from Spain for defending the right to regional expression. The centrality of being Catalan was a sentiment shared by almost all inhabitants of Catalonia, including immigrants, for whom expressing a regional identity operated as a means to integration in an otherwise hostile environment. But Catalan nationalism did not come to constitute a major force for direct opposition.

Basque nationalism, in contrast, went on to become a law-and-order problem for the dictatorship. The Basque nationalist movement did not perceive itself by the mid 1960s, nor was it perceived, as merely fighting for the right to cultural expression. ETA, the most important vehicle for the expression of Basque nationalism in the 1960s, constituted a threat to the unity of the Spanish state itself. ETA emerged in 1958 out of the group around the Basque cultural journal, *EKIN*, formed in 1952 as a result of dissatisfaction with the cautious and moribund leadership of the Partido Nacionalista Vasco (PNV, the Basque Nationalist Party) in exile. Initially, the young people of *EKIN* were concerned with rediscovering their Basque inheritance after a generation of suppression. But *EKIN* was also involved with the need to take action in order to preserve all that was Basque in defiance of the Francoist state. ETA grew directly out of this renewed activism and as a response to the repression of regionalism by the dictatorship. The movement was to maintain a fairly anti-communist line until 1964, but thereafter was influenced by Marxist theories of underdevelopment and national liberation which led it to adopt armed struggle in 1968 and to incorporate a class analysis into its nationalist philosophy.[28]

Until the mid 1960s, possibly even up until 1968, the Francoist regime registered regionalism as only a sporadic problem, to be solved through reactive repression. After that date, it responded by creating systematised methods of repression in the Basque country which intensified Madrid–Basque hostility. There is evidence indicating that the regime was well informed about Basque and Catalan Nationalist politics though it chose to do little about regionalism. The regime knew that the PNV counted for little politically, and that new groups were appearing which favour 'direct action'. A report pointed out that these new groups had the capacity to 'operate through youth groups who use nineteenth century forms of opposition, such as raising the flag in a church tower or sabotaging a train. They have a clandestine organisation, ETA, which has recently become active'.[29] The report indicated that the nationalists counted on the sympathy of Basques, whose complaints against Madrid centralism were recognised as 'often justified', and on the absences of arenas in which to express Basque culture due to the suspicions of the state. It recognised than many Basques wished to practise a regional identity without separating from Spain and it urged the government to take action in order to prevent an escalation of the problem. Franco, however, chose to do nothing. And, indeed, it would have proved impossible for the government to accept manifestations of northern regionalism without incurring the hostility of the armed forces.

A new activism was also apparent in the labour movement in the early 1960s. It is important, however, to avoid a mechanistic approach to the emergence of labour protest after 1959. The independent unions which emerged, the Workers' Commissions (*Comisiones Obreras*), were not a result of industrialisation alone. Changes to the system of wage bargaining created the context in which the new union activity of the Workers' Commissions developed. And independent labour militancy had never completely ceased, despite the repression of the dictatorship. There was therefore also a sense of continuity with the past. In 1962, the most widespread series of strikes in Spain since 1939 broke out in Asturias, the Basque provinces, Madrid and Catalonia. As a result, the government was forced to recognise the legitimacy of economically motivated strike activity in the Law of Collective Disputes. This legislation was an almost inevitable corollary to the 1959 Law of Collective Bargaining. In practice, however, labour organisation was still restrictive and the government retained the official union structure through the Organización Sindical Española (OSE).

The monopoly of the OSE in representing labour was challenged by the expansion of the Workers' Commissions. Initially the commissions were *ad hoc* shop-steward movements and rank-and-file committees in Asturias and Catalonia, which brought together Catholic activists with communists, socialists and even some Falangists, and which counted on the support of many workers on the shop floor who had no ties to political parties. But in 1964 there was an attempt to create a permanent organisation out of the Commissions. The OSE adopted what seems at first the strange tactic of tolerating the Commissions. In fact, the Falangists had co-operated with them in the hope of increasing their power within the regime through control over the union movement. As a result, the elections for union delegates in 1966 were more open than ever before. While some union activists were wary of the elections which were run by the OSE, for fear of collaborating with the regime, the Workers' Commissions nonetheless took the decision to participate as a way of spreading the union movement. As a result of their participation, the official candidates for union offices did badly while the non-official candidates (mostly from the Workers' Commissions) did well. In the newly industrialising town of Sabadell, for example, in the engineering union, 33 of the 36 new union delegates were from the Commissions.[30] Not surprisingly, the results shocked the dictatorship. Instead of favouring regime candidates as officials had expected, the new policy of openness had led to their defeat. As a result, the policy of tolerance of the Commissions came to an end. In 1966 the government unleashed a wave of repression against the unofficial unions which indicated that the period of liberalisation had been perceived as unsuccessful. Thereafter, demonstrations of union strength were followed by repression.

Between 1959 and 1966, then, opposition to the dictatorship increased. However, it was weakened in terms of its political impact by its lack of unity. Protests were local, social and sectoral. And while a consciously anti-Francoist opposition was to emerge at the end of the 1960s, it was always riven by ideological divisions. Indeed, some of the strength of social opposition in this period lay precisely in its ability to rise above ideological divisions. For example, the extraordinary strength of the Workers' Commissions lay in their ability to unite a range of ideological currents against the official candidates of the regime. But its strength was also to prove its weakness. The emerging opposition from civil society could not be backed up by political parties. The only party to have any real organisational presence within Spain was the Communist Party. In fact 1960 constituted the nadir for the traditional parties of the Republic, such as the socialists and the Basque National Party. All the parties were still dominated by figures from the civil war period and they were increasingly out of touch with the daily life and changing reality of the dictatorship. The early 1960s witnessed some tentative moves towards party resurgence and activism, but these were embryonic. The most significant event was the meeting in Munich of 118 Spaniards associated with the non-communist opposition, including the monarchists Gil Robles, ex-head of the CEDA, and Alvarez de Miranda, the socialist Rodolfo Llopis and the social Christian and ex-Falangist Dionosio Ridruejo. It was an inconclusive meeting, the significance of which lies in the fact that it occurred at all, in view of the deep divisions between the participants. Inside Spain, there were also some small indications of the formation of a political opposition. In 1959, for example, monarchists grouped together in the Unión Española under the leadership of Joaquín Sastrústegui, who attended the meeting in Munich, had held a meeting with a group of intellectual socialists clustered around the university professor Enique Tierno Galván. But the political impact of these meetings was small and party organisation was weak. Yet without the political parties, it was difficult to challenge the dictatorship and offer a credible alternative to it. So the strong local and sectoral protests which emerged were unable to damage the regime seriously enough to threaten its survival.

CONCLUSION

At the beginning of this chapter, we identifed the key questions facing the regime as stability and succession. The dictatorship weathered the 1950s and sailed into the 1960s, able to relax somewhat the iron hand of repression. The state was institutionally strong. It was also protected by the international climate of the Cold War which structured the global order in a way that was favourable to anti-communist dictatorships. Could it therefore have been said to have become stable? At one important level, it is difficult to see the regime as a stable system of government, even in the 1950s when it was least challenged, and despite its longevity. For a political system to be stable, it is necessary that the mechanisms are in place that ensure its continuity. Yet how the regime would become institutionalised was a permanent source of division within Francoism.

Indeed, the paradox of the dictatorship was that it was both strong and fragile at the same time. Its strength lay in the broad consensus generated amongst the rightist groups which made up the authoritarian alliance about the figure of Franco and around the need for dictatorship. It could also draw on a long-established state apparatus. Finally, the regime was strong because it could draw on long-established cultural traditions of religious belief and the deep-rooted practice of social deference as ways to manufacture social consent. Yet the regime was fragile in that its survival came to depend exclusively on Franco himself, who was the only legitimate figurehead to all the groups within the authoritarian camp. Since the dictatorship was not in fact personal, in that policy depended on the relationship between social actors and the state, this created disjunctures within it. For, while the state was becoming more bureaucratic in its operation, its very existence was tied ultimately to an individual. This problem was to become more acute as the mechanisms which had guaranteed the survival of the regime gradually broke down through the 1960s, and as the Francoist alliance began to fall apart.

NOTES

1 G. Collier, *Socialists of Rural Andalusia* (Stanford, 1987), p. 168.
2 Juan Linz, 'An Authoritarian Regime: The Case of Spain', in Erik Allardt and Yrjo Littunen, eds., *Cleavages, Ideologies and Party Systems* (Helsinki, 1974).
3 A. Shubert, *A Social History of Modern Spain* (London, 1990), p. 222.
4 D. Gilmour, *The Transformation of Spain: From Franco to the Constitutional Monarchy* (London, 1986), p. ix.
5 M. González García, 'The Armed Forces: The Poor Relations of the Franco Regime', in P. Preston, ed., *Spain in Crisis* (Hassocks, 1976), pp. 23–47.
6 F. Lannon, *Privilege, Persecution and Prophecy. The Catholic Church in Spain, 1875–1975* (Oxford, 1987).
7 On the church and Francoism, see R. Gómez Pérez, *Política y religión en el régimen de Franco* (Barcelona, 1976); and G. Hermet, *Los católicos en la España franquista* (Madrid, 1985). On the role of Opus Dei, see D. Artigues, *El Opus Dei en España 1982–1962* (Paris, 1971) and Hermet, *Los católicos*.
8 S. Payne, *The Franco Regime, 1936–1975* (Madison, 1987).
9 Consejo Nacional del Secretaría General del Movimiento, 'Acción Política y Cultural para Superar Conceptos Nacionalistas Disagregadores, 1961', Archivo General de la Adminstración Central (AGAC) Presidencia de Gobierno, Caja 9835.
10 S. Ellwood, *Prietas las filas: historia de Falange Española 1933–1983* (Barcelona, 1984).
11 L. López Rodó, *La larga marcha hacia la monarquía* (Barcelona, 1977), p. 121.
12 López Rodó, *La larga marcha*, p. 199.
13 López Rodó, *La larga marcha*, p. 155.
14 F. Silva Muñoz, *Memorias políticas* (Barcelona, 1993).
15 Consejo Nacional del Secretaria General del Movimiento, 'Notas de Orientación Política para el Curso que Empieza, 1958', AGAC, Presidencia de Gobierno, Caja 9835.
16 López Rodó, *La larga marcha*, p. 155.
17 López Rodó, *La larga marcha*, p. 155.
18 P. Preston, *Franco: A Biography* (London, 1993).
19 A very detailed account of these events can be found in Payne, *The Franco Regime*.
20 'Notas de Orientación'.
21 'Notas de Orientación'.
22 For a thorough discussion of the internal tensions within the SEU in the mid 1950s, see

Elena Hernández Sandoica, 'Reforma desde el sistema y protagonismo estudiantil: la Universidad de Madrid en los años cincuenta', in J. Carrera Ares and M. Ruiz Carnicer, eds., *La Universidad Española bajo el régimen de Franco* (Zaragoza, 1991).

23 S. Balfour, *Dictatorship, Workers and the City* (Oxford, 1989).

24 López Rodó, *La larga marcha*, p. 136.

25 For a discussion of the reforms and their political context, see L. López Rodó, *Memorias*, vols. II and III (Esplugues de Llobragat, 1991 and 1992).

26 See Balfour, *Dictatorship*.

27 J. Linz 'Early State-Building and Late Peripheral Nationalism against the State: The Case of Spain', in S. N. Eisenstadt and S. Rokkan, eds., *Building States and Nations* (London, 1973) and S. Giner, 'Centro y periferia: la dimensión etnica de la sociedad española', S. Giner, ed., *España. sociedad y política* (Madrid, 1990). On Basque nationalism, see J. Linz, *Conflicto en Euskadi* (Madrid, 1986); Alfredo Pérez-Agote, *La reproducción del nacionalismo: el caso Vasco* (Madrid, 1984): and J. P. Fusi, *El Pais Vasco* (Madrid, 1984). On Catalan nationalism, see N. Jones, 'The Catalan Problem Since the Civil War', in P. Preston, ed., *Spain in Crisis*.

28 J. Grugel, 'The Basques', in M. Watson, ed., *Contemporary Minority Nationalism*, (London, 1990).

29 'Acción Política y Cultural para Superar Conceptos Nacionalistas Disagregadores'.

30 Balfour, *Dictatorship*, p. 92.

4

The Death of the Regime, 1966–1976

This chapter charts the complex politics of the final years of the dictatorship. It explores the debates which took place between Francoists about the future after the death of Franco and about the nature and direction of the regime. For some Francoists, this simply meant how to ensure the survival of the authoritarian state. For others, however, the succession was a more open question, with certain Francoists admitting that substantial political change would have to be introduced once Franco had gone. It was no longer a question of 'after Franco, who?', but rather 'after Franco, what?' The number of authoritarians prepared to discuss opening up the system was growing. Indeed, José María de Areilza, a committed authoritarian who recanted in 1964, claimed that by the mid 1960s not even ministers believed that Francoism could outlive Franco.[1] During this period, then, a political right outside the dictatorship cautiously began to emerge.

By the 1960s the state possessed some considerable autonomy from the social groups which had brought it to power and legitimised it. While this guaranteed the fairly efficient running of the country, it also distanced the regime somewhat from its own supporters. This process was progressive and it contributed decisively to the fragmentation of the authoritarian alliance, as some groups moved away from the core. By the late 1960s, partly as a result, a new political right was in the process of formation. It recognised its origins within Francoism, but it was no longer intimately connected to it nor so concerned with the dictatorship's survival. Some of the new right moved away from the regime and established contacts with opposition groups. Others simply distanced themselves in order to await events. Individuals who had separated themselves from the authoritarian alliance in these ways were to form part of the right which would collaborate in the peaceful dismantling of the dictatorship after the death of Franco, under Adolfo Suárez.

Other groups within Francoism resisted change. Admiral Carrero Blanco was the incarnation of the immobilist tendency within the state until his assassination in 1973. He wished to use the institutions of the state and its distance from society to preserve authoritarianism without concessions. After his death, the die-hard authoritarians tried, ultimately unsuccesfully, to hold back the tide of liberalisation which followed. These internal conflicts heightened the atmosphere of tension in the country, as the political responses of the 'ultra' authoritarians became unpredictable and increasingly aggressive. Rising violence from rightist groups became a regular feature of politics as the dictatorship moved towards collapse.

The fact was that the regime was condemned by its long association with the figure of Franco himself and by its origins in the civil war, an event now part of history for many Spaniards. As late as the 1960s, the legitimacy of the dictatorship still rested ideologically on the Nationalist victory of 1936 and on Franco as the architect of that victory. This meant effectively that it was legitimate in the eyes of those social and political groups which identified themselves with the uprising of 1936 and who continued to see its relevance to present-day politics. But it could never lay claim to being a legitimate regime in the eyes of all Spaniards. In the 1960s, attempts had been made to find new bases of support through economic modernisation. This had accentuated the identification of the regime with the propertied classes and with labour repression, however, because industrialisation occurred within the confines of authoritarianism. Thus, the regime remained tied to defending the social and political privileges of the wealthy, and failed to create new institutions which might have linked it more closely to wider society. The social tensions generated by industrialisation were attributed overwhelmingly to the existence of the dictatorship.

Like all authoritarian regimes, the Francoist state attempted to eliminate social conflict, and regularly turned to repression. The social and economic problems which confronted Spain in the 1960s, and which to a greater or lesser extent were typical of western Europe – labour militancy, the revival of sub-state nationalism, student protest – were dealt with differently in Spain from the way they were dealt with in its democratic neighbours. In Franco's Spain, these problems were identifed with the politics of the Republican left of the 1930s. As in 1936, they were regarded as symptoms of decadence and national disintegration; those involved in these activities, therefore, were enemies of the country. As such, the mechanisms adopted for dealing with protest in the 1960s were essentially similar to those used in the 1930s and 1940s although the social and political context was quite different. The ways in which the state responded to challenges from within society intensified the depths of the protests themselves, thereby creating a cycle of protest and repression which was not modified until after the death of Franco.

Some of the complexity of politics in this period, therefore, lies in the internal disagreements within the authoritarian coalition and its disintegration when it came to making strategic political choices. But the background to this disintegration was the process of broader changes occurring within society. For the first time since the Republic, social movements recovered their dynamism.

The government was put on the defensive and forced to react to multiple demands so opposition groups were able to take the offensive and shape the political agenda.

THE POLITICAL CRISIS OF LATE FRANCOISM

Dissent within Francoism over liberalisation began after the passing of the Organic Law of 1967. This law was designed to draw together all previous efforts at codifying the regime. Its importance was that it offered the prospect of modifying the legal basis of the state. Various groups internal to Francoism therefore hoped to establish their dominance within the dictatorship through the new law. Francoism had always been a coalition of elites, of course. Not only their interests but, perhaps more importantly, their ideology, belief systems and what we might call the moral underpinning of their politics, were also different. What was significant now, however, was that some sectors of Francoism hoped that the new law would contain the seeds of a limited pluralism and modernisation. Individuals wishing for this outcome felt drawn ideologically to the democratic ideologies of the right-wing parties in the rest of Europe, especially in Germany, Italy, Britain and France and feared that Spain was being left behind. They argued that the dictatorship must cast off the remnants of its totalitarian past and 'modernise'. Indeed, these former and dissident Francoists saw modernisation of the dictatorship as the only way to preserve the gains made for the social groups represented within Francoism after the Caudillo's death. For, by the mid 1960s, as Franco's health declined and opposition increased, the survival of the regime and the fate of its supporters after Franco were the overwhelming concerns of all the elites within the authoritarian alliance.

The decision to introduce a new law of this type had been the subject of internal disputes within the Francoist state from the early 1960s. When it finally emerged, the regime presented the Organic Law as an attempt to deepen participation within the political system. Indeed, Franco himself called it 'a broad democratisation of the political process'.[2] But, in the end, the promised overhaul of the Francoist legislation turned into a mere codification and reordering of existing legislation along with some administrative reform. It reaffirmed the role of the four main institutions of the state: the monarchy, the Council of the Realm, the National Council of the Movement and the Cortes. It stressed the importance of the National Movement, not as a powerhouse of ideas and direction for the regime, but rather as an organisation which was to reflect and balance the different tendencies inside the regime. Membership of the National Council of the Movement was increased to 108, though the direction of the Council was still controlled by the fact that Franco himself appointed 40 members. (Another 50 came from the provincial organisations and the rest from the Cortes.) The role of the Council of the Realm was also extended and its numbers expanded to 16. The vertical syndicates were abolished and the OSE was declared autonomous from the government, though union structures outside the OSE remained illegal. The Cortes remained unable to introduce legislation and was largely outside the legislative procedures. The number of its representatives was expanded and for the first time a percentage were 'elected', in accordance with a corporatist model of democracy, through the family representatives. But, ultimately, the reform could be described as democratisation only from the peculiar perspective of organic democracy which aimed to represent and aggregate the interests of the nation or national communities such as the family or sectors of production. The individual person was, as the Organic Law made clear, subordinate to the state. It was therefore very different from the ideas of liberal democracy, which conceives of the individual as possessing a set of inalienable social and political rights.

Manuel Fraga, a key figure pushing for reform from within Francoism, ascribed the failure of the regime to change the political structures to the fact that the government was cautious and slow in its decision-making, combined with the fact that events in the country moved beyond the control of the government:

> I believe that, from 1953, Franco searched, slowly and prudently as was natural in him, for ways to change the [dictatorship]. He would not have authorised the Press Law of 1966 if he had planned on remaining a military dictator all his life. What happened was that the years went by and in the end, by 1969, everything came to a halt.[3]

Regime supporters such as Fraga presented unreformed authoritarianism and indeed the increased repression of the 1960s as simply a 'failure of the regime to evolve'.[4] But what kind of evolution was possible? Evolution, as Fraga understood it, required not a move towards democracy, but an internal reformulation of power between regime forces. It would not have altered the authoritarian core of the regime. That this was unacceptable more broadly to the Spanish people was indicated by the vehement anti-regime protests of the 1960s and 1970s.

Other groups who had formed part of Francoism were prepared to go further than Fraga. They argued for a dismantling of the regime and the erection of a set of very different political structures. This meant, effectively, deserting the authoritarian coalition and attempting to form a new right. As a result, by the 1970s, it was clear that the regime could no longer lay claim to representing all right-wing opinion. This was a very significant development. An organised liberal right was in the process of formation and it was to emerge more strongly after the death of Franco. But conservative groups outside Francoism were in the political wilderness until the 1970s, neither acceptable to the regime nor part of the opposition.

These splits and divisions on the right and within the regime weakened it by reducing its legitimacy. The number of groups the state could call upon to fulfil government functions was steadily eroded. This contributed to another problem; namely, due to the length of time the regime had now lasted, many of the key figures within it were old, tired and in ill-health. While there had been a generational renewal in the economics ministries, key positions in the Ministry of the Interior in particular were held by civil war veterans. In 1969, when Carrero Blanco urged Franco to form a new cabinet, he cited the fact that some in the existing cabinet were simply too old to deal with the demands of government.[5] Indeed, the very language the government spoke sounded outmoded by the 1960s.

Alongside these difficulties, there was the pressing issue of the succession, or what would happen after Franco's death. The monarchy appeared the only realistic option but, from the perspective of the Francoists, there was still no obvious candidate. Don Juan refused to relinquish his rights to the throne, but by the mid 1960s it was looking unlikely that he would ever become acceptable within the regime, in view of the increasingly liberal approach to politics he endorsed. Rather than being the king of an authoritarian state, Don Juan's followers dared to argue that the monarchy should be constitutional and democratic, and thereby act as a rallying point for all Spaniards. They saw the monarchy as a means to heal the divisions of the civil war which Francoism kept alive. This was hardly an approach designed to endear Don Juan to the ultras within the regime. In contrast to his father, Juan Carlos appeared prepared to unite the monarchical tradition with the preservation of authoritarianism. Given that he was generally silent about politics, it was not unsurprising that he was trusted by regime supporters. Carrero Blanco and López Rodó pushed hard from within government for a solution to the problem of succession, phrasing it as an issue of regime stability.[6] According to Powell, 'it is generally believed that Franco finally took the decision to nominate Juan Carlos in the course of the summer and early autumn of 1968'.[7] But it was not until July 1969 that Juan Carlos was informed that his nomination was to be sent to the Cortes for formal ratification. As a compromise, it was agreed that he would use the title 'Prince of Spain' until he acceded to the throne, rather than the more usual title to designate the heir to the throne, 'Prince of Asturias', since this would have implied that there was in fact a king reigning in Spain. As was to be expected in Franco's docile parliament, the nomination was approved. Four hundred and ninety-one votes were cast in favour and 19 against, with the only real opposition coming from some of the monarchists themselves, both supporters of Don Juan and the Carlists. In recogition that the monarchy was emerging from the dictatorship, Juan Carlos swore an oath of loyalty to the fundamental principles of the regime.

The nomination of Juan Carlos, however, came too late to save the regime. In fact, by 1969, only regime adherents and monarchists thought, or feared, that resolving the question of the succession could save the Francoist state. Few in the opposition believed that Juan Carlos could be separated from the regime, the very existence of which they opposed. For the most part, therefore, the opposition was Republican. Resolving the question of succession did not solve the immediate problems facing the dictatorship, which were caused by the rising tide of protest and popular dissatisfaction. Nor did making Juan Carlos the official heir to Francoism clarify exactly the powers the monarchy would enjoy on Franco's death, or the nature of the political system that would accompany this transition.

Juan Carlos's nomination was not entirely unconnected to the rising tide of Opus Dei influence in the government and to the emergence of technocratic, conservative forces within the authoritarian state, a development which continued through the 1960s. As Catholic conservatives, Opus Dei members tended to favour monarchical government in principle. López Rodó, in particular, who had established early on in his career an excellent relationship with the key figure of Carrero Blanco and whose main concern was the continuity of the authoritarian state, played an important role in promoting the monarchy as a solution to the problem of succession. Indeed, members of Opus Dei even penetrated the structures of the National Movement, which was less and less under Falangist influence, especially since the Falange could attract so few young members. This trend had begun as early as 1961 when Opus Dei member Fernando Herrero Tejedor became vice-secretary general of the National Movement, a position he occupied until 1966. Other Opus Dei members began to occupy positions in the provincial organisations of the National Movement. The dominance of Opus Dei in the government reached its height in 1969, when the tradition of balancing elite interests was broken and a cabinet named which was effectively an Opus Dei cabinet. This was referred to as the 'monocolour' cabinet.[8]

The background to this important cabinet restructuring was the MATESA affair, which broke over the summer of 1969. This implicated high-ranking Opus Dei officials and even possibly Opus Dei government members in corruption. Francoists hostile to Opus Dei's political influence tried to use the scandal to push them out of government. The manoeuvre failed.[9] What appears to have happened was that a leading Spanish company, MATESA S.A., obtained considerable export credits from the government, without having first obtained the necessary orders abroad, which was the condition under which they could be granted. The company claimed that the circumstances surrounding their credit application were well-known within government circles and that it was accepted by officials that firms would apply for export credits without having the requisite orders abroad first. The affair was denounced by the director of Spanish customs, a Falangist, delighted to implicate Opus Dei associates in scandal. His motivation appears to have been primarily political and it was hoped by the Falange that the scandal would throw into doubt the management skills and even the honesty of Opus Dei members. The affair was investigated by a commission of the Cortes and, unusually, it was widely reported in the press. Allegations were also made that Opus Dei used MATESA to send money abroad in order to finance their operations outside Spain. At the very least, it seems that Opus Dei members had allowed the rules to be broken and had seen the legislation, to some degree a left-over from the earlier economically nationalist period, as an obstacle to be circumvented. The interest kindled by the MATESA affair was not due to the fact that financial corruption was a rare event in Spain. It owed its prominence to the fact that reformists around Fraga and the Falangists within the National Movement were prepared to use their access to the press to attempt to discredit Opus Dei and it is an indication of how tense relations were between the Francoist families. The scandal failed to dislodge Opus Dei members from positions of authority, however. In fact, this would have required removing Carrero Blanco himself. He protected the group and was, by 1969, the leading figure within the government. Additionally, it would have left the government without a cohesive economic team, and would have raised questions internationally about the stability of the regime's economic policies. By 1969, the international dimension constituted an important constraint on policy choices and this undoubtedly weighed in the decision to retain the Opus Dei team. Finally, several prominent Opus Dei members were close to Franco's own family circle, making it even less likely that they could be removed.

The result was a reshuffle in October 1969, which actually strengthened the hand of Opus Dei within the cabinet. The new cabinet was composed almost exclusively of Opus Dei members or other prominent Catholics, and Fraga, Solís and Nieto Antuñez were removed. The Foreign Minister, Fernando María Castiella, was also dropped, as his foreign policy was becoming difficult to reconcile with closer integration into Europe and a more consensual approach to the US. Alonso Vega, Minister of the Interior, was retired on the grounds of his age and replaced by Tomás Garicano Goñi. Carrero Blanco remained as vice-president, a position which he had occupied since 1967. López Rodó was retained as Minister without Portfolio, Silva Muñoz as Minister of Public Works, Antonio María de Oriol as Minister of Justice and José Luis Villar Palasí as Minister of Education. Torcuato Fernández Miranda, who had been a tutor to Juan Carlos, became secretary of the National Movement, a cabinet position, where he was able to exercise considerable influence. Enrique García Ramal, was put in charge of the Syndical Organisation and Gregorio López Bravo moved to Foreign Affairs. The new Finance Minister, Alberto Monreal Luque, was close to Opus Dei in economic matters, and the new Minister of Information, Alfredo Sánchez Bella, was identified with the ultra-conservative anti-conciliar Catholic movement. In 1970, Silva Muñoz, the only minister left in the cabinet identified with liberalisation, was removed and replaced by Gonzalo Fernández de la Mora, a right-wing Catholic integrist, fiercely hostile to all expressions of political liberalism. So, in sum, the final result of the MATESA scandal was a clear shift to the right within the cabinet.

As vice-president, Carrero effectively ran the day-to-day business of government. His influence over the ailing figure of Franco increased to the point where he was regularly referred to as the Caudillo's *alter ego*. His long memoranda to Franco provided the analyses of the political situation on which many key, non-economic government decisions were based. This in itself points to the decay within Francoism. It had failed to generate new cadres and effective politicians outside the economic sphere. Carrero represented an adamant commitment to continuity without significant change. He recognised the importance of maintaining the support of social elites and institutions, but his vision of the state was that it was entrusted to guide Spain and was above the actors in the society it protected. For Carrero, preservation of the authoritarian state and its autonomy was the primary goal of government. Relations with the different forces inside Francoism were a secondary concern in the 1960s. He believed that no changes of real sigificance had taken place since 1936 and was unwilling to recognise that pro-regime groups should have any influence over policy.[10] In a memorandum to Franco in 1968, for example, he attributed the problems of government to a lack of unity within the cabinet and advised the formation of a new cabinet under the control of Franco, without considering the impact this would have within the regime or whether it would upset the balance of forces within the dictatorship.[11] In another memorandum of 1969, he showed himself prepared to antagonise the official unions, which, he suggested, enjoyed too much freedom. He also appeared to be opposed to the liberalising tendencies of Fraga, Minister of Information, and went on to advise Franco to appoint only individuals of proven moral character to the cabinet.[12] Carrero urged the government to take action to stop even the criticisms of dissident Francoists and he pressed the cabinet to reform the Press Law and end freedom of the press. Although he lost that particular battle, since by 1968 the rest of the cabinet and Franco himself recognised that it would be impossible to tighten the press laws further in that it would have provoked too much protest from society, he never ceased in his campaign to urge the government to act decisively to protect the Spanish people from the vitiating influences of freedom, democracy, atheism, communism and freemasonry.

Not surprisingly, then, the internal tensions which had always characterised cabinet meetings were not eliminated by the reshuffle. By now, events in Spain were moving so rapidly, due to increased pressure from the opposition and the failing health of Franco himself, that policies had to be made and remade and established decisions reconsidered as well as new ones taken. This process, as might have been foreseen, split the new cabinet. Once again, the divisions which emerged were between hard-liners and moderates who saw the need for some degree of *rapprochement* with elements of civil society. In May 1973, Garicano Goñi, a moderate, was dismissed, following his suggestion that ultra-right elements were undermining the regime and were in fact protected by some ministers. He argued that his position had become 'intolerable', and that participation in government with hard-liners now raised moral issues even for right-wingers. In later interviews with the press, Garicano claimed that the consensus within the cabinet had been fundamentally broken during the trial in 1970 of ETA militants, known as the Burgos trial.[13] The trial brought Spain under the intense, critical and sustained scrutiny of international observers for the first time since the 1940s and raised a number of moral questions about the methods which the regime used to deal with opposition.[14]

In 1973 the cabinet was once again reshuffled. Now, for the first time, Franco gave the active running of the cabinet to Carrero Blanco, who became president of the government, with Franco remaining as head of state. It was a symbolic move that indicated that the regime was attempting to create a framework which would be maintained after the Caudillo's death. Payne alleges that the cabinet was chosen for the most part by Carrero Blanco, with only Carlos Arias Navarro as Minister of the Interior, the position Garicano's removal had left vacant, suggested by Franco.[15]

The key issue facing the new cabinet was the government's relationship with society. The question was how the government would respond to the growing demands for greater participation and accountability and for democracy itself. It was an issue which could no longer be ignored. Fernández Miranda, as Minister of the National Movement, was put in charge of analysing the channels for political participation within the system and was given the brief of finding ways in which they could be made to respond to demands for change without undermining the dictatorship. His response was to concentrate on the identification of the National Movement exclusively with the authoritarian regime and with Franco personally, as figurehead and as Caudillo. He argued that, for the regime to survive, the Movement must be rendered more dynamic and it must also be able to exist without Franco. In order to bring about the necessary changes, Fernández Miranda proposed that the National Movement be slowly brought round to identifying itself with the monarchy. He pointed out that the Movement would not be able to govern without depending on the monarchy but, equally, he argued that the monarchy would not survive without the institutional support which the Movement offered. The way forward, therefore, was to tie the two together: 'The Movement must be renewed with an eye towards the future. We must now organise the King's Movement. It was Francoist in origin but now it will be the King's.'[16]

The debate about participation and the role of the National Movement was not destined to go far, however. It came to an abrupt halt with the spectacular assassination by ETA of the president of the government, Carrero Blanco. He was blown up by a car bomb on 20 December 1973. The assassination was part of ETA's strategy to force the government to move towards repression and thereby reveal the sham of its liberalisation attempts. ETA hoped that increased repression would radicalise the population, who would mobilise in rejection of the dictatorship and bring it to an end. The political climate at the time of the assassination was rendered even more tense, in that it took place on the day that the trials of leaders of the independent unions, the Workers' Commissions, were due to begin. This seemed to indicate that the government was even more likely to crack down on opposition activities and turn even further to the right. In the event, however, ETA's calculations about the government response were wrong and Fernández Miranda, who automatically became president of the government following Carrero's death, refused to give orders for widescale repression. ETA's strategy, therefore, in the short term, failed. Taking a longer perspective, however, the removal of Carrero Blanco ended the illusion that the regime would be able to survive the death of Franco and contributed decisively to the collapse of the dictatorship.[17]

The assassination of Carrero Blanco had made obvious what had, in fact, been a reality in Spain since around 1969: that despite the relatively smooth running of government on a day-to-day basis, the political agenda was being shaped by the growing waves of social protest of different kinds and by a political opposition which was in the process of recomposition. There were three distinct oppositional forces in particular which presented serious problems to the authoritarian regime: industrial labour; ETA; and the student movement. The political parties on the left, by contrast, were as yet poorly organised, did not present a serious challenge to the regime and did not control the social movements which had sprung up to protest against the dictatorship. They did, nonetheless, continue to issue condemnations of the regime from exile, and had begun to rebuild the parties inside Spain. In addition, the regime faced severe criticisms from sectors of the Catholic church, and occasional confrontations with other organised groups, such as the terrorist group Frente Revolucionario Antifascista y Patríota (FRAP).

Labour militancy was a continual problem for the regime, as strikes mushroomed from 931 in 1973, to 2990 in 1974 to reach 3156 in 1975. This signified more hours lost in strikes in Spain than in France or the UK, where union activity was legal. But, despite the undoubted impact of labour opposition, ETA was the most spectacular of the oppositional forces. It counted on growing support from Basque youth, and a more general climate of tolerance within the Basque country which was due to widespread nationalist sentiment in the region, as well as being a consequence of state repression. The government adopted the policy of suspending civil liberties in the Basque provinces as a result of nationalist activity and of trying suspected terrorists in military courts, on the presumption that they had committed war crimes. The high point of this policy was the Burgos trial, effectively a court martial, of ETA members in 1970. In fact, government policy served only to exacerbate the problem and the dynamic of confrontation–repression between Madrid and the radical Basque nationalists was a lasting legacy bequeathed to post-Franco Spain.[18]

INTERNAL DISAGREEMENTS AND THE DEVELOPMENT OF A 'CIVILISED RIGHT'

The Francoist regime consisted of an alliance between the political and social forces which made up the Spanish right. It had been forged in the uprising of 1936. The authoritarian state, however, had never fused these groups into a composite movement, despite the creation of a single party. Francoism was therefore a flexible coalition, in which power flowed between clearly identifiable, though overlapping, elites. Its success until the end of the 1950s lay in its ability to accommodate all the different social and political groups on the right. In the 1960s the unity of the right, and therefore of the Francoist alliance, fractured decisively and irreparably over questions of goals and strategy. The first stage in the dissolution of the alliance was the Organic Law of 1966.

Disaffected Francoists saw the Organic Law as the last opportunity for the regime to liberalise from within. Ex-Francoist Alvárez de Miranda claims that even reformers within the government attempted to push the proposals further than Franco accepted. He wrote later in his memoirs:

> The greatest expectations surrounded the announced Organic Law, which Federico Silva explained to me personally as a decisive step towards political pluralism ... I am convinced that Silva also saw that law as a decisive step in the political evolution of the regime.[19]

Notwithstanding Alvarez de Miranda's claims, Silva himself, Minister of Public Works in the government, makes no mention of any dissatisfaction of his own over the contents of the Organic Law. Indeed, he claims that he was responsible for certain aspects of the final text.[20] Nonetheless, with hindsight, Silva recognised it was an error of the dictatorship to attempt to perpetuate itself in power through the single-party structure which the Organic Law upheld. This position was shared also by the technocrats, most vocally by López Rodó. Unlike ex-Francoists who had moved towards genuinely liberal positions, rightists like Silva argued that the regime needed to change for instrumental reasons, in order to satisfy international actors, above all the US:

> We are living in an American-dominated century ... and the American philosophy is democracy. So it was important to find a viable democratic formula for us. We had the opportunity to do this with the attempt at institutionalising the regime.[21]

The disappointment provoked by the Organic Law proved a point of departure within Francoism. It crystallised the emergence of a tendency which Linz describes as 'semi-opposition'.[22] These were groups of dissident Francoists, generally either monarchists or Christian Democrats. The regime tolerated their activities for the most part and, in return, they opposed the regime without attempting to mobilise Spanish society against it. Individuals rather than organisations were important and opposition was expressed through newspaper articles or in journals, taking advantage of the press liberalisation, or in small elitist discussion groups. To move outside these tolerated arenas for opposition, however, meant incurring penalties. Newspapers which took too critical a stand found themselves closed. Even *Madrid*, under the editorship of Rafael Calvo Serer, member of Opus Dei and ex-regime supporter, was closed in 1972 after it became evident that his shift to the left was putting him beyond the political pale. In exile in Paris, as if to prove the point, he drifted towards collaboration with the communists.

The example of Calvo Serer notwithstanding, most dissident rightists were unwilling to throw in their lot with the Republican groups which had opposed the dictatorship from its beginnings. The furthest they could go was to make contact with individuals from the moderate opposition. Additionally, they wished to preserve many of the privileges they had enjoyed under the dictatorship. They retained an identification with the uprising of 1936, they did not offer a revisionist version of the 'official' history of the Crusade, and they did not question the original legitimacy of the regime. Crucially, they avoided populist calls to broader elements within society to organise mass opposition and overthrow the dictatorship. Hence the regime in turn was generally respectful of these groups, many of whose supporters were personally known to government members and who inhabited the same social and cultural world. On the few occasions when who individuals from the semi-opposition were detained, they were treated better than perceived leftists were treated.[23]

For all of these reasons, Preston is suspicious of regarding these groups as part of the 'opposition' to Franco.[24] He argues that they offered a kind of 'creative discord' and that disagreements represented merely internal quarrels and a jostling for position and power within the state. They could not be considered as representing a threat to the regime. Of course it was the goal of these groups to change the regime rather than end it. But to overemphasise this aspect of their activities is to miss the significance of the transformation that many Francoists and ex-Francoists underwent, albeit in many cases for instrumental reasons, in the final years of the dictatorship. The drift of important supporters of the regime towards the possibility of accommodating (at least some of) the opposition was to prove a crucial feature of the transition to democracy. This trend, in fact, constituted a *sine qua non* of the transition. The emergence of a semi-opposition indicates that the forced duality of two Spains, regime and opposition, which had sustained the dictatorship since the civil war, was breaking down. By the end of the 1960s, Spanish society was no longer divided into two mutually exclusive categories.

Dissident Francoists and ex-Francoists followed different routes. Some, like Fraga, 'represented a kind of loyal dissidence, whose goal was the modification of the cabinet rather than changing the structures of the regime'.[25] Fraga hardly moved from this position until after the new democratic constitution was promulgated in 1977. Others, however, broke more decisively with the regime in the 1960s and early 1970s. One such figure was José María de Areilza.[26] He had held important offices under Franco, including mayor of Bilbao after the civil war, ambassador to Argentina in the 1940s and, more latterly, France. In 1964, Areilza resigned to take up the cause of the monarchy. As secretary to Don Juan, Areilza worked to convert the monarchy into a liberal institution which would be an alternative to authoritarianism. His broader project, however, was the creation of what he termed 'a civilised right', a term he first used in 1968. Areilza realised that liberalisation in Spain depended not only on the introduction of a degree of genuine electoral participation within the country but, more fundamentally, on a profound process of change within the Spanish right. The right would have to learn to separate itself from the dictatorship and live with the elements of uncertainty that are intrinsic to democratic politics. This new understanding of the role of the right in politics is the clearest indication of the distance he travelled from Francoism. The logic of his reflections was as follows:

> The right had won militarily the civil war, and it had won absolutely, without pacts or negotiations with the enemy. Since then, it had been in government in Spain. It is true that politics under Franco contained ingredients of social reform . . . but it is also true that a very significant percentage of our ruling class considered itself installed for life and protected by an authoritarian system which gave them advantages and status, exclusive access to the centres of decision-making and considerable benefits. This privileged situation lasted until the final day of the Francoist regime. And to speak of 'civilising the right', sounded in many ears as an impertinence which meant the destruction of a system which had functioned efficiently for many decades.[27]

The liberal monarchists were the first sector of the original authoritarian coalition to separate their cause from that of Franco. The Unión Española (UE) was founded as early as 1957, under the leadership of Joaquín Sastrústegui. Representing a tendency on the right rather than an active political organisation, UE proclaimed itself to be Catholic but tolerant of other religions, and respectful of regional identities. There were early contacts between the UE and some socialists inside Spain, notably those grouped around Tierno Galván. But the UE was unusual in that it was prepared to repudiate the regime openly. In 1959, Sastrústegui asked: 'Can a civil war constitute the foundations of a political regime? I and others . . . participated in the uprising from the beginning, but we believe that a civil war is an enormous tragedy on which the future cannot be built.'[28]

Sastrústegui consistently argued that the role of the monarchy was to effect national reconciliation. It had to separate itself from authoritarianism and identify itself as democratic in order to carry this out. He was therefore highly suspicious of Juan Carlos, whom he perceived as collaborating in the creation of an authoritarian monarchy. He wrote to Juan Carlos in 1969, shortly after the latter had been named Franco's successor:

The monarchy that the King [i.e. Don Juan] offers the Spanish people is one which would make possible the evolution of the country towards a stable and peaceful harmony and democracy in line with the principles of the post-conciliar Church . . . . This kind of monarchy could have been established years ago, if the monarchy, as an institution, had not been identified with political tendencies that are incompatible with that democratic evolution. This is the immobilist monarchy to which Your Highness has been summoned. The two concepts are inherently contradictory. Your Highness will agree that the only reason for the elimination of the King [Don Juan] is that he genuinely wishes to represent a monarchy that can evolve. His displacement . . . points to the fact that those of us who trusted in the liberalisation that monarchy would effect in order to overcome the divisions of the civil war and ease our entry into Europe will be disappointed.[29]

Despite the outspoken tone which UE adopted, its impact was always greater in terms of transforming the attitudes of the right and in signalling the potential existence of a 'civilised right', rather than in directly challenging the regime. The UE could offer little effective opposition to the regime and was a loose grouping of like-minded upper-class individuals. In terms of an impact on society, the more significant section of the ex-Francoists to move into opposition was the Catholics who moved towards Christian Democracy, as a result of their radicalisation by the social concerns of the teachings of the Catholic church and later by the Second Vatican Council. These were to form the Democracia Social Cristiana (DSC) under the presidency of Gil Robles, ex-head of CEDA and convinced monarchist. The DSC was identified with Don Juan and participated in the opposition meeting in Munich in 1962.[30] A second Catholic group emerged in the shape of the Izquierda Demócrata Cristiana (IDC), which had developed out of the student movement of 1956. Identified with ex-minister Manuel Giménez Fernández, the IDC had a national presence in universities in the 1960s and was closer ideologically to Spanish socialism in its hostility to communism and its suspicions of the monarchy and Don Juan. The Catholic opposition was strengthened by the appearance of *Cuadernos para el Diálogo* in 1963, edited by Joaquín Ruiz Giménez, ex-Minister of Education. But it was also hindered by the tendency towards schisms and disagreements which prevented the Christian Democrats from organising effectively.

Rather than constituting a direct challenge to the dictatorship, then, these dissident groups were important in that they undermined the legitimacy of authoritarianism. As a result of the number of Francoists leaving the fold, the running of the government was entrusted more and more to Admiral Carrero Blanco, whose loyalty to the values of the 1936 uprising was unquestionable. In complete contrast to the reformist or moderate Francoists, Carrero Blanco was aware of no relevant changes which had taken place in Spain since 1936 which might render the dictatorship, or the form the dictatorship assumed, outmoded or inadequate. His world vision remained set in a framework which blamed the Freemasons, the communists and, perhaps most strangely of all, even the British, for most of the problems affecting the country; in 1969, he even suggested that it was likely that the money to finance ETA came from the British government, determined to distract the Spanish from the problem of Gibraltar.[31] It was evidence of the erosion of support and the absence of internal renewal within Francoism which the defection of important parts of the right had contributed to.

THE POLITICS OF OPPOSITION

There was an escalation of opposition to the dictatorship from within society after 1966. The opposition movements which developed around this time operated more openly than in the earlier years and used the spaces created by the partial liberalisation which had taken place. The independent union movement, the Workers' Commissions, had set a precedent in this direction as early as 1962. Operating openly and competing in syndical elections had allowed the Commissions to make a significant impact on the political scene. But there were dangers associated with openness too, as the fate of the Commissions themselves made clear. In 1967 the regime's tolerance of union activity outside the official union structures suddenly ended, and the Commissions were pronounced illegal and subversive organisations and completely proscribed. Officials from the Workers' Commissions were detained and many of the shop stewards who had organised the movement at the base level were also arrested, making it difficult for the Commissions to maintain the momentum they had built up. As this example shows, the government response to oppositional social movements was cyclical and selective. This kept the opposition in a state of uncertainty and obscured the limits of their activities. It forced a kind of self-censorship onto the opposition which was never sure how far it would be able to go. The openness with which the Commission leaders operated, which was a strategy imposed by the Communist Party, was in fact criticised by some unionists, since it exposed individuals to the possibilities of arrest and repression, and left many without work because they were dismissed.

There were three main types of social opposition to the dictatorship which emerged at this time: from labour unions, from regional nationalists, especially the Basques, and from students. Labour demonstrations and strikes involved more Spaniards in active protest against the Franco regime than any other sort. The dynamics of labour protest against the dictatorship were twofold. On the one hand, there was the logic of collective action against employers, in order to improve wages and working conditions. State legislation and actions had consistently shaped labour relations in favour of the employers. On the other hand, there was a logic of political protest. The two dynamics of workers' action were of course in practice intertwined. In research based on interviews with union leaders, Maravall claims that politically motivated strikes increased in number after 1967 compared to those related to economic demands.[32] 'Collective bargaining was used by the secret organisations to stimulate sets of demands that became increasingly political, bringing the labour-repressive institutions to the centre of the struggle'.[33] Working-class militancy after 1967, therefore, was the result of a combination of factors, including the process of industrialisation and the disciplinary and productive regime under which workers were employed, as well as a rejection of the authoritarian regime. But its impact was overwhelmingly political.

The workers' movement was more militant by the late 1960s than it had been in the early years of the decade. But it remained fragmented, due to the scale of police repression after the Workers' Commissions had been made illegal. For some workers, this initially silenced them like the harsh and systematic repression of the 1940s had silenced their parents. Others have described graphically how they had to overcome fear and confront family pressure in order to participate in anti-regime movements:

> What I've always felt in my family was that they desperately tried to keep me away from any kind of political activity. You see, I've always been aware of the great terror, a terror which existed amongst the people, as a consequence of the war – the only ideology that I got from my family was fear: 'Don't get involved in anything', that's what they always said.[34]

The working-class movement remained fragmented in the late 1960s for cultural reasons as well. Militancy was in part due to the new social and economic conditions engendered by industrialisation. The main centres of workers' protests and strikes were the cities. Many of those participating in strike activities were newcomers to the city who had migrated in search of employment as a result of the economic expansion of the 1960s. This did not make them necessarily any less militant than workers whose families had been in the cities for a generation or more. But it did mean that the cultural links which bind people into their communities and make possible collective social actions were rather more fragile. In other words, the rapidity of urbanisation meant that there had not been sufficient time for the cultural consolidation of working-class ties. The net result of this was that continuity in terms of protest and opposition was sometimes a problem.

In view of these barriers to organised protest, the scale of working-class activity was remarkable. Labour militancy even spread to areas of production which had no history of union activity under Franco or even before the civil war. Originally, militancy had been associated with metalworkers, miners, etc. – those groups which had a history of union organisation that predated the existence of the authoritarian regime. By the late 1960s, it encompassed middle-class professionals in banking, teaching and the administration. It had also spread to the new industries like the motor vehicle industry. In October 1971, the state-owned SEAT car factory in Barcelona, the largest industrial plant in the country, was brought to a standstill as 8000 people stopped work in support of a group of union militants who had been dismissed because of their political activities. SEAT refused to negotiate with the workers and the police were called to clear the factory. It took them 13 hours to gain control of it and in the process several workers were shot and one was killed. In the days following, rallies and demonstrations were held throughout Barcelona, indicating broad support across the city for the SEAT workers. So, although it proved impossible to organise nationwide general strikes against the dictatorship, local activities were undertaken effectively. In certain regions such as Catalonia, the workers were aided by the new social movements then emerging to present a broad front of rejection to the dictatorship. The protests, strikes and stoppages were also supported by a new generation of lawyers who had specialised in labour law and assisted the unions in contesting the Francoist legislation in the courts.

In the early 1970s, these kinds of general strikes confined to a small area were to prove particularly effective against the regime. All workers in all branches of production would stop working in a particular area. In 1973, there was a localised general strike in Pamplona, two in Sabadell and three in Baix Llobregat. They were called for political reasons, either in solidarity with dismissed workers, who had been on strike, or because of police repression. In 1974, 80 per cent of workers in the Basque provinces came to a halt in solidarity with Basque political prisoners who were on hunger strike. It was a particularly effective political protest since it made it difficult for the regime to single out individuals against whom it could take reprisals. Nevertheless, the workers' capacity to take action was limited by government repression of Worker' Commissions, which had organised most of the protests. In 1973, the government arrested and tried many of the national leaders of the Commissions in a celebrated and publicised trial known as Proceso 1001. This was the trial that opened on the day that Carrero Blanco was assassinated.

The most spectacular opposition to the dicatorship came not from the unions, however, but from the Basque separatist movement, ETA. The leadership of the traditional party of Basque nationalism, the Partido Nacionalista Vasco (PNV), had been forced into exile after the creation of the dictatorship. By the early 1960s, its support was so reduced that it was unable to organize any opposition to the regime. Yet the centralist and Castile-centred discourse of Francoism intensified nationalist sentiments within the Basque provinces. The dictatorship engaged in active repression of the Basque language, culture and identity. It has been argued, in fact, that the degree of repression in the Basque provinces was unique. According to Stanley Payne, Francoism consistently commanded less support from Basque political elites than from those in other regions of Spain and recruitment to the security forces was lower than elsewhere, with the result that the paramilitary police force, the civil guard, took on for Basques the character of an army of occupation.[35] And, significantly, the repression actually increased in the last years of the regime, with torture of detainees commonplace and states of emergency almost continually in force.

The harshness of the dictatorship, combined with the weakness of the PNV as a vehicle for opposition, brought about a dramatic change in the nature of Basque nationalism: for the first time it took on radical and Marxist elements. ETA, formed in 1958, adopted the armed struggle ten years later. It went on to constitute a challenge to the Franco regime and to the Basque industrial and financial elites, who were seen as collaborators in the economic and cultural policies of Francoism. The new radical nationalism of ETA, therefore, was directed as much against the pro-Spanish groups within the Basque provinces as it was against Madrid. This accounted for some of the confusion about ETA's goals within the rest of the opposition at the time. ETA was praised and even aided by the Spanish Communist Party in its campaigns during the dictatorship.[36] However, ETA was always more concerned with liberating the Basques from Spain than with liberating Spain from Francoism, although until 1977 this distinction appeared rather an academic one.

ETA's activities constituted a serious problem for the authoritarian regime. But the challenge ETA presented was not so much a result of its organisational sophistication or its capacity to carry out armed actions. Until 1971, the movement was weak and rent by internal divisions and disagreements over strategy and tactics. Clark estimates that, between 1968 and 1977, 119 people were killed in ETA-connected events, of whom 57 were members of the organisation, generally, though not always, killed by the police.[37] Most of ETA's targets in this period were designed to avoid major civilian casualties and were attacks on government offices or the private homes of government officials, large financial institutions and the mass media. In contrast, therefore, to the activities of the state, the violence employed by ETA in pursuit of their nationalist goals did not appear great. And because the state employed the whole weight of its repressive apparatus against ETA, and allowed rightist groups to act outside the law with impunity, ETA became a rallying point for Basques and indeed Spanish people in general. The challenge which ETA represented to the regime, therefore, was rather that it unmasked the authoritarian and repressive methods used by the dictatorship in the attempt to wipe out opposition.

The government's response to ETA was twofold. Firstly, it attempted to eliminate support for ETA by repression of the Basque people generally. It introduced states of emergency throughout the Basque provinces and occasionally throughout the country in response to ETA actions. This involved a suspension of civil liberties, including freedom of movement, residence and association. Perhaps most importantly, it suspended habeas corpus, which meant that individuals detained by the police could be held indefinitely without charge. States of emergency – declared six times in the Basque country between 1960 and 1977 – also created the conditions in which right-wing terror could be employed since it gave citizens few legal rights of protection. The Guerrilleros de Cristo Rey, a right-wing terrorist group, carried out 85 actions, including two that resulted in the deaths of their victims, in the Basque provinces during the state of emergency which lasted from spring 1975 to autumn 1976.[38]

Secondly, where possible, the government attempted to bring suspected ETA members to trial. The most important trial of ETA militants was the Burgos trial of December 1970, in which 16 members were tried by a military court. Two of the accused were priests. It followed a police offensive throughout 1969, which had severely disabled the movement. However, the trial worked in favour of ETA, in that it placed the organisation at the centre of political events. In this way it backfired on the government, for instead of terrorising the Basques into abandoning ETA, it produced a wave of support for the movement and of condemnation of the regime both in Spain and abroad. The defence of the accused was skilfully conducted by a number of opposition lawyers, including Gregorio Peces-Barba, a socialist and later a prominent figure in the transition. They used the trial to illustrate to a national and international audience the social and political exploitation and repression of ordinary Basque and Spanish people. Defendants consciously made use of their access to international public opinion – the trial was well covered by foreign journalists – in order to win support for their cause. As a result, the image of the Franco regime abroad was considerably damaged, as foreign television channels and newspapers extensively covered not only the allegations of abuse and torture made at the trial but also the protests and demonstrations in support of the defendants. It was not surprising that, although nine of the defendants were condemned to death, the government decided to commute the sentences to life imprisonment in order to avoid further international attention.

Regular protests by university students were another feature of politics in the main cities of Spain in the 1960s. Student protest had not disappeared after the events of 1956. It centred initially on winning independence for the students' union. Between 1962 and 1964, independent candidates won university elections in Madrid, Bilbao and Barcelona. Students protested against the state's interference in university affairs and in favour of academic freedom. Based around these demands, an independent student movement gradually built up, extending its influence to other cities, including Oviedo, Valencia, Pamplona and Santiago. Violent confrontations with the police led to the abolition of the official student union, the SEU, in 1965, and in the early 1960s their cause was strengthened by the support of some prominent intellectuals such as José Luis Aranguren and Enrique Tierno Galván of the University of Madrid. In 1968, however, student protest increased in tempo and reached an unprecedented level of activity. The police were called into the universities regularly thereafter to repress student demonstrations and sit-ins, and did so using considerable violence. As a result, the universities became a major site for anti-regime mobilisation and political activity. Police repression increased and the police began to occupy the universities as a pre-emptive measure whenever a state of emergency was declared. In turn, this intensified the physical violence which characterised university protest between 1968 and 1975.

Student protest was significant for a number of reasons. Firstly, it was important because of the role of the university in Spanish culture and politics. Secondly, the sheer size of the student population meant that it was impossible to ignore them. By the time of Franco's death there were around 400 000 university students in the country, all located in large towns. This was a population larger than that of most cities in Spain at the time. The numbers had grown dramatically in the early 1970s as a result of social and demographic change in Spain and as a consequence of government plans to increase the university population. Thirdly, the student protests indicated that the regime had failed in one of the central tasks it set itself. It had failed to depoliticise the generation who did not remember the civil war. Young Spaniards, who had grown up without access to a free press or without the freedom to join a political party of their choice, were turning to Marxism and to radical political thought, and were demanding free elections, representative democracy or even revolution. It was quite a shock to the dicatorship, which blamed external influences for corrupting the young. And, finally, the protests signified that Spain could not stand outside the trends of European politics. Student radicalism was a feature of the late 1960s throughout Europe. Spain was not, after all, different. In fact, despite its impact, the movement was also weaker than it seemed because it was deeply divided ideologically. Disputes developed between the communists, the socialists, the Catholic-inspired groups and the smaller parties on the extreme left over tactics and organisation. Sometimes they dominated student politics and actually prevented the movement from offering more effective opposition. Still, student protest created a climate of mobilisation and an image of widespread rejection of the dictatorship which made it impossible for the regime to control society.

THE DISINTEGRATION OF THE REGIME, 1973–1976

Following the death of Carrero in December 1973, Franco appointed Carlos Arias Navarro, Interior Minister in the previous cabinet, as president of the government. It was a surprise appointment, and passed over the acting president, Torcuato Fernández Miranda, a lawyer and academic who was regarded as having managed the tense situation well. A possible reason for choosing Arias was that, as a hard-liner himself, he was acceptable to the law-and-order Francoists who were demanding a tough response to the assassination. He was also seen as having been an effective administrator in previous positions such as when he was mayor of Madrid. But he was given an impossible brief: to maintain public order, to take control of the political situation and to seize the initiative from the opposition. As if this were not enough, the Spanish economy began to enter a critical phase of development as a result of the international economic crisis which was just beginning, making the task of governing even more difficult.

The new government included more bureaucrats whose origins were within the state structures than ever before. The Opus Dei personnel largely disappeared and the traditional families also slipped into the background. It was, therefore, largely an administrative, technical and 'non-political' cabinet, which tried to present a united front to the opposition and satisfy the army that the crisis following Carrero Blanco's death would be controlled. But as might have been predicted, it was to prove impossible by this time to satisfy all sectors of Francoism. As a result, the new government wavered between promising a political opening in an effort to take the political initiative and conciliating moderate rightists and instituting repression to please the ultras and the army. Arias took a liberalising line in his speech to the Cortes which set out the programme for government. But there was little chance of implementing this programme, since hard-line Francoists openly went on the offensive from outside government in a way which had never occurred before. The hard-liners, given the name 'the Bunker' because of their willingness to retreat, like Hitler, to a bunker rather than surrender or change, were vociferous in demanding an increase in repression. The neo-fascist party Fuerza Nueva, organised by Blas Piñar and the Confederación de Ex-Combatientes, now led by ex-Minister José Antonio Girón, were supported by the newspapers *El Alcazar* and *Arriba*. These newspapers had a significant circulation within army barracks. Indeed, it was the fear of retaliation from the armed forces that was to operate as the most important check on how far liberalisation could go. By June 1974, only six months after taking office, Arias was trying to retain the image of liberalisation without giving it any content.[39]

Tensions over whether to liberalise or repress surfaced constantly. In October 1974, Pío Cabanillas was dismissed as Minister of Information for adopting too liberal a line. His dismissal was followed by the resignation of other government figures, including Francisco Fernández Ordóñez, president of INI and Marcelino Oreja, under-secretary at the Ministry of Information. After this, Arias pinned the government strategy of limited liberalisation to the promotion of 'political associations'. These had been proposed as a vehicle for a limited kind of political organisation and the idea had been under discussion within the government and the National Council of the Movement since the end of the 1960s. However, the proposal was rejected by the cabinet as being too difficult to control and it was decided that any participation would have to occur within the framework of the authoritarian system. Instead, the National Movement was entrusted, once again, with looking at the issue of participation. The analysis carried out by the National Council of the Movement revealed both the decay of the regime structures of participation and its separation from civil society.[40]

In the report to government, the National Movement showed itself to be aware of these problems, though it was at a loss as to how to address them. The report reveals that the Movement was almost moribund in terms of active membership and that participation in many areas was impossible due to the collapse of local organisation through 'either a lack of interest or a lack of means'.[41] It also criticised the leadership at local level which it described as 'barely capable of leading the base harmoniously and from the general perspective'.[42] In less flattering words, this meant that the cadres the Movement could attract lacked intelligence and dynamism. The analysis of the situation, then, was realistic. The solutions proposed, however, were optimistic to say the least. The National Council suggested that participation could be increased in the Movement by making local level meetings open to the public and by consciously appealing to those individuals who had so far kept outside active politics. The report claimed, bizarrely, that these individuals were 'susceptible to political indoctrination', something the Movement appeared to believe was necessary to participate actively in the formal structures of the regime. It goes on to present these proposals as 'taking note of the demographic changes which have taken place in Spain as well as the changes in social structure and thought within the country'.[43] It is altogether an extraordinary document, indicating the bankruptcy of regime options for repairing its relationship with Spanish society.

Nevertheless, it constituted part of the justification for the new government initiative, a statute of associations, which was passed in December 1974. This allowed for political groups to register for the first time outside the Movement. The idea was a failure. The hard-liners denounced the arrangement as the beginning of the end and the return of political parties, and the associations were ignored by the opposition, dismissed as an attempt at pseudo-democratisation with the intention of forestalling the changes which were increasingly seen as inevitable on the death of Franco himself. The failure of the project effectively put an end to the idea of liberalisation from within. This became apparent with the resignation of the Minister of Labour, Liciano de la Fuente, in February 1975, when a liberalisation of labour legislation was blocked by the cabinet.

This led to the formation of a new cabinet in March 1975. The most important change was the introduction of Fernando Herrero Tejedor, a member of Opus Dei who had important contacts in the National Movement, into the cabinet. His appointment was significant in that he was also a close advisor to Juan Carlos. He brought with him a young protégé, Adolfo Suárez, later a key figure in the transition. But any liberalisation which Herrero Tejedor might have been planning came to an end in June, when he was killed in a road accident. In any case, these changes in personnel were unlikely to be taken seriously in the country, as a result of mounting opposition and increasing defections from the authoritarian camp. The opposition continued to seize the political initiative. Furthermore, by 1974, the political parties were becoming more active within the opposition. After years of bitter fighting among themselves, the parties began to co-ordinate their efforts. In 1974, the Junta Democrática was formed, which included the communists, the small Popular

Socialist Party of Tierno Galván, and a mixed group of independent figures. A year later, the Plataforma de Convergencia Democrática brought together the socialists, a group of Social Democrats, Christian Democrats, the PNV and the Carlists, who had been part of the Junta Democrática, but who now defected.[44] Meanwhile Franco's health continued to deteriorate, amid rising political violence. A novel feature of the violence was that much of it now came from organised right-wing terrorist groups. Despite this, the new anti-terrorist legislation of August 1975 was applied only to the left-wingers from ETA and FRAP. In September 1975, Franco signed the death warrants of five revolutionaries in spite of international pleas for clemency, including interventions from the Pope and from Juan Carlos himself.

One consequence of all of this was that pragmatic Francoists became more aware than ever that the regime would not survive the death of Franco intact. In particular, those individuals tied to the Francoist state whose livelihoods depended on public employment were aware of the need to compromise with at least sections of the anti-Francoist opposition. The degree of institutional reform they were prepared to offer was not clear and was recognised as a matter for negotiation. Eventually, the party of the transition, the Unión de Centro Democrático (UCD), came to represent those ex-Francoists prepared to negotiate and institutionalise reform.[45] But if the civil bureaucracy was open to reform, this was not the case with the army, which remained, some exceptions notwithstanding, the guardian of the authoritarian state.[46] Fear of retaliation from the Armed Forces was a factor in conditioning reform projects from 1975 onwards.

Hence, as Maravall and Santa María point out, the crisis of Francoism 'cannot be entirely explained away by the structural transformations undergone by Spanish society since the late 1950s or by the political changes and contradictions experienced within the state organisation from the 1960s onwards'.[47] The decomposition of Francoism, which was revealed with the assassination of Carrero Blanco and which continued under Arias Navarro, was not straightforwardly a result of economic and social change within Spain. Neither was it merely a result of the paralysis of state organisations and errors of government. It came about as a consequence of a set of interrelated factors: demands for change from within Spanish society; a willingness to co-operate with political change on the part of social and economic elites; and the decay of the authoritarian institutions, which forced elites to look for an accommodation with the new social and political forces which had emerged in the 1960s. Self-interest, therefore, played an important role for the Francoist political class situated within the state.

Franco died on 20 November 1975, following a final illness aged 82. He had long suffered ill-health due to Parkinson's disease and his symptoms had worsened considerably during his last few years. His health took a turn for the worse in October and he was never seen in public again. Juan Carlos became king just two days later, on 22 November 1975. Arias Navarro was confirmed as president of the government six days after Franco's death. His cabinet this time, in contrast to the previous one, included some dissident Francoists and rightists who favoured reform, including Areilza and Antonio Garrigues, a liberal corporate lawyer. Fraga was appointed Minister of the Interior. However, contrary to the expectations of some, Fraga turned out to be a hard-liner as minister and ordered the police to repress demonstrations and strikes. But even with liberalisers in the cabinet, the new government was unable to take control of the political situation. The opposition kept up the momentum for democratisation – or democracy 'without adjectives' as it came to be known. Waves of strikes continued throughout 1976. Public services were brought to a halt. Demonstrations took place to demand the release of political prisoners and in the Basque country and Catalonia there were demands for autonomy from Madrid. In March 1976, five workers were killed by the police in particularly violent clashes in Vitoria. ETA's activities gave an air of urgency to the situation, since they continued unabated and largely uncriticised from the opposition.

Relations between Arias and Juan Carlos deteriorated as the government floundered. The king, yet to make clear his views on the political system he would like to see take shape in the future, and suspect to many in the opposition in view of his long association with the authoritarian state, sought a rapid solution to the political crisis. In June, in an important speech to the American Congress, he proclaimed his intention of presiding over a democratic Spain. Back at home, the Cortes rejected even the timid reforms offered by Arias, leading to a complete impasse. As a result, Arias resigned at the beginning of July.

Partly as a result of the patronage of Torcuato Fernández Miranda, who had taken him up on the death of Herrero Tejedor, the young Adolfo Suárez, ex-civil governor of Segovia and previously director-general of the state-run television service, was included in the list of three names submitted to the king, from which the new prime minister was to be selected. Suárez, to everyone's surprise, was chosen. It was undoubtedly a strange choice in that he was relatively unknown and his politics were not completely clear. Areilza would have been a clearer option for reform but he was kept off the list, precisely, it was presumed, because of his commitment to change. The appointment of Suárez, although he was in fact to be the architect of change in Spain, was greeted with suspicion from the opposition. By contrast, it was greeted happily by the old guard. In fact, Suárez was to implement rapid measures towards creating a new democratic framework for the country. His lack of clear association with any ideological camp within or outside the authoritarian state, his ambition, and his knowledge of the Francoist bureaucracy, all proved to be advantages at a moment when unfettered pragmatism and negotiating skills were more important than massive social or political support.

Although we shall look at the transition in more detail in the final chapter, it should be noted here that, from July 1976 when he was appointed, until the first democratic elections held almost a year later in June 1977, Suárez pushed through a series of reforms including the Law for Political Reform in October, which was passed by the old Cortes and effectively meant the *procuradores* voting for their own dissolution. This was perhaps the most significant reform of all. It indicated a break with Francoist institutions, though not necessarily the establishment of full democracy. Many in the Cortes were thought to have voted for their own dissolution in the belief that a new party of the right would be formed which would win a majority in a new parliament and therefore that their positions would be saved. They were proved wrong, but by then it was too late. Other key reforms followed, including the disbanding of the National Movement, the legalisation of political parties, the release of political prisoners, the introduction of new electoral laws, and the legalisation of the Communist Party. The last, perhaps more than anything else, indicated the government's irreversible commitment to democracy. It was a difficult reform to introduce because of the possibility of opposition from the army. As a result, the decree legalising the Communist Party was passed during a holiday period when it would be difficult for the army to organize opposition. All of these reforms were passed against a background of popular mobilisation and demands from the left for a rapid transformation of politics. As the pace of reform increased, so did police and right-wing violence. In just one week in January 1977, two students and five communist lawyers were killed. Violence from ETA did not cease either, with the police figuring as their main targets.

Suárez governed mostly by decree, with few formal negotiations with the opposition. According to Gunther, he offered only dialogue, not negotiations about the shape of the future political system.[48] This was democratisation from the top down. In terms of style and political management, the government of Suárez had inherited an authoritarian, not a consensual, approach to policy-making and he did not break with that tradition. Nevertheless, the democratisation of the formal political system went ahead remarkably rapidly. On 15 June 1977, the first open parliamentary elections since 1936 took place in Spain. The main task of the new parliament was to write a democratic constitution. Suárez's rapidly-formed UCD won 34.8 per cent of the vote to become the largest single party. He was returned, therefore, as the first elected president of the government since the civil war.

CONCLUSION

By 1977 the disintegration of the authoritarian regime, which had set in irreparably during the 1960s, was complete. Having failed to stabilise the alliance between forces within the authoritarian state, the regime fell to pieces from within as dissidents deserted Francoism and as the bureaucratic class opted, mainly for instrumental reasons, to preside over a process of democratisation. The new system was to be cemented in place by the king, Juan Carlos, who had chosen democracy when he selected Suárez as president of the government. The disintegration of authoritarianism and the transition were also driven by the immense clamour from within Spanish society for political change. The mobilisation of large sections of society was a characteristic of the politics of opposition in the 1960s and 1970s, in contrast to the weaker presence of the political parties. The democratisation of the formal political system was completed in 1977 and free elections were held. The democratisation of the culture and practice of politics is, however, in its very nature a slow and incremental process everywhere. How far Spain has progressed in that direction, and what the legacy of the dictatorship is, will be analysed in the final chapter of this book.

NOTES

1 J. M. Areilza, *Crónica de la Libertad* (Barcelona, 1985), p. 55.
2 S. Payne, *The Franco Regime* (Madison, 1987), p. 515.
3 M. Mérida, *Testigos de Franco* (Esplugues de Llobragat, 1977), p. 66.
4 Mérida, *Testigos de Franco*.
5 Note from Carrero to Franco, 7 May 1969, 'Consideraciones sobre la situación política', in L. López Rodó, *La larga marcha hacia la monarquía* (Barcelona, 1977), pp. 650–3. Carrero returns to the same point regularly in his correspondence with Franco. See also 21 October 1969, 'Consideraciones sobre la conveniencia de proceder a un reajuste ministerial', López Rodó, *La larga marcha*, pp. 654–9.
6 López Rodó, *La larga marcha*.
7 C. Powell, *Juan Carlos of Spain. Self Made Monarch* (Basingstoke, 1996), p. 35.
8 See Payne, *The Franco Regime* and J. P. Fusi and R. Carr, *Spain: Dictatorship to Democracy* (London, 1979) for further details.
9 A good description of the political context of the MATESA scandal can be found in P. Preston, *The Triumph of Democracy in Spain* (London, 1986), p. 23.
10 R. Soriano, *La mano izquierda de Franco* (Barcelona, 1981). For the relationship between Franco and Carrero Blanco, see also P. Preston, *Franco* (London, 1993).
11 Note from Carrero Blanco to Franco, 'Consideraciones sobre la situación política', López Rodó, *La larga marcha*, p. 650.
12 López Rodó, *La larga marcha*, p. 656.
13 See A. Bayod, ed., *Franco visto por sus ministros* (Barcelona, 1981), pp. 193–205.
14 For different perspectives on the Burgos trial, see Lurra, *Burgos juicio a un pueblo* (San Sebastian, 1978) and F. Ateaga, *ETA y el proceso de Burgos* (Madrid, 1971).
15 Payne, *The Franco Regime*, p. 587.
16 López Rodó, *La larga marcha*, pp. 456–7.
17 I. Fuente, J. García and J. Prieto, *Golpe mortal: assesinato de Carrero y agonía de franquismo* (Madrid, 1983).
18 For a discussion of the legacy of Francoism in the Basque country, see M. Onaindía, 'Transición democrática en Euskadi', *Leviatan* 21 (Otoño, 1985) pp. 12–27.
19 Fernando Alvarez de Miranda, *Del 'contubernio' al consenso* (Barcelona, 1985), p. 53.
20 F. Silva Muñoz, *Memorias políticas* (Barcelona, 1993).
21 Silva Muñoz, *Memorias*, p. 150.
22 J. Linz, 'Opposition To and Under an Authoritarian Regime: The Case of Spain', in R. Dahl, ed., *Regimes and Opposition* (New Haven, 1973). For an evaulation of Linz's contribution to the study of the opposition to Franco, see M. Gómez-Reino, F. Orizo and

D. Vila Carro, 'Spain: A Recurrent Theme for Juan Linz', in R. Gunther, ed., *Politics, Society and Democracy: The Case of Spain* (Boulder, 1993) and J. Cazorla, 'The Theory and Reality of the Authoritarian Regime', in R. Gunther, ed., *Politics, Society and Democracy*.

23 Alvarez de Miranda, *Del 'contubernio'* gives a perceptive account of what it meant to belong to the semi-opposition.

24 P. Preston, 'The Anti-Franco Opposition: The Long march to Unity', in P. Preston, ed., *Spain in Crisis* (London, 1976).

25 Preston, 'The Anti-Franco Opposition'.

26 Areilza has written extensively about his own role in politics, the dictatorship and the transition. See especially *Diario de un ministro de la Monarquía* (Barcelona, 1977), *Cuadernos de la Transición* (Barcelona, 1983) and *Crónica de la Libertad*.

27 J. M. Areilza, *Crónica de la Libertad*, p. 119.

28 Javier Tusell, *La oposición democrática a franquismo* (Barcelona, 1977), p. 344.

29 López Rodó, *La larga marcha*, p. 639.

30 For Gil Robles' period as secretary to Don Juan, see J. M. Gil Robles, *La Monarquía por la que yo luché: páginas de un diario, 1941–1954* (Madrid, 1976). For a description of his activities in the 1960s, see Tusell, *La oposición democrática al franquismo*.

31 Note from Carrero Blanco to Franco, 'Consideraciones sobre la situación política'; López Rodó, *La larga marcha*, p. 652.

32 J. M. Maravall, *Dictatorship and Political Dissent: Workers and Students in Franco's Spain* (London, 1978), p. 37–8.

33 Maravall, *Dictatorship*, p. 38.

34 Maravall, *Dictatorship*, p. 93.

35 S. Payne, *The Basques* (Reno, 1975).

36 See L. Falcón, *Viernes y trece en la calle de correo* (Barcelona, 1981) for a description of how the communists assisted ETA in the assassination of Carrero Blanco.

37 R. Clark, *The Basques: The Franco Years and Beyond* (Reno, 1979).

38 Clark, *The Basques* p. 171.

39 See Carr and Fusi, *Spain Dictatorship to Democracy* and Preston, *The Triumph of Democracy* for accounts of this period.

40 Consejo Nacional del Secretaría General del Movimiento, 'Participación y Movimiento Nacional, April 1974', (AGAC) Presidencia de Gobierno, Caja 9835.

41 'Participación y Movimiento'.

42 'Participación y Movimiento'.

43 'Participación y Movimiento'.

44 J. Tusell, *La Oposición Democrática*.

45 C. Huneeus, *La Unión de centro democrático y la transición a la democracia en España* (Madrid, 1985).

46 For an excellent review of the military at the end of the dictatorship and in the transition in comparative perspective, see F. Aguero, *Soldiers, Civilians and Democracy* (Baltimore, 1995).

47 J. M. Maravall and J. Santa María, 'Political Change in Spain and Prospects for Democracy', in G. O'Donnell, P. Schmitter and L. Whitehead, eds., *Transitions from Authoritarian Rule* (Baltimore, 1986).

48 R. Gunther, 'Spain: The Very Model of the Modern Elite Settlement', in J. Higley and R. Gunther, eds., *Elites and Democratic Consolidation in Latin America and Southern Europe* (Cambridge, 1991), p. 52.

II

THE POLICIES OF FRANCOISM

5

The Political Economy of Francoism

The period of Francoist rule saw a transformation of economic life in Spain. Between the end of the civil war and the fall of the regime, output in all areas of the economy and average income per head rose enormously. Economic growth was also accompanied by major structural changes. From a predominantly rural society in the 1930s the country had become industrialised and urbanised by the 1960s. Yet Francoism did not offer a smooth path to a developed society after a long period of economic failure. Instead, the regime directly contributed to nearly 20 years of economic stagnation through its early policies. These brought to a halt movements towards modernisation that peaked in crisis during the Republic and the civil war. A policy of autarky (self-sufficiency) and economic intervention served to guarantee the interests of the dictatorship's supporters at the expense of its enemies, but it was a failure in wider terms. By the end of the 1950s the weakness of the economy came to threaten the survival of Francoism, prompting a turn to a more liberal approach to economic affairs. At a time of worldwide economic growth, this allowed Spain to enjoy rapid development that finally transformed the country. However, while this gave the regime a new lease of life, the stresses produced by growth and the expectations that were heightened by it became increasingly difficult to contain. Even before the downturn of the early 1970s, the dictatorship showed itself to be incapable of dealing effectively with the problems of development. By the time of Franco's death almost every economic interest in Spain was ready to abandon the regime.

DEVELOPMENT AND CRISIS: THE ECONOMIC BACKGROUND TO FRANCOISM

Far from being overwhelmingly backward as is often suggested, by the 1930s Spain had moved from steady economic growth in the nineteenth century to rapid development from around the time of the First World War, reaching a highpoint in 1929. Between 1900 and 1929 agricultural output grew by a total of 65 per cent at an annual rate of 1.13 per cent according to a recent estimate, outstripping a population increase of 0.77 per cent. Industry performed more modestly until the 1920s when growth leapt to over 5 per cent a year. The economy not only grew in terms of output but also experienced structural changes. By 1929 the proportion of the active population engaged in agriculture had fallen to 45.5 per cent from 66 per cent in 1910. Over the same time period the proportions engaged in industry and services rose from 15.8 to 26.5 and 18.2 to 28 per cent respectively. Spain seemed to be moving steadily towards becoming an industrial and urban society. However, economic change was by no means straightforward or unproblematic.[1]

The most deep-seated problems arose within Spain's mosaic of rural societies. In the central, northern and Mediterranean regions, there was a preponderance of family farms (*minifundios*). Many, particularly in the north, were too small to adequately support a household, and peasant families lived a precarious existence. Lacking economies of scale, greater output and productivity were only possible through harder work. This left migration to find urban employment on a full-time or seasonal basis as the only alternative. The cereal growers of central Spain and livestock farmers of the north formed the bulk of those leaving the land but they also increasingly sought protection for their livelihoods. Along the Mediterranean, the main problem was not strictly production – diversification into high-value export crops such as wine, citrus fruits and nuts made this the most successful region of the country – but rather escalating disputes over the terms of leases between households and landowners. The bitterest and most intractable economic conflicts were found, however, in the southern regions of Extremadura and Andalusia. Here great estates (*latifundios*), controlled by the most powerful of Spain's agrarian elites, were a dominating feature. Commercial arable and livestock production on the estates relied on a mass of rural labourers and sharecroppers. Overpopulation led to fierce competition for scarce work and leases, keeping incomes at a low level and profits correspondingly high. This produced one of the most deeply divided agrarian societies in Europe.[2]

Industrial Spain was not immune to similar problems. Development was also highly regionalised and uneven. Established industries, such as textiles in Catalonia, steel-making and shipbuilding in the Basque country and mining in Asturias were only partially modernised and were uncompetitive in world terms. Industrialists in these areas pressured for tariff protection, often using regional nationalism as a vehicle. During the 1920s rapid economic change gave a boost to these older industries and stimulated the development of new enterprises outside the core industrial areas. Metallurgy, cement-making, construction, electricity, automobiles, railways, processed foods and consumer durables all became established. Many businesses served the expanding urban population. In this way cities such as Madrid, Valencia, Seville and Valladolid became manufacturing centres in their own right. Services also developed in tandem, with banking, insurance and retailing showing particularly strong growth. However, investment was erratic and firms were often precariously small. In both established and newly developed industries, wages and working conditions were often poor, employment insecure and living conditions in the expanding cities primitive.[3]

In many respects, therefore, economic change was destabilising, creating deep tensions within society. This was the background to the rise of powerful movements in the countryside and cities that sought to redistribute rising wealth and struggled for improvements in living and working environments. Leaseholders' organisations in the Mediterranean regions campaigned for better contracts, while in the south revolutionary anarchist and socialist peasant movements were only kept in check by the use of force on the part of the landed elites. Meanwhile, urban working-class movements – anarchists predominating in Catalonia and socialists elsewhere – struggled for improvements. Economic and social tensions became increasingly explosive. Government responses in the first three decades of the century oscillated between seeking a measure of social reform and the repression of discontent in support of the economic elites. A three-year revolutionary crisis at the end of the First World War (the so-called *trienio bolchevique*) culminated in military intervention. This was followed by attempts under the Primo de Rivera regime to appease both workers, through an alliance with the Socialist Party, and employers. The crumbling of this pact and the withdrawal of elite support, were instrumental in the fall of the regime and the creation of the Republic in 1931.[4]

Pent-up conflict over economic affairs finally came to a head during the Republic, and formed a significant factor in the outbreak of the civil war. Although Spain was spared the worst of the world depression, the economy was increasingly paralysed as it became the central battleground of the new regime. For the first time, Spain had governments committed to a series of fundamental reforms on both economic and social grounds. These were a mix of measures that included an eight-hour working day, compulsory wage arbitration, security of tenure for leaseholders and sharecroppers, and agrarian reform to redistribute the large estates. There was little co-ordination of policies and some – agrarian reform in particular – were inept and ineffective. But alongside the enormous increase in labour agitation produced by the open conditions of the Republic, reform threatened to undermine property rights and alter the balance of economic power. Not surprisingly, conservative economic interests led by the agrarian and industrial elites fought back. After 1933 the reforms were reversed under right-wing governments, only to be reapplied even more forcefully with the victory of the Popular Front in 1936. With waves of strikes and land invasions underway, the economy stood virtually at a standstill as rural and urban employers abandoned production. When military intervention against the Republic began it was welcomed by a broad range of economic interests: most prominently the elites but also by many peasant farmers and small businessmen.[5]

THE ECONOMIC FOUNDATIONS OF THE NEW STATE

Like much else under the Franco regime, the New State's approach to economic affairs was strongly shaped during the civil war and its aftermath. Its guiding principles of autarky or national self-sufficiency and economic intervention were not in themselves new, but the war convinced a wide range of Nationalist opinion that they were a necessity. The idea of economic independence from foreign goods and markets, and freedom from the pressures of foreign competition, were supported by most of the rightist political groups. This was reinforced by the disruption to trade caused by the civil war, the effects of the allied blockade during the World War, and the boycott of Spain afterwards. Likewise, state direction of the economy had a powerful attraction as a means to protect the national economic interest – as defined by the regime. Furthermore, many of the military and civilian leaders of the Nationalist camp felt that the state must take the lead internally as well as externally in order to make up for the perceived deficiencies of a liberal economy. The market was seen as both too individualistic, promoting selfish interests, and too prone to degenerating into class warfare. Political leaders of all shades of opinion, with Falangists particularly vehement, argued that economic mismanagement by the elites was partly to blame for the development of a revolutionary threat. Accordingly, the promotion of economic efficiency and social harmony required direction from the state. Thus, from the start, political and economic aims were closely intertwined in regime policies.[6]

Above all, there seemed to be a solid military logic shaping autarky and intervention. The leadership of the Nationalist side saw the protection and direction of the economy as a vital part of winning the war against the Republic and maintaining national security afterwards. As such, economic forces needed to be commanded as much as any other aspect of life in Spain. The economy was to be run, literally, on military lines; objectives were to be identified and the necessary factors of production brought together, almost like an army logistical exercise. Such primitive notions – held most strongly by Franco himself – rejected any place for professional economic expertise. This was perhaps not so surprising given that the Republic had relied so heavily in its reform policies on just such experts. Consequently, economic policy during and after the war was placed largely in the hands of the military. At all levels of economic policy-making and implementation men in uniform abounded. Army and naval engineers were seen as particularly suitable candidates for economic posts both during and after the war.[7]

Beginning during the war, a bewildering array of bodies at national and provincial levels was created to supervise every aspect of economic life. The intention that this would be a permanent system, not just a wartime necessity, was proclaimed by regime leaders. Attempts at economic direction had been tried in the past by very different regimes – most recently by both the Primo de

Rivera dictatorship and the Republic. They had almost all fallen foul, however, of resistance led by the agrarian and industrial elites. Yet no such veto was exercised by the powerful coalition of conservative interests that rallied to Francoism, despite the New State's rejection of unrestrained capitalism, leaving the regime to exercise unprecedented control over economic affairs. The reason for this reversal was that the regime's supporters accepted everyday intervention in their affairs in return for the preservation of their basic economic interests. During the war both land and industry had been confiscated and collectivised in large parts of the Republican zone, threatening the destruction of private property rights. In this respect regime policy was never destined to be even-handed. Instead it was underpinned by an economic 'cleansing' that went hand in hand with the political restructuring of Spain in the early years of the Franco regime. The elites and middle classes were united in their approval of ruthless class-based actions that altered the fundamental balance of economic power well beyond a simple return to the pre-1931 situation.

The civil war was fought by the Nationalists in defence of private property and as an all-out economic assault on their Republican opponents. Land and businesses expropriated through legal reforms and by collectivisation in the Republican zone were returned to their former owners as the Nationalist army captured them. The main beneficiaries here were the southern agrarian elites and the industrialists.[8] This respect for property did not extend, however, to those labelled opponents of the Franco regime. Towards them the regime presided over a ruthless stripping of economic assets that complemented its political repression. Like the repression as a whole, this began spontaneously and was then given a 'legal' basis and systematised. Sharecroppers and tenant farmers were driven from their lands, shopkeepers and artisans forfeited their businesses, homes were lost, even farm tools, looms and sewing machines were taken in retribution. Impoverishment ensured that the sheer hardship of survival sapped their capacity to resist the new order. Meanwhile these assets were kept, given or sold to regime supporters in a transfer of wealth of incalculable proportions. Under the Franco regime in its early years it was truly the case that those who had received yet more, and those who had not lost even the little they had.[9]

The position of property-holders was further entrenched by the regime's labour policies. As the section of society identified as the greatest revolutionary threat, the working class received the harshest treatment. Independent trade unions and working-class parties were destroyed as the fomenters of a divisive class struggle that undermined the national interest. Instead the regime offered the alternative of a corporate state on the lines of fascist Italy, as laid out in one of the first major pieces of legislation produced in 1938. In theory the *Fuero de Trabajo* (Labour Charter) proposed a permanent partnership between capital and labour, united in the common good, following the fascist idea of a 'third

way' between capitalism and socialism. Official syndicates (unions), based
around the small pre-war Falangist union movement and run as the preserve of
the Falange Español Tradicionalista (FET), were created for each trade. With
everyone engaged in each area of the economy enrolled in a syndicate,
representatives from both employers and the employed were supposed to act
together to ensure harmonious labour relations. In practice, while all workers
were dragooned into the syndicates, employers successfully demanded exemp-
tion and the official organisations became devices for disciplining the labour
force. With strikes and collective bargaining outlawed, the syndicates controlled employment, and set wages and conditions of work. Not surprisingly, it
was the interests of employers that were mainly favoured. Republican prisoners
were also forced into labour battalions in order to 'redeem themselves through
work': in other words to labour without payment. As a consequence real wages
in both agriculture and industry plummeted throughout the 1940s. Women
were forced out of paid work wherever possible, in line with the regime's policy
of putting them back into the home. The politically suspect were denied work
while regime supporters received their jobs.[10]

In other respects the policies pursued by the regime were more ambiguous,
if not contradictory. Self-sufficiency, for instance, was a double-edged sword.
Tariff walls, trade controls and an overvalued peseta certainly protected
Spanish agriculture and industry from competition – as the economic elites had
long campaigned for. However, they also prevented exports and access to
imported food, raw materials and equipment. The only trade allowed was in
imported oil, itself severely rationed by the Allies during the Second World
War, and with the German holding companies created in exchange for military
aid to exploit Spanish mineral resources.[11] Similarly, the intentions of domestic
intervention were far from clear. On the one hand, the dictatorship adopted a
strident rural rhetoric aimed at its most powerful and numerous backers among
the agrarian elites and propertied peasantry of central and northern Spain. The
land and its people were declared to be the backbone of the nation, and the
production of foodstuffs was portrayed as the most noble activity. On the other
hand, industrialisation was set as a goal of strategic importance. This was partly
an attempt to appeal to the industrial elites and urban business interests. But
armaments were also needed to win the civil war and protect the regime
afterwards, and only an industrialised state could achieve the greatness claimed
for Spain by the Francoists.[12]

How exactly to achieve self-sufficiency and maximise domestic output,
without regard to costs, was a matter of some debate within the regime. In
practice, individual ministries and the bodies responsible for different sectors
of the economy tended to go their own way, creating a confusing array of
different initiatives. Many began, particularly in wartime, as stopgap measures
to meet a particular need or crisis and then became permanent. Some were
indirect in nature, offering incentives to encourage greater output. But what

characterised the overwhelming majority of them was excessive interference in every stage of the production processes. In both agriculture and industry permission was needed for such details as the purchase of raw materials, seeds and fertiliser, and investment in new buildings and machinery. Eager to justify their existence, the armies of poorly paid bureaucrats involved themselves in decisions as diverse as the choice of crops, prices, sales and marketing.[13]

SPAIN'S ECONOMIC WINTER, 1939–1950

The result of autarky was a rupture with the previous pattern of development. Intervention worked during the war in the sense that the Nationalists managed to run the economy in their zone slightly less badly than the Republicans. Ironically, given their goal of self-sufficiency, they were also more successful in attracting material and financial help from abroad for the duration of the conflict.[14] But the real test came with peace and the need to reconstruct the economy as a whole. In fact the civil war was far less economically destructive for Spain than the World War was for the rest of Europe. Although there was an average yearly fall in national income of 6 per cent, this represented a disruption of economic activity rather than the effects of material destruction on a large scale. Despite the catastrophic effect of the conflict on the population in general, with half a million dead or exiled, Spanish industry and agriculture emerged largely intact materially. Yet recovery was painfully slow and the economy stagnated for over a decade. GDP per head did not recover to the levels of the peak year of 1929 until 1954.[15]

Agriculture was the sector of the economy hardest hit. Output did not reach the level of 1929 until 1958. The regime resorted to blaming 'persistent drought' (*la pertinaz sequía*) and the activities of the 'previous Marxist government'. More important were the results of its own interventions which misguidedly caused a retreat towards traditional patterns of production rather than reinforcing change. Staples such as wheat and olives were encouraged in order to favour the broadest mass of rural producers who supported the regime. Along with difficulties of exporting, this stifled the move towards the production of higher value crops such as fruits and nuts where Spain had an international advantage. New machinery, fertilisers and draught animals were all in very short supply due to the regime's import restrictions. Those that were available could often only be secured by bribing officials. Not surprisingly, productivity and yields declined markedly from pre-war levels.[16]

Also disastrous was the creation of a National Wheat Service (*Servicio Nacional de Trigo*) in 1937 to protect cereal growers by purchasing and distributing the whole of the national crop. The pressure for cheap bread meant that prices were consistently fixed too low for producers to cover their real costs. Farmers reacted by switching to other crops, cutting production and trading on the rapidly developed black market, known as the *estraperlo*, which grew larger than the official market. Southern estate owners, in particular, took advantage of the illegal market, using their political protection to avoid prosecution. Ironically, the wealth of the landed elites was secured by subverting the economic policies of the regime that they overwhelmingly backed politically. Considerable profits were made from black market operations, which became the largest source of private capital accumulated during the 1940s. The elites were also the main beneficiaries of the halving of agricultural wages from pre-war levels under the impact of the regime's labour policies. Smaller producers fared less well, unable to evade the low prices set by the regime for staples. The situation of northern livestock farmers was worst of all, as meat and milk production was ignored completely.[17] Although by 1950 the poor performance of agriculture reduced its share of GDP to just above 30 per cent, Spain actually re-ruralised in terms of its active population. Migrant peasants from the central provinces returned to the countryside, forced back by the regime's controls over labour and by the difficulties of city life in the 1940s. The increase in the agricultural workforce to 47.6 per cent of the total thus represented a reversal of the considerable productivity gains made for labour before the war.[18]

Agricultural stagnation also reversed the positive contribution the rural sector had made as a market and supplier of labour and capital to industrial development before the civil war. Industry suffered from many of the same post-war problems imposed by autarky. Raw materials, capital goods and energy were all in chronically short supply because of the policy of import substitution. Here, as well, bribery and corruption flourished as the only way to obtain vital new machinery or replacement parts from abroad. Restrictions on investment, control of prices, shortages of skilled labour and the overvalued peseta also reduced output and restricted trade. Consequently, industrial production did not reach the level previously achieved in 1929 until 1950, and its share of GDP did not overtake the pre-war level until the mid 1950s.[19]

This poor performance occurred despite the high priority the regime placed on industrialisation. State intervention in industry was on a far greater scale than in agriculture and took a different form. Whereas the dictatorship sought (and largely failed) to protect rural producers and reinforce the status quo, it actually aimed to encourage new development in manufacturing. In 1941 this led to the creation of a state holding company, the Instituto Nacional de Industria (INI). Modelled on an Italian fascist example, this was led for two decades by Franco's boyhood friend, Juan Antonio Suanzes, a naval engineer like many of those entrusted to directing the economy at this time. Incentives were offered to new and existing enterprises, particularly in 'strategic' sectors such as vehicles, metals, chemicals and armaments. INI specialised in supporting heavy industry, either through partnerships with private enterprises or by setting up its own companies.

However, once again the results were often counter-productive. Decisions were often taken without regard to real costs. Many firms remained too small and undercapitalised. Too many projects were undertaken for prestige reasons rather than as part of a co-ordinated strategy. Consumer goods were both neglected and priced too low, leading to another flourishing black market. Rather than stimulating entrepreneurship, subsidies were pocketed by the industrial elites and the regime's own supporters. Even members of the military, for instance, used their influence to be granted monopoly rights over certain products or received grants for fictitious businesses. Productivity remained chronically low, while profits relied on the lowering of wages. The numbers of workers employed in industry fell and urbanisation was stopped in its tracks.[20]

A generation of economic development and material well-being was sacrificed during the 1940s under the regime's forlorn attempts at self-sufficiency and half-baked interventions. National income per head eventually recovered to pre-war levels by the end of the decade, but real purchasing power was seriously undermined by rampant inflation, leaving overall living standards pitifully low. Shortages of basic foodstuffs left average calorific intakes at subsistence level, giving rise to the description of the period as 'the hungry forties'. Cut off, by the nature of the regime, from the Marshall Aid, which was boosting European post-war recovery, the only respite from abroad came from Argentina which gave credits of $264 million between 1947 and 1949 that were used for food imports.[21]

However, the suffering was not equally shared and in some senses it actually benefited the regime as the worst privations fell, once again, on its perceived enemies while supporters were protected. Food, fuel, housing and clothing rationing favoured regime supporters, particularly the families of Nationalist war veterans, while known Republicans were often denied supplies entirely. Meanwhile, in the absence of a welfare state, charity and poor relief used basic necessities as a means of social control. Both regime organisations such as Auxilio Social, an aid organisation created during the war and controlled by the Women's Section of the FET, and Catholic bodies expected conformity to political and religious orthodoxy in return for their help. Moreover, the rampant black market also benefited regime supporters, as it could only exist with the involvement of its functionaries. Local Falangists, policemen and soldiers were often engaged in supplying and protecting black market operations while being officially responsible for their suppression. The scale of activity was often large, even to the extent that the Madrid Metro functioned as one of the main supply centres to the city. The customers were naturally the friends and acquaintances of the marketeers, leaving those without good contacts literally out in the cold. As a result hunger, particularly widespread in the cities and the southern countryside, was the preserve of the losers in the war and further weakened their will to resist.[22]

THE BREAKDOWN OF AUTARKY, 1951–1959

There were increasing signs that the tightly restrictive policies of the dictatorship were economically and socially unsustainable. Sporadic strikes broke out
in the industrial regions of the Basque Country and Catalonia in the winter of
1946–7. Although Republican organisations were blamed for this agitation, it
was clear that conditions had reached such a low level that workers were
prepared to take action despite the risks. Intervention by the regime quickly
suppressed the protests by force, but the underlying problem remained. In
1951 an even more serious strike wave hit Catalonia, beginning with a stoppage
by Barcelona tram drivers that spread to other workers. Thousands were
involved, but more worryingly for the regime the strikes were backed by many
of the Falangist 'official' unions – suggesting that there were limits beyond
which those responsible for controlling labour felt they could not go in ignoring
the interest of their members in support of government policy.[23] Meanwhile,
complaints from producers about shortages of equipment and supply bottlenecks and objections to the meddling of officials grew. The road and rail
systems were in a state of collapse. By the 1950s evasion of government
regulations was so widespread that the black economy was effectively becoming
the real economy.

Even at the highest ranks of the regime, where lifestyles were very comfortable to the extent of regular indulgence in imported wines and cigars, it was
obvious that government policy was unsustainable.[24] Faced with growing
economic dissatisfaction the regime was forced to modify the most constraining
features of its policies. The cabinet reshuffle in July 1951 brought in two new
economic ministers, Manuel Arburúa at Commerce and Rafael Cavestany at
Agriculture. Both had been internal critics of government policy, not to the
extent of rejecting the political aims of autarky and intervention, but arguing
against the means of achieving them. Consequently, they approved the relaxa-
tion of many internal controls on prices and investment, and allowed selective
imports where shortages were acute. They also took measures to deal with
specific structural problems that had been ignored in the 1940s, particularly in
agriculture.[25]

The immediate situation was also cushioned by closer relations with the
United States as the Cold War progressed. In 1950 the US congress granted a
loan of $62.5 million while a full package of economic and military aid secretly
signed with the Eisenhower administration in 1953 brought in $625 million by
1957. The real economic significance of these agreements was that they granted
Spain access to international markets to make good economic shortages. Profits,
particularly from agriculture which remained the chief source of capital during
the 1950s, could also be used via the banking system for investment in raw
materials, energy and new equipment.[26]

The objective, therefore, of the new cabinet was not to overturn existing policies but to make them work more effectively. There was no serious questioning of the need to protect the economy through autarky nor any commitment to retreat wholesale from internal control. For the Francoist leadership, including Franco himself, these remained a political necessity vital to the security of the regime. Of course, the fundamental continuation of policy was also in the interests of the economic bureaucrats and Falangist union officials whose job prospects would be threatened by any reversal. Even so, it was clear that some real economic growth and a more general rise in living standards was also required if the regime was not to stoke up serious resentment against it from both enemies and friends alike. Partially released from its straitjacket, the economy did indeed return to a pattern of significant growth and structural change.[27]

Recovery in agriculture was the most pressing need. Cavestany and his successor Cirilo Cánovas allowed price rises that gradually eliminated the attractions of the black market and encouraged producers to extend the area under cultivation. Meanwhile, Arburúa granted sufficient foreign currency and licences to allow the importation of new farm machinery and fertilisers by larger landowners. Under these stimuli agriculture finally overtook pre-war levels of production by the end of the decade. Food supply improved sufficiently to allow the suspension of rationing by the middle of the decade. Productivity of labour also improved and significant emigration to the cities began once again. By 1960 over a million people had left the countryside, mainly from central Spain but also for the first time from the south, thereby reducing agriculture's share of employment irreversibly to 42 per cent. Despite this, the supply of labour remained abundant, keeping agricultural wages relatively low. Landowners and small farmers alike considered the 1950s as something of a golden age for agriculture. In many respects this was indeed the case, though it only signified a return to the position of 20 years before. Traditional agriculture did reach its high point at this time, but it also finally entered a period of decisive change that would sweep the old economic order on the land away.[28]

The regime also adopted policies that addressed some of the deep-seated problems of land productivity. Significant advances were made in irrigation, particularly in the south where a large-scale programme of dam construction was undertaken. A scheme to encourage the consolidation of smallholdings into larger units, known as *concentración parcelaria*, redistributed some 250 000 hectares of land in the centre and north by 1959. However, this represented only a small part of the problem and even the new holdings remained too small to take real advantage of economies of scale in production.[29] No matter that the quality and variety of foodstuffs remained poor – the hungry did not complain. The regime also continued to reward its rural supporters with subsidies for staples while higher value livestock and export crops continued to be ignored.

The performance of industry and services was even more impressive. Industrial production almost doubled between 1951 and 1959, with average yearly increases of 6.6 per cent in the first half of the decade and 7.4 per cent in the second. Once again the granting of import licences and access to foreign currency allowed manufacturers to replace antiquated machinery. The importation of raw materials, particularly energy, and semi-finished products also eliminated many bottlenecks in production. Those industries which benefited most were iron and steel, shipbuilding, vehicles and the production of cement and chemicals. Mineral extraction and consumer goods grew at a lesser rate. The service sector also expanded after remaining flat since the 1930s, with retailing and banking particularly reflecting increased disposable incomes and greater circulation of capital. The return to increased urbanisation also sponsored a corresponding expansion in housing construction.[30]

This pattern of development reflected the regime's continued emphasis on heavy industrial and engineering projects. Licences for imports and the allocation of foreign currency went overwhelmingly to those areas. INI also maintained its concentration there. By the end of the 1950s some 30–40 per cent of public investment was being directed into INI-controlled firms. The relative lack of interest in the production of consumer goods meant that Spain lagged well behind the move towards a consumer economy in the rest of western Europe. Imports in this area remained even more rigidly controlled than for the rest of industry, showing that the aim of self-sufficiency continued to be a central priority of the dictatorship. This also affected the levels of investment available for industry. The capital that provided for growth in the 1950s came overwhelmingly from internal sources, mostly from the accumulated profits of agriculture. Despite the links with the United States, foreign investment was still strongly restricted, cutting Spain off from the industrial booms taking place elsewhere.[31]

In many respects economic growth actually accentuated the limitations of autarky and intervention rather than overcoming them. Renewed inflation undermined higher living standards. Workers in expanding industries that were short of skilled labour were able, despite the regime's suppression of independent organisation, to demand and receive wage rises. Although rural workers remained quiescent, illegal wildcat strikes continued in the established industrial regions in support of these claims. Almost two decades after the end of the civil war this reflected the extent to which workers, often of a new generation, felt more confident in defying the regime, at least in pursuit of their immediate material needs.[32]

Unrest was also the product of changes within the officially recognised union organisations. These had actually been initiated from within the regime by the announcement in the late 1940s that elections to workplace councils (*jurados de empresa*) would take place. This attempt to mobilise genuine support amongst workers for the syndical apparatus – heavily resisted by employers – was a belated recognition that low productivity was partly a product of resentment at the heavy-handed actions of the regime. However, illegal opposition parties, particularly the communists but also socialists, seized the opportunity presented by the elections to infiltrate the official unions. By the late 1950s, when elections really became widespread, their presence was beginning to be felt. At the same time, legal Catholic union organisations, the Hermandades Obreras de Acción Católica (HOAC) and Juventud Obrera Católica (JOC), previously of little significance, took more of a stand against regime policies on behalf of labour. Together with disillusioned radical Falangists in the OSE, these forces presented the regime with the first stirrings of a new workers' opposition.[33]

THE ECONOMIC FOUNDATIONS OF THE NEW STATE

Beyond a return to widespread repression, which was increasingly impossible without starting a mini civil war within Francoist ranks, the regime had no adequate response to economic discontent. Attempts to reimpose price controls in order to combat inflation were heavily resisted by producers, particularly in agriculture. This situation was compounded by the mid 1950s by an even more direct threat to the dictatorship's control of the economy from a growing balance-of-payments problem. A tide of imports was simply not offset by a growth in exports from Spain's protected industries. This was partly due to the inferior quality of Spanish goods but mainly it was the result of government spending to protect an artificially overvalued peseta, payment of continued subsidies, and the use of central funds to pay for many imports of capital goods. National bankruptcy threatened.[34]

The response to growing economic instability was a further cabinet reshuffle in December 1956 which brought in a new team of economic ministers and advisors. Most were closely associated with the Catholic lay organisation Opus Dei and all were trained in economics and business administration. The key figures were Alberto Ullastres, appointed to the Ministry of Commerce, Navarro Rubio, who went to Finance, and Laureano López Rodó, already in place as Technical Secretary of the Presidency. Their technocratic outlook contrasted strongly with those previously in positions of economic responsibility whose backgrounds were the military, engineering and the 'traditional' professions such as law. As such they represented the upper level of a new generation of regime functionaries, mostly in their early forties, who had grown to maturity under the dictatorship. Broadly liberal in economic outlook, which is to say in favour of market solutions, they remained strongly authoritarian in social and political attitudes. In fact, they had no particularly fixed ideas about how to solve Spain's economic problems when placed into office, except to realise like many others that the previous policies were finally exhausted.[35]

The technocrats presided over a fundamental shift in the economic orientation of the regime. This grew initially out of crisis management and the need, first and foremost, to deal with external economic relations. Spanish isolation was ended and the fantasy of national self-sufficiency at all costs was finally abandoned. Currency and import controls were relaxed and the peseta was devalued to improve the balance of payments. Furthermore, with the sponsorship of the United States, Spain joined the main international economic organisations: the Organisation for European Economic Co-operation, (now the Organisation for Economic Co-operation and Development (OECD)), the International Monetary Fund (IMF) and the World Bank. Only attempts to join the nascent European Economic Community (EEC) foundered, as membership of this democratic club was denied to the dictatorship. These moves to integrate Spain into the international economy were justified to reluctant traditionalists within the cabinet, Franco included, as the only possible means of breathing new economic life into the regime.[36]

Concerns that foreign influences would weaken the control of the dictatorship turned to alarm when a raft of further measures was proposed by the technocrats in 1959. The so-called Plan for Stabilisation and Liberalisation aimed to reduce inflation and to liberalise foreign trade and investment. Public spending would be slashed by nearly 75 per cent, and there would be sharp rises in the prices of utilities, the taxes on tobacco and petrol, and in interest rates for borrowers. Import controls were to be abolished. Tariffs, taxation and exchange rate systems would be reformed. There was to be a range of incentives for foreign investors to bring much-needed capital into the economy. Direct subsidies for producers, particularly in agriculture, were to be curtailed.

The old guard recognised correctly that with this package of measures a watershed had been reached in the political economy of the dictatorship. Led by Franco they strongly resisted the plan, fearing that the introduction of market mechanisms implied a fatal weakening of the regime and a move towards a capitalist economic model that was indistinguishable in substance from the norm in democratic western Europe. For those whose mentality was firmly fixed in the 1930s, this seemed all too much like a dangerous step back towards the Republic. In a series of meetings with Franco, Navarro Rubio assured the dictator that the technocrats were as committed as he was to the political continuation of the regime. However, this was now only possible if the economy functioned more effectively. Moreover, it was pointed out that there really was no other choice but to opt for the plan, backed by the World Bank, the IMF and the OECD, given the depth of the crisis in the first half of 1959. Eventually, even the economically illiterate Franco grasped that Spain faced imminent economic collapse due to the balance-of-payments deficit. Reluctantly, the Liberalisation Plan was accepted.[37]

In fact the technocrats did not intend that the regime should completely reject all attempts at economic control. While trade and foreign investment were liberalised, the general principle of internal direction was retained. However, the form and objectives of intervention were changed from those under autarky. In 1962 the technocrats announced that economic planning, loosely based on the indicative system used by France since 1945, was to be introduced. The priority was industrial development at all costs. Protection from imported foodstuffs and guaranteed prices for agriculture were largely abandoned. Instead, under the first plan of 1964–7, publicly owned industries were given production targets to meet, while private firms were encouraged by a system of credits and tax breaks to reach output agreements with the Industry Ministry. At the same time, in this and the two subsequent plans, attempts at detailed control of prices and wage rates were abandoned and market mechanisms were allowed a greater influence. Even so, the regime retained the system of regulations over labour and employment through the OSE. These changes showed that the liberalisation of economic policy, at least internally, had its limits.[38]

The result of these changes was to consolidate in power and influence a new group of interests. The technocrats were confirmed as the prime economic decision-makers within the regime. López Rodó became Head of Planning and his Opus Dei colleagues dominated the major ministries. This did not leave the former interventionist bureaucrats on the streets; there were plenty of posts to be had under the new scheme of things and the Syndical Organisation remained a Falangist fiefdom still employing over 100 000 people during the 1960s. Businessmen and bankers, rather than landowners, became the main concern of economic policy for the first time.[39] Within agriculture there was a mixed response to the demotion of rural interests. For the agrarian elites it made little difference to their fortunes: they were well placed to take advantage of the liberalisation of food production and had also become well integrated with urban interests. The situation was far more serious for the peasantry of central and northern Spain – a bedrock of regime support now abandoned to their fate and unable to protest. They had to take their chances in the new economic climate that opened up in the 1960s.[40]

DEVELOPMENT AND CRISIS, 1959–1975

The promise made by the regime in its new policies was for an 'economic miracle' to match that of post-war northern Europe. Dreams of a fortress Spain, protected from international developments, were dropped in favour of a rhetoric of growth. The wider economic justification for the existence of the dictatorship was that it could deliver prosperity. The favourable international climate during the 1960s ensured that this could happen. Although the Liberalisation Plan was fiercely deflationary, it did not deliver an economic slump. It was countered by a stream of new investment generated from abroad, mostly linked to the economic boom in western Europe. The largest part came from a massive expansion in the tourist trade which by the end of the 1960s brought over 30 million northern Europeans a year to Spain. Much of the new holiday infrastructure which transformed formerly peaceful fishing villages into booming tourist complexes on the Costa del Sol and Costa Brava was built by foreign investors who were allowed to repatriate a sizeable proportion of their profits. Similar arrangements pertained in the case of industrial investment which, though not large by European averages, created an important sector of foreign-owned companies and joint ventures. Finally, the domestic economy also benefited from the remittances sent home by over a million Spaniards who were allowed to migrate to work abroad.[41]

New investment allowed an even greater expansion in the importation of foodstuffs, raw materials, energy and capital goods without creating a financial crisis. The result was sustained economic growth at rates above those achieved in the 1950s and rapid structural change. Overall GDP grew at 7.5 per cent per year between 1960 and 1973, an expansion in world terms second only to Japan. The effect of planning on economic performance was marginal, if not negative. Rapid development was mostly due to the release of untapped potential in the economy following greater participation in general European growth after 1959. Expansion was, in fact, greater before planning began in 1964 than afterwards. The more important effect of the various plans was that they allowed the regime to claim direct responsibility for growth. The fact that average income per head trebled between 1960 and 1974 gave a certain plausibility to these assertions.[42] However, there was a marked disparity in the contribution of the main sectors of the economy during this final leap to an industrialised society.

During the 1960s the traditional rural economy was swept away and the countryside ceased to be the chief source of wealth. By 1965 the contribution of agriculture to GDP had declined to 18.5 per cent. At the same time, production finally began to shift away from staples to provide more meat and milk products which vastly improved Spanish diets, while export crops became an important speciality of many regions. Many longstanding problems of productivity were overcome. Although agriculture achieved only a yearly growth of 2.3 per cent, irrigation, mechanisation, fertilisers and more intensive husbandry raised output and productivity on medium-sized and large farms. For the first time on southern farms the costs of investing in mechanisation were less than those of employing manual labour. This was due to a dramatic rise in rural wages, itself the product of an increasing scarcity of workers. By 1970 almost two million male workers had left the land since 1960, halving the rural workforce, and those left behind accounted for 22.8 per cent of the total active population. The government aided this vast population movement, after decades of discouraging it, by setting up emigration offices in most rural provinces. However, it was the availability of large numbers of new urban jobs that was the real motor driving this flight from the land. Some found work in northern Europe, but the majority joined an expanding force of unskilled labour sucked into the industrial and service sectors of the economy. The effects on the countryside were dramatic, particularly in central and northern Spain where many smallholders were unable to respond to change and went bankrupt. In the two Castiles, the phenomenon of villages deserted, apart from the elderly who were unable to migrate, became commonplace.[43]

Growth in the industrial sector was spectacular, at an average of 10.2 per cent a year. Driven by foreign investment and imports, paid for by remittances and tourism earnings, there was expansion in most areas of manufacturing. Heavy industries such as shipbuilding, steel-making, cement and mineral extraction grew rapidly, as well as textiles and the finishing of imported semi-finished goods. Consumer goods such as cars and household appliances, as well as pharmaceuticals and plastics, became important industries. Full industrialisation was matched by the export of goods, mainly to the rest of Europe. Competitive prices for Spanish products were guaranteed by relatively low wage costs – though these rose by an average of over 40 per cent in real terms between 1960 and 1974 – and a policy of export subsidies by the government. By the 1970s industry accounted for almost 40 per cent of GDP and employed 300 000 more workers, both male and female, than it had a decade earlier.[44] Although industrial development boosted the existing regions of manufacturing, particularly the Basque Country and Catalonia, it also led to the growth of industrial suburbs in cities such as Madrid, Valencia, Seville, Alicante and Zaragoza.

But by far the greatest structural change in the Spanish economy during the development years was the shift towards services. Between 1960 and 1974 the service sector expanded at some 6.7 per cent, with tourism, banking and services to the new urban centres accounting for the largest proportion. By the 1970s Spain had joined the so-called 'tertialised' economies, with services accounting for nearly 50 per cent of total GDP. In employment terms, as well, services boomed. Almost 1.5 million new jobs were created in the 1960s in labour-intensive enterprises. The largest number were in tourism, producing a rush to the coastal resorts as well as the cities, followed by construction and public services. Building the concrete apartment blocks which mushroomed around the old city centres at this time, as well as the road and rail infrastructure to serve them, soaked up many unskilled rural labourers. At the same time the demands for health care, education and welfare provoked by urbanisation led to a doubling of the number of nurses, doctors, school and university teachers, and civil servants.[45]

Breakneck development was incredibly uneven. Standards of living rose for nearly everyone, creating a true consumer economy, but inequalities actually increased. Many new fortunes were made at the time in industry and finance, joining existing ones in agriculture, and a comfortable urban middle class of managers, professionals and white-collar employees fully emerged. They were the new bedrock of economic support for the regime, which guaranteed their interests through low taxation and career preferment. In contrast, the urban working class – particularly its newest recruits – bore the main burdens of change. Unskilled workers and their families fresh from the countryside faced a host of difficulties: coping with the new disciplines of factory or tourist jobs, finding accommodation and fitting into urban life. Even skilled workers in well-established industries found themselves faced by long working hours and poor conditions of employment. Ordinary public sector employees – including army officers – found that their pay failed to keep up with price increases, and many of them took second jobs to compensate. Rural incomes also continued to lag well behind, leaving the remaining labourers and peasant farmers firmly at the bottom of the economic heap.[46]

Such differences provided the background for a continuation rather than diminution of labour unrest. A chief feature of this was the emergence of a new, organised workers' movement. This grew from the activities of regime opponents in the elections to factory committees. From this the formation of clandestine illegal groups, known as Workers' Commissions (Comisiones Obreras), was a natural step. Communists and Catholic reformists linked to HOAC and JOC were the main leaders, but there was often considerable overlap with the official Syndical Organisation. The result was a blurring of legal and illegal activity, and the sparking of a conflict within the official unions between reformist and reactionary Falangists. First formed in Asturias in 1958, by the early 1960s the Commissions were active in new waves of strikes protesting at low wages and poor conditions of work. In 1962 there was a major upsurge in strike activity in the Basque Country and Catalonia, which continued throughout the 1960s. Organisation and action were aided by relatively full employment and scarcity of labour. As the decade progressed, organisation spread even to the southern countryside where rural labourers became active for the first time since the civil war.[47]

The response of the regime and employers to industrial unrest was deeply confused. On the one hand there was an attempt to maintain the status quo. Strikes remained illegal, and a wide range of punishments was in force against those involved. Although the regime had promoted collective bargaining as a means of solving industrial disputes, the Commissions remained banned. Meanwhile, the leadership of the Syndical Organisation, under Ruiz Solís, tried to revive the floundering unions and to root out opponents from positions on factory committees. Heavy-handed treatment of strikes and arrests of leaders continued to occur. However, at the same time, the counter-productive results of repression were also evident – serving to politicise disputes, producing low productivity and even industrial sabotage. The result was that employers increasingly began to negotiate secretly with the Commissions to resolve disputes, ignoring the official apparatus. The regime also turned a blind eye to many 'illegal' strikes and refrained from prosecuting activists. This was most evident in the case of the leading figure in the Commissions, Marcelino Camacho. Employed by the British engineering firm of Perkins Diesels in

Madrid, his activities were closely monitored and reported on by informants. Yet no action was taken against him until the end of the 1960s, when regime policy lurched back towards repression as the numbers of strikes continued to mount.[48]

Although unrest was sporadic and many areas of the economy were unaffected, it was clear that neither the stick of repression nor the carrot of greater rights within the OSE could tame an increasingly alienated workforce. By the early 1970s strike action became less spontaneous in character and increasingly more organised and effective. The Workers' Commissions were well established in the main industrial centres and had become an important base for the Communist Party, though Catholics, socialists and dissident Falangists still had a presence. Strikes in Madrid, Barcelona, and the Basque Country paralysed factories and were successful in winning concessions over pay and conditions from employers. Unable to turn the clock back to the fierce discipline imposed on labour after the civil war, and unwilling to take radical steps to accommodate workers' interests that would have undermined the dictatorial nature of the state, the regime was effectively sidelined.[49]

Growing social divisions were sharpened even further by the failure of the regime to develop welfare policies to cope with an industrial society. Public services were simply overwhelmed by the pressures of rapid urbanisation. Basic needs such as housing, sanitation, health care and education could not be catered for without high levels of public investment. Increases in state provision simply failed to keep pace with the growth of demand, as the necessary increases in taxation were vetoed as likely to alienate regime supporters who were able to make use of private services. Rampant corruption in the awarding of public sector contracts – the most lucrative form of graft after the elimination of the black market – made things even worse. Ghetto developments by private speculators to house workers and the lower middle classes often failed to meet the set standards, resulting in the collapse of some Madrid apartment blocks in the 1960s. Money for schools and hospitals was siphoned into private bank accounts and the buildings were never constructed. Secure jobs as teachers and university lecturers often went to those better qualified politically than academically.[50]

Corruption was one of the features of uncontrolled development which came back to haunt the regime. In 1969 a major financial scandal became public, known as the MATESA affair after a multi-national textile conglomerate. The firm's director, Juan Vilá Reyes, was accused of illegally obtaining export credits. Given the extent of such practices, this was nothing out of the ordinary on face value. However, it became an opportunity for traditionalists, particularly in the National Movement, to strike back at the Opus Dei technocrats. The scandal dragged on for a number of years, costing the jobs of the finance and commerce ministers and throwing the wider government into disarray. In other respects economic policy was also faltering. By the early 1970s, the old difficulties of inflation and an adverse balance of trade had re-emerged. Meanwhile, following the resignation of Suanzes in 1963, INI had become a bloated white elephant, subsidising loss-making coal mines and steel works rather than forging dynamic new industries. With no real regional policy to speak of, uncontrolled growth left some regions as economic wastelands while others were overburdened. Pollution, massive environmental damage, urban blight and rural decay were all evident.[51]

Any remaining expectations raised by over a decade of sustained economic growth were shattered by a renewed crisis in the 1970s. In particular, an economy dependent on imports of capital goods, raw materials and energy proved highly vulnerable to sudden rises in commodity prices in 1973, particularly the huge increase in the cost of petroleum. The recession throughout the rest of Europe also had its effect, reducing the flow of finance and tourists to Spain. A serious downturn in trade occurred, which particularly affected agricultural and heavy industrial exports. Inflation and unemployment rose rapidly, while living standards were eroded. As a result, all the rosy predictions of the third plan (1972–5) were completely blown off course and the regime's economic policy was thrown into turmoil. This was even further compounded by the cabinet changes after the death of Carrero Blanco in 1973, which swept all the Opus Dei ministers, including López Rodó, from office.[52]

The paralysis of the regime in the face of these deep economic problems helped convince its own chief supporters that the dictatorship was now an obstacle rather than an aid to the pursuit of their interests. With strikes growing in their intensity and overt political purpose, employers abandoned the official syndical apparatus to deal directly with the 'illegal' unions. Police repression, particularly in the Basque country, was both ineffective and exacerbated tensions. Industrialists and financiers, now the most powerful economic elites in Spain, also saw the regime as a serious barrier to economic recovery. In particular, repeated failure to join the European Economic Community cut the regime off from concerted measures to preserve trade and restore energy supplies. Community states made it absolutely clear during negotiations in the late 1960s and early 1970s that Spain could never hope to become a member while the Franco regime remained in power.[53]

CONCLUSION

By the time of Franco's death in 1975, almost all sections of society were united in looking beyond the regime in support of their economic interests. This marked a complete reversal of the situation that had pertained 40 years before, when economic problems had provided an important backdrop to civil war and the creation of the dictatorship. Of course, economically Spain was a very different country in the 1970s compared to the 1930s and 1940s. The regime had presided over the most important economic transformation in Spanish histoɪy into a fully industrialised and urban society. Yet it had at first actually delayed this process through its reactionary policies, and had then chosen to manage change badly, eventually making itself redundant in the process. For its supporters it had been a vital defence of their interests and the guarantor of economic stability: by the 1970s its existence seemed to threaten both.

NOTES

1 On agriculture see James Simpson, *Spanish Agriculture: the Long Siesta, 1765–1965* (Cambridge, 1995), pp. 25–8. Even higher figures for growth are given by Grupo de Estudios de Historia Rural, 'Notas sobre la producción agraria española, 1891–1931', *Revista de Historia Económica*, 1 (1983), pp. 185–252. See also J. I. Jiménez Blanco, 'Introducción', in Ramón Garrabou *et al.*, eds., *Historia agraria de la España contemporánea, vol. 3: El fin de la agricultura tradicional (1900–1960)* (Barcelona, 1986), pp. 9–141 and Jesús Sanz, 'La agricultura española durante el primer tercio del siglo XX: un sector en transformación' in J. Nadal *et al.*, eds., *La economía española en el siglo XX* (Barcelona, 1987), pp. 237–57. On industry the most reliable source of performance is the index of industrial productivity produced by Alberto Carreras. Originally published in 1982, he has modified it in a number of ways since then: see *Industrialización española: estudios de historia cuantatitiva* (Madrid, 1990) esp. pp. 23–54, 65–88. A. Carreras, 'La producción industrial en el muy largo plazo: una comparación entre España e Italia de 1861 a 1980', in Leandro Prados de la Escosura and Vera Zamagni, eds., *El desarrollo económico el la Europa del Sur: España e Italia en perspectiva histórica* (Madrid, 1992), pp. 173–210 and A. Carreras, 'La industria: atraso y modernización', in Nadal *et al.*, eds., *La economía española*, pp. 280–312 give another view and discuss rival figures. Attempts at quantification are a matter of great dispute between practitioners. We have tried to follow the most widely accepted, and to give alternatives in the notes. Readers should be aware, however, that while there is much dispute on exact figures, historians are generally agreed on the general trends in output and productivity under Francoism. For recent overviews of development before the 1930s, see L. Prados de la Escosura, 'Crecimiento, atraso y convergencia en España e Italia: introducción', in Prados de la Escosura and Zamagni, *El desarollo económico*, pp. 27–55 esp. table 1.5 and Prados, *De imperio a nación: crecimiento y atraso económico en España (1780–1930)* (Madrid, 1988); Gabriel Tortella, *El desarrollo de la España contemporánea: historia económica de los siglos XIX y XX* (Madrid, 1994); J. L. García Delgado, ed., *Lecciones de economía española* (Madrid, 1996) and Nicolás Sánchez Albornoz, ed., *The Economic Transformation of Spain, 1830–1930* (New York, 1987).

2 On the problems of agriculture in general, see A. M. Bernal, 'Resistencias al cambio económico en el sector agrícola, 1880–1930', in J. L. García Delgado, ed., *España entre dos siglos, 1875–1931: continuidad y cambio* (Madrid, 1991), pp. 141–56. Simpson, *Spanish Agriculture*, Chapter 2 gives an overview of regional differences. For the distribution of rural property, see E. E. Malefakis, *Agrarian Reform and Peasant Revolution in Spain* (New Haven, 1970). On the social consequences, J. Rodríguez Labandeira, *El trabajo rural en España (1876–1936)* (Madrid, 1991) is a useful introduction.

3 J. Maluquer, 'De la crisis colonial a la guerra europea: veinte años de economía española', in Nadal *et al.*, eds., *La economía española*, pp. 62–104 outlines the structural changes. On

the negative effects of protectionism, see Pedro Fraile Balbín, *Industrialización y grupos de presión. La economía política de la protección en España, 1900–1950* (Madrid, 1991). Alvaro Soto Carmona, *El trabajo industrial en la España contemporánea (1874–1936)* (Madrid, 1990) considers urban working conditions.

4 On rural unrest, see Malefakis, *Agrarian Reform*; Tim Rees, 'Agrarian Power and Crisis in Southern Spain: The Province of Badajoz, *1875–1936*', in R. Gibson and M. Blinkhorn, eds., *Landownership and Power in Modern Europe* (London, 1991), pp. 235–53; G. A. Collier, *Socialists of Rural Andalusia* (Stanford, 1987); Temma Kaplan, *Anarchists of Andalusia* (Princeton, 1987). Urban conflict is outlined in B. Martin, *The Agony of Modernization: Labor and Industrialization in Spain* (Cornell, 1990) and Adrian Shubert, *The Road to Revolution in Spain: The Coal Miners of Asturias, 1860–1934* (Chicago, 1987). For the policies of the Primo de Rivera regime see Shlomo Ben-Ami, *Fascism from Above* (Oxford, 1983).

5 On the economic problems of the Republic, see Jordi Palafox, *Atraso económico y democracia: La Segunda República y la economía española, 1892–1936* (Barcelona, 1991) and Juan Hernández Andreu, *España y la crisis de 29* (Madrid, 1986). On the struggle for reform see Malefakis, *Agrarian Reform*; A. López López, *El boicot de la derechas a las reformas de la Segunda República* (Madrid, 1984); Paul Preston, 'The Agrarian War in the South', in P. Preston, ed., *Revolution and War in Spain, 1931–1939* (London, 1984), pp. 159–81; Mercedes Cabrera, *La patronal en la II República: organizaciones y estrategia* (Madrid, 1983).

6 On the general thinking behind regime policies, see J. Ros Hombrevella *et al.*, *Capitalismo español: de la autarquía a la establización (1939–1959)*, vol. 1 (Madrid, 1973), Chapter 1; M.-J. González, *La economía política del franquismo (1940–1970)* (Madrid, 1979), Chapter 1; J. L. García Delgado, 'Notas sobre el intervencionismo económico del primer franquismo', *Revista de Historia Económica*, 3 (1985), pp. 135–45.

7 On the military and engineering domination of autarky, see Carlos Velasco Murviedro, 'El "ingenerismo" como directriz básica de la política económica durante la autarquía (1936–1951)', *Información Comercial Española*, 652 (1987), pp. 13–27 and 'El orígen militar de la "autarquía" y su significación económica', *Perspectiva Contemporánea*, 1 (1988), pp. 117–33; Juan José Martínez Gutiérrez, 'Economía de guerra después de la guerra', in Javier Tusell *et al.*, eds., *El régimen de Franco (1936–1975)* (Madrid, 1993) pp. 317–30.

8 M. J. González, 'La autarquía económica bajo el régimen de Franco: una visión desde la teoría de los derechos de propiedad', *Información Comercial Española*, 676–7 (1990) is interesting on the relationship between property and autarky. The relationship between economic power and the regime is explored in Carlos Moya, *El poder económico en España (1939–1970)* (Madrid, 1975).

9 The organised dispossession of opponents initially began through locally organised *comités de incautación de bienes* (committees for the seizure of goods). Their functions were taken over directly by the Tribunals of the Law for Political Responsibilities in 1939. Economic punishments were a very important part of the repression, and in fact became the dominant element after 1945.

10 Miguel Aparicio, *El sindicalismo vertical y la formación del estado franquista* (Barcelona, 1980) is the key work. Also interesting is Sebastian Balfour, *Dictatorship, Workers and the City: Labour in Greater Barcelona since 1939* (Oxford, 1989), Chapter 1. For the rural syndicates, the *hermandades agrícolas* (agricultural brotherhoods), see J. Foweraker, *Making Democracy in Spain: Grassroots Struggle in the South, 1955–1975* (Cambridge,

1989), part 2 and M. Ortiz Heras, *Las hermandades de labradores en el franquismo. Albacete, 1943–77* (Albacete, 1992). On work and the position of women see Chapter 6 below.

11 On economic relations with the Allies and Axis see Denis Smyth, *Diplomacy and Strategy of Survival: British Policy and Franco's Spain, 1940–1941* (Cambridge, 1986); Angel Viñas, *Guerra, dinero, dictadura: ayuda fascista y autarquía en la España de Franco* (Barcelona, 1984); C. Leitz, *Economic Relations Between Nazi Germany and Franco's Spain, 1936–1945* (Oxford, 1996). The problems of trade barriers and overvalued currency are discussed in Jordi Catalan, 'Reconstrucción, política económica y desarrollo industrial: tres economías del sur de Europa, 1944–5', in Prados de la Escosura and Zamagni, eds., *El desarrollo económico*, pp. 359–95.

12 For the mixed messages of the regime, see C. Velasco, 'El pensamiento agrario y la apuesta industrializadora en la España de los cuarenta', *Agricultura y Sociedad*, 23 (1982), pp. 233–73; Eduardo Sevilla Guzmán, *La evolución del campesinado en España* (Barcelona, 1979), Chapter 5; J. M. Areilza and F. M. Castiella, *Reivindicaciones de España* (Madrid, 1941).

13 On the functioning of the system, see P. Tedde, 'Economía y franquismo: a propósito de una biografía', *Revista de Historia Económica*, 4, (1986), pp. 57–65; Ros Hombrevella *et al.*, *Capitalismo español*, pp. 99–128; García Delgado, 'Notas sobre la intervencionismo económico'.

14 For a comparison of the wartime economies, see E. Malefakis, 'La economía española y la guerra civil', in Nadal *et al.*, eds., *La economía española*, pp. 150–63. See also Viñas, *Guerra, dinero, dictadura*.

15 Alberto Carreras, 'Depresión económica y cambio estructural durante el decenio bélico, 1936–45', in J. L. García Delgado, ed., *El primer franquismo: España durante la segunda guerra mundial* (Madrid, 1989), pp. 3–33; Leandro Prados de la Escosura and Jorge Sanz, 'Growth and Macroeconomic Performance in Spain, 1939–1993', in Nicholas Crafts and Gianni Toniolo, eds., *Economic Growth in Europe since 1945* (Cambridge, 1996), p. 356 for GDP. Catalan, 'Reconstrucción, política económica y desarrollo industrial' gives an unfavourable comparison with post-war reconstruction elsewhere.

16 For an overview of the impact of Francoism on agriculture, see Carlos Barciela, 'Introducción', in Garrabou *et al.*, eds., *Historia agraria*, pp. 383–454; J. M. Naredo, *La evolución de la agricultura en España: desarrollo capitalista y crisis de las formas de producción tradicionales*, 2nd edn. (Barcelona, 1974); Simpson, *Spanish Agriculture*, pp. 244–9.

17 Carlos Barciela, 'La España del "estraperlo"' in García Delgado, ed., *El primer franquismo*, pp. 105–22 and 'El mercado negro de productos agrarios en la posguerra, 1939–1953', in Josep Fontana, ed., *España bajo el franquismo* (Barcelona, 1986), pp. 192–205; J. M. Naredo, 'La incidencia del estraperlo en la economía de las grandes fincas del sur', *Agricultura y Sociedad*, 19 (1981), pp. 81–115 and 'La agricultura en el desarrollo económico', in Garrabou *et al.*, eds., *Historia agraria*, esp. pp. 461–5.

18 Figures from Simpson, *Spanish Agriculture*, p. 28. Carreras, 'Depresión económico y cambio estructural', p. 29 estimates an increase in the agricultural population from 44.6 per cent in 1940 to 50.3 per cent in 1945.

19 Carreras, 'La industria: atraso y modernización'; J. L García Delgado, 'La industrialización y el desarrollo económico de España durante el franquismo', in Nadal *et al.* eds., *La economía española*, esp. pp. 165–9.

20 J. L. García Delgado, 'Estancamiento industrial e intervencionismo económico durante el primer franquismo', in Fontana, ed., *España bajo el franquismo*, pp. 170–91; J. Donges,

La industrialización en España: políticas, logros, perspectivas (Barcelona, 1976). For different views of INI see P. Martín Aceña and F. Comín, *INI: 50 años de industrialización en España* (Madrid, 1991) and 'El estado en la industrialización de posguerra: el Instituto Nacional de Industria', in Prados de la Escosura and Zamagni, eds., *El desarrollo económico*, pp. 421–44, and Pedro Schwartz and Manuel Jesús González, *Una historia del Instituto Nacional de Industria, 1941–76* (Madrid, 1978). On the weakness of consumer goods see the case study by J. S. Miranda Encarnación, 'La industria del calzado española en la posguerra: los efectos del intervencionismo sobre una industria de bienes de consumo', *Revista de Historia Económica*, 2 (1994), pp. 317–39.

21 On post-war living conditions, see Rafael Abella, *Por el imperio hacia Dios: crónica de una posguerra (1939–1953)* (Barcelona, 1978). Barciela, 'Introducción' gives figures for calorific intakes. On Argentinian aid, see A. Viñas *et al.*, *Política Comercial exterior de Franco, 1931–1975*, 2 vols. (Madrid, 1979). See also Chapter 7 below.

22 F. Albuquerque, 'Métodos de control político de la población civil: el sistema de racionamiento de alimentos y productos básicos impuesto en España tras la última guerra civil', in Manuel Tuñón de Lara, ed., *Estudios sobre la historia de España* (Madrid, 1981).

23 Balfour, *Dictatorship, Workers and the City*, pp. 8–30 gives details, including estimates of living conditions for workers in Barcelona.

24 The Archivo de la Administración Central contains copies of the orders granting import licences for these luxuries.

25 For Arburúa's views, see his memoir *Cinco años al frente del Ministerio de Comercio* (Madrid, 1956).

26 On aid, see E. Fanjul, 'El papel de la ayuda americana en la economía española, 1951–57', *Información Comercial Española*, 577 (1980), pp. 159–65; A. Viñas, *Los pactos secretos de Franco con Estados Unidos: bases, ayuda económica, recortes de soberania* (Barcelona, 1981). On the recycling of profits, see J. L. Leal, *La agricultura en el desarrollo capitalista español*, 1940–1970, 3rd edn. (Madrid, 1986), part 1.

27 See Chapter 3 above.

28 Simpson, *Spanish Agriculture*, pp. 28–9, 249–51; Barciela, 'Introducción', pp. 416–25.

29 Barciela, 'Introducción', pp. 425–31.

30 Carreras, *Industrialización española*; García Delgado, 'La industrialización y el desarrollo económico', pp. 170–6.

31 See Donges, *La industrialización en España*. Fraile, *Industrialización y grupos de presión* argues that the intervention agencies had effectively been taken over by producers by the 1950s and used for their own short-term benefit.

32 On inflation and wage rises, see González, *La economía política*, pp. 49–81. On labour unrest, see Balfour, *Dictatorship, Workers and the City*, pp. 30–6 and José Maravall, *Dictatorship and Political Dissent: Workers and Students in Franco's Spain* (London Tavistock, 1978), Chapters 2 and 3.

33 Balfour, *Dictatorship, Workers and the City*, pp. 14–20; Maravall, *Dictatorship and Political Dissent*, pp. 26–9; Robert Fishman, *Working-class Organisation and the Return to Democracy in Spain* (Ithaca, 1990); B. López García, 'Discrepancias y enfrentamientos entre el estado franquista y las asociaciones obreras católicas', *Anales de Historia Contemporánea*, 5 (1986), pp. 177–87.

34 Donges, *La industrialización en España*; Ros Hombrevella, *Capitalismo español*.

35 On the shift in outlook, see E. Fuentes Quintana and J. Requeijo, 'La larga marcha hacia la política inevitable', *Papeles de Economía Española*, 21 (1984), pp. 3–39; pp. 134–7 points out their lack of concrete plans.

36 Viñas, *et al.*, *Política Comercial exterior de Franco*. On the so-called 'pre-plan' period, see González, *La economía política*, Chapter 3; Ros Hombrevella, *Capitalismo español*, Chapter 4.

37 On the plan and the depth of the crisis, see González, *La economía política*, Chapter 4; E. Fuentes Quintana, 'El plan de estabilización económica de 1959, veintecinco años después', *Información Comercial Española*, 612–3 (1984), pp. 25–40; E. Fuentes Quintana, 'Tres decenios de la economía en perspectiva', in J. L. García Delgado, ed., *España, economía* (Madrid, 1989), pp. 1–75. On Franco's reluctance, see S. Payne, *The Franco Regime* (Madison, 1987), p. 470.

38 On planning and the limits of liberalisation, see R. Tamames, 'Los planes de desarrollo, 1964–75', *Información Comercial Española*, 676–7 (1989), pp. 57–65. For the objectives of the plans, see Rosa Alsina, 'Estrategia de desarrollo en España, 1964–75: planes y realidad', *Cuadernos de Economía*, 15 (1987), pp. 337–70.

39 See Moya, *El poder económico* and Richard Gunther, *Public Policy in a No-Party State* (London, 1980), esp. Chapter 8.

40 See Naredo, *Evolución de la agricultura*, Chapter 7.

41 For a good overview see Prados de la Escosura and Sanz, 'Growth and Macroeconomic Perfomance', pp. 369–72.

42 Donges, *La industrialización en España*; Tamames, 'Los planes de desarrollo'; Alsina, 'Estrategia de desarrollo en España'; González, *La economía política*, Chapters 5 and 6, remarks on p. 321; F. Estapé and M. Amado, 'Realidad y propaganda de la planificación indicativa en España', in Fontana, ed., *España bajo el franquismo*, pp. 206–13.

43 Simpson, *Spanish Agriculture*, pp. 249–62; Leal, *La agricultura en el desarrollo*, part 3.

44 See Carreras, 'La industria: atraso y modernización'; Fuentes Quintana and Requeijo, 'La larga marcha'; García Delgado, 'La industrialización y el desarrollo'.

45 See J. R. Cuadrado, 'La expansión de los servicios en el contexto del cambio estructural de la economía española', *Papeles de Economía Española*, 42 (1990), pp. 98–120.

46 Balfour, *Dictatorship, Workers and the City*, Chapter 2; J. Foweraker, *Making Democracy in Spain: Grassroots Struggle in the South, 1955–1975* (Cambridge, 1989).

47 Balfour, *Dictatorship, Workers and the City*, Chapter 3; Foweraker, *Making Democracy*; Maravall, *Dictatorship and Political Dissent*, Chapter 4.

48 On the attitudes of employers, see Robert Martinez, *Business and Democracy in Spain* (London, 1993).

49 Fishman, *Working Class Organisation*.

50 Fuentes Quintana, 'Tres decenios de la economía'.

51 See the report of Fundación FOESSA, *Efectos queridos y no queridos en el desarrollo español* (Madrid, 1968).

52 G. de la Dehesa *et al.*, 'Spain', in D. Papapeorgiou *et al.*, eds., *Liberalising Foreign Trade: the Experience of New Zealand, Spain and Turkey* (Cambridge, 1991) gives a good summary of the problems of dependence.

53 J. L. García Delgado, *Economía española de la transición y la democracía* (Madrid, 1990).

6

Culture and Society under Francoism

The New State that the victorious Franco regime proposed to create was a cultural and social enterprise, as much as an economic and political one. The insurgents in the civil war had seen themselves as fighting to establish a new moral order in Spain. This went beyond opposition to the social reforms pursued by the centre-left governments of the Republic, and included – in theory at least – a complete rejection of the liberalising trends which had emerged in Spain in the nineteenth century. In many respects the democratic regime was itself held to be a symptom of the supposed 'decadence' into which the country had fallen by the 1930s. The Republic and its supporters represented a threat to property, religious values, the social order, and the integrity of the nation state. These were taken by all sections of Nationalist opinion to be the products of a deep-rooted cancer in Spanish society.

In this sense the Nationalist rhetoric of 'true Spain' and 'anti-Spain' was as much directed at cultural and social forms and practices as at political ones. This holistic approach also suggested that simply suppressing the organisations that sustained the ideologies of liberalism, anarchism, socialism, communism and regionalism would not be enough. Society had to be rebuilt in such a way as to eliminate the possibility of their resurgence. Constructing the New State was therefore not merely a response to an immediate threat; it was an attempt to wield cultural and social power in order to rewrite the evolution of Spain and make Francoism an unquestioned part of the natural order of things.

THE FRANCOIST VISION OF SOCIETY

The vision of society projected in Nationalist discourse during and after the civil war appeared at first glance to be profoundly reactionary. This was due, first and foremost, to the all-pervasive influence of the Catholic church, which provided the most important component of Francoist social thought. In fact, it was a particular type of integrist Catholicism that became strongly linked to the Nationalist cause. Deep dissatisfaction with modernity was its defining characteristic. Even before the Republic, most church leaders had been uncomfortable with the non-confessional state despite the privileged position it gave to Catholicism. Under the monarchy, Catholicism was the sole religion recognised by the state, public funds supported the clergy, the church played the major role in school education, only religious marriages were recognised, and Catholic teaching was incorporated into many areas of public policy. On most issues the positions taken by the church were such that social and political conservatism and Catholicism became virtually synonymous in most people's minds. For the middle and upper classes, in particular, the defence of property, national unity, traditional morality and the social order were indistinguishable from the defence of the church. Left radicalism and anti-clericalism, or even anti-Catholicism, tended to go hand in hand. The church was resented for its control of education and charity, the only real welfare system that existed in the country. Among the working class and for liberal intellectuals, in particular, hatred of the church, its servants and followers, ran very deep. As the popular saying had it: 'Every Spaniard follows the church, with either a candle or a club.'[1]

This conflict came to a head with the Republic, when the church came under direct attack from reformers within the new regime. Church and state were completely separated in the new constitution, state subsidies were withdrawn and Catholic control of education was ended. Furthermore, laws for civil marriage, divorce and eventually abortion hit at the heart of Catholic teachings on morality and the family. Attempts to encourage experimentation in the theatre, literature and cinema, and the abandonment of censorship, scandalised much of Catholic opinion. In addition, members of the Society of Jesus (the Jesuits) were expelled from Spain and, in the early months of the Republic, there were physical assaults on churches and monasteries by anti-clerical mobs. Although theoretically reduced to a private organisation dealing exclusively in spiritual matters, harassment of the church even affected everyday religious practice and freedom. While most Catholics rejected the Republic from the start, these measures ensured that the alternative currents that did exist within the church were marginalised. Dissenting voices that had called for a rethinking of the position of the church were largely silenced. The few Catholic republicans were effectively denounced as traitors to a cause under siege. Meanwhile, Basque and Catalan Catholics were forced to chose between their support for a regional identity and their attachment to the values of a Castilian-dominated church. With the deaths of clergy in the Republican zone at the outbreak of the civil war criticism became an impossibility and the church was bound to rally to the Nationalist cause.[2]

Not surprisingly, the desire to return to a supposedly better past infused church views on the war. In many ways this was not a straightforward reaction, but a utopian vision that used nostalgia as a means to propound an image of society as it should be. Moreover, it was one that dovetailed perfectly with the broader themes of the Nationalist war effort. The ideal that was upheld, strongly influenced by the nineteenth-century polemicist Menéndez Pelayo, was of the 'golden age' of Ferdinand and Isabel. This suggested that the church and its traditional teachings were essentially responsible for the past greatness of Spain. The reconquest and unification of Spain, and the creation of an empire, were all identified as 'Catholic' projects, designed principally for the spread of the true religion. In contrast, national decline as an economic and political power was equated with the weakening of church influence and the rise of secular and anti-clerical ideologies such as liberalism and socialism. A 'truly Spanish character and social order' was postulated that was Catholic by definition. Its fundamentals were the family, a fixed social hierarchy and orthodox notions of morality that accorded with church teachings – particularly in matters of marriage, gender relations and sexuality.

More modern Catholic teaching on social relations was incorporated, but in forms that tended to complement rather than challenge the emphasis on tradition. The most important was social Catholic doctrines which were influential in Catholic Action – the array of lay organisations dedicated to influencing society in accordance with church teachings. Despite talk of creating harmony between the classes, and appeals to the charitable duties of the privileged, the approach to social problems even before the civil war was decidedly reactionary. Catholic trade unions and rural syndicates were largely controlled by the propertied and powerful, attracting the support of the middle classes and smallholding peasantry rather than converting the urban and rural proletariats from anarchism and socialism. Much the same was true of other lay organisations, such as the National Association of Catholic Propagandists (ACNP) with its extensive network of newspapers and Opus Dei which aimed to create a modern Catholic educational and political elite. Both attempted to use modern methods of propaganda and influence, but for highly traditional goals.[3]

These bodies also bridged the divide the church proclaimed between its wholly spiritual mission and the wider diffusion of Catholic ideas in the supposedly separate secular world of society and politics. Even before the civil war this was a decidedly blurred line, as the church's lay associations provided the indispensable underpinning for the mobilisation of the mainstream political right during the Republic. Nevertheless, the church maintained its formal apoliticism and attachment to purely religious causes even during the civil war. Nor was this entirely a fiction. As Frances Lannon has argued, the church lent its support to the Nationalist rising but was not its originator. Many, if not most, religious participated in the war effort and approached the peace with a genuine belief in the re-Christianisation of Spain, a spiritual reconquest on a par with earlier crusades. Certainly church leaders hoped to regain what they saw as the proper position of Catholicism in society, but in concert with the state rather than by becoming directly incorporated into it. In these circumstances, the support of the political movements incorporated into the single party was crucial for translating church doctrines into regime policies.

All the political tendencies represented in the FET espoused the defence of the church and support for its teaching to a greater or lesser degree. For the different monarchist groups, as well as the conservatives of CEDA, Catholicism stood at the heart of their beliefs. The Carlists were the most wholeheartedly traditionalist in outlook, with almost medieval views on culture and society. Almost equally integrist was Renovación Española, whose followers saw the restoration of church privileges and control over matters such as education, public morality and family policy as an essential aim. Both groups had received the support of the clergy and lay associations before the war. When the rising began in Navarre, the Carlist stronghold, local priests proved to be amongst the most active in the fighting and in the campaigns that followed. But before the war, CEDA had been the main beneficiary of church backing. Indeed, the lay organisations of the church, particularly the press network controlled by the Propagandists and its agrarian syndicates, had been the backbone of CEDA's struggle to defend religion within the Republic. Although there were clearly differences between these groups, by 1936 they shared support for a dictatorial corporate state that would defend the church, suppress alternative ideas and impose Catholic values on society. With the formation of the single party in April 1937 these groups became the chief standard-bearers of political Catholicism within the new regime, often aided by their strong support within the army.[4]

More qualified support for Catholic doctrines came from the Falange. Its attachment to the so-called 'national syndicalist revolution' seemed to run counter to the reactionary message of the church and its supporters. In fact, this was not completely the case. Many Falangists saw Catholic values as central to their own cultural and social programme, and as a feature of their ideology which differentiated the Spanish version of fascism from its Italian and German counterparts. However, in many respects this was due to a recognition of the extreme nature of integrist Catholicism rather than an example of the 'moderation' of Falangism. Certainly, Falangists had no argument with the church's endorsement of a dictatorial state, strong centralism, and, perhaps above all, with its ultra-nationalist and imperialist vision of a nation reborn. As Ernesto Giménez Caballero, a main proponent of this view, argued: 'The fascism for Spain is not fascism, but Catholicism.'[5] Others accepted Catholicism as part of a general Spanish tradition, but were more influenced by secular and more openly radical models of society, in particular modernist fascist ideas of the 'new man' and the 'third way', of a people and a society neither capitalist nor socialist. Criticism of the status quo, including calls for a redistribution of rural property, was part of their rhetoric. Falangists also used the language of totalitarianism, meaning the connection of all aspects of life, including religion, to the state as the highest expression of national unity.[6]

The possibility that the church might be subordinated to the state was the main fuel to the rivalry between Catholics and Falangists in the early years of the regime. In most respects the differences over doctrine, though significant to the protagonists, were slight in reality. However, orthodox Catholics harboured the particular fear that if the Falangists dominated all aspects of cultural and social policy they might wield that power in ways of which the church disapproved. In areas such as education and public morality, seen as of special concern to the spiritual mission of the church, there was a strong determination to exclude Falangist influence. Given that it was the national syndicalist strand that was most prominent in the FET immediately after its creation, this fear had some substance. The struggle that followed for cultural and social control within the regime was never completely resolved, but a rough division of labour had emerged by 1945.[7]

The church achieved most of its aims. These were secured under a series of Catholic ministers who successfully pursued the church cause. The most important were the successive education ministers, Pedro Saínz Rodríguez and José Ibáñez Martín, and the Foreign Minister Alberto Martín Atajo who resigned as head of Catholic Action when he took office in 1945. Church–state relations were formally defined by a temporary agreement with the Vatican in 1941, during the regime's most national syndicalist phase, and finally by the 1953 concordat, when overt fascism was being buried. This fell far short of the theocracy that some Catholics would have liked. Many lay bodies were incorporated into state organisations, particularly the Catholic unions and rural syndicates. But Catholic Action remained outside the state, as did the ACNP and Opus Dei. National Catholicism, as it was known, made Spain a confessional state, gave the church a religious monopoly, and reinstated subsidies for the clergy and Catholic organisations. Furthermore, all legislation was to conform to church teaching, particularly on matters such as the family. The existence of church schools and religious dominance in higher education was secured. Finally, the clergy were given a major role in the supervision of public morality and in censorship.[8]

Although the single party, and particularly the Falangists, were the losers, this did not mean that its control over cultural and social affairs was negligible. After 1945, the National Movement was the main link between the regime and society at large. It had authority over everything the church did not and in many cases had an overlapping mandate to intervene. Like the church, the party had a strong physical presence through its block structure, which placed one of its representatives in every village, neighbourhood and apartment building. Favourable reports from such people – along with that of the local priest – were vital for individuals involved in all kinds of public matters, from defending themselves in cases brought under the Law of Political Responsibilities to applications for local authority jobs. Aside from this brief to watch over society, the FET received more specific tasks. It controlled the means of communication, apart from the religious press, and directed the propaganda of the regime. Although the single state education system favoured by most

Falangists was not created, the party retained some say through its control of political instruction and influence over the content of school textbooks. Outside the classroom and lecture halls the official university student's union (Sindicato de Estudiantes Universitarios) and broader Youth Front (Frente de Juventudes) placed children of both sexes and male adolescents under party control. Control of the activities of female adolescents and mature women of all ages was under the authority of the Women's Section of the FET (Sección Femenina), headed since its creation in 1934 by Pilar Primo de Rivera, sister of the founder of the Falange. There was no all-embracing men's organisation, as in a sense the whole of the FET, apart from the Women's Section, was a male preserve. Perhaps the closest thing were the Movement's organisations for ex-combatants and the so-called Franco's Guard, which mixed welfare functions with political activities. Taken together, therefore, the party also undertook a wide range of social responsibilities and had enormous powers to intervene in society.[9]

MAKING SOCIETY FRANCOIST, 1936–1957

The policies adopted by the Francoist New State in the two decades after the civil war could not be completely monolithic in nature. Apart from the different priorities of the two main agencies involved – the church and party – utopian intentions could not be translated into unambiguous social realities. No regime with 'totalitarian' ambitions has been able to achieve domination of all aspects of society, or to penetrate completely into private life. Even so, the regime's policies did define and shape social realities in Spain. The main goal was to isolate the country from pernicious cultural and social influences, to cleanse society of them and finally to rebuild. Close parallels with economic autarky were evident, and in many respects the approach taken towards society was a necessary corollary to it. Regime rhetoric echoed similar calls for national unity, a return to national greatness and an imperial mission. The elimination of social conflict, through a return to properly Catholic and truly Spanish ideals of family life and morality, and a respect for hierarchy, were the means. Recognition of an unchanging, uniquely Spanish, character – the regime's version of racial superiority – was the basis for reasserting influence in the world after a period of decline.

Tremendous emphasis was placed on the family as a source of social stability. It was idealised as the basic fixed unit of society, in which all proper social relationships were founded. The family was a sacred institution according to the church, and a model of society in microcosm. In contrast, class and other differences were either superficial in importance or fantasies created by Marxists eager to tear down the social order. The family was perceived on an authoritarian model, commanded by a patriarch just as Franco commanded the 'family' that was Spain. As in society at large, everyone had their proper place within the family, which functioned to reproduce the nation as a source of morality and a barrier to deviance and illicit passions of all kinds.[10]

While the civil war still raged, the Republic's legislation relating to the family was overturned by the Nationalists. Divorce and civil marriage were banned: separated couples were forced back together under threat of punishment, while others who thought themselves married suddenly found that they were not. Anyone divorced and remarried was in a very difficult situation indeed. The regime also reinforced male authority within the family by reintroducing the 1889 Civil Code, later incorporating it into the *Fuero de los Españoles* of 1945. This gave legal status to a male head of the household (*cabeza de la familia*), making him officially in charge of all other family members and the representative of the family in the public sphere. Women and children, including minority males, were firmly confined to the private sphere of family life. While women might own property, only men as fathers, husbands or brothers could control it. Heads of household also had authority over sexual relations, which of course were only supposed to occur within the confines of marriage. A stark legal double standard was reintroduced, whereby men were allowed to physically punish women for any adulterous or pre-marital liaisons, but they were not held liable for any of their own. However, this was not a complete licence for men to behave as they wished. According to the regime, men had to be strong, controlling and virile, if the nation was to be the same. Therefore, homosexuality, though not lesbianism which the regime seemed to assume could not exist, was fiercely repressed – most publicly and tragically in the case of the playwright and poet Federico García Lorca, who was murdered in Granada at the start of the civil war.[11]

The overall result of regime policies was that, in the name of the family, all the rights won by women before the civil war were rolled back, to be replaced by an extreme form of patriarchal rule based on an ideology of separate spheres. Women had to be driven back into the home, to fulfil their biologically determined destiny as wives and mothers. In fact the obsessive interest of the regime in the control of women reflected the special status given to them in Catholic and right-wing thinking. Women were seen as both the source of all virtue and of all vice in society. On the one hand there was the ideal woman, dedicated to marriage and motherhood (*la perfecta casada*), faithfully fulfilling her domestic duties as the 'angel of the home' by not only cooking and cleaning but also by imparting religious values, love of nation and respect for (male) authority. At the same time, there were dangerous women who tried to step outside their 'natural' sphere to meddle in public affairs for which they were mentally unfitted, or who undermined the family by offering sexual temptation to men.

In promoting this version of family values, the regime found itself in a dilemma over the degree to which women could themselves be enlisted in the cause. This focused in particular on the role of the Women's Section of the

Falange. Founded in 1934, from the start it supported a 'traditional' interpretation of the role of women. However, after the single party was formed in 1937, there was considerable debate among the Nationalist leadership as to whether it should be abolished. The main reason was that it actually offered to women just the kind of public role that they were not supposed to have. Although it was decided to retain the organisation, this ambiguity could never really be overcome. If anything, it was most acute in the leading figures of the section, all of whom were required to be single (married women could certainly not be seen outside a domestic role). In fact, Pilar Primo de Rivera never married – despite a bizarre plan at one point to match her up with Adolf Hitler – and she remained a highly visible figure, the only woman to hold a Cortes seat during the life of the regime. This ambiguity was also evident in the choice of role models presented to women. The cult of the Virgin Mary was seen as highly suitable, but historical figures beloved of the church and the right, such as Queen Isabel and Saint Teresa of Avila, presented more of a problem given that they could be read as examples of women with a powerful public role.[12]

This sense of some women (as well as men) telling others to do as they said rather than as they did was at its strongest in the pro-natalist policies of the regime. The production of children was seen not just as part of church teaching on the family and women's role but also as part of the fantasy of Spain's imperial future, in which a surplus population to export abroad was required. To achieve this aim, the half a million deaths and exiles of the civil war needed to be made up and a long-term decline in birth-rates reversed. With a population of just under 26 million according to the 1940 census, the regime was convinced that rapid growth was required. Accordingly, abortion and contraception were banned, with stiff penalties for anyone found guilty of practising or promoting either. To encourage procreation, family allowances (*subsidio familiar*) were introduced in 1938 and family bonuses (*plus de cargas familiares*) in 1945. Both were paid to male heads of household, and only for 'legitimate' children. A system of prizes (*premios de natalidad*), as well as further material support for exceptionally large numbers of children, was also created. Particularly fecund families were featured in the newspapers of both the party and church as shining examples. Despite these efforts, however, the policy was a clear failure. Throughout the 1940s and early 1950s the birth-rate continued to decline as couples continued to limit the size of their families. Overwhelmingly this was a response to the poor economic conditions of the time: more children could not be afforded.[13]

The corollary of driving women into the home was to force them out of work. To this end the 1938 Labour Charter stated that women were to be 'freed from the workplace and the factory' and in 1942 a law was introduced stating that all married women should be dismissed with the compensation of a marriage dowry. However, such a policy had limits which the regime could not easily overcome. In some areas of the wage economy women's work was a necessity.

For instance, this was the case in agriculture and in the food-processing industries which required women and children for their operation. In fact, this was particularly the case amongst the regime's strong supporters in the independent peasantry. Family farms could only operate if all family members engaged in agricultural work. Many other industries, from textiles to cigar-making, relied upon female labour. Even the concession that unmarried women could engage in paid work was not enough to overcome these economic obstacles. Although the law was applied with rigour in state-controlled enter-prises, in privately owned concerns it was not prosecuted with the same zeal because of employers' objections. Even so, many married women who needed paid work found themselves deprived of employment. Perhaps the most acute cases were of women married to Republican prisoners of the regime or men in hiding or exile. Not surprisingly, in these circumstances women became an important part of the black economy of the post-war years. Another recourse was to prostitution, which the regime hypocritically tolerated until the mid 1950s and did little to suppress thereafter, despite a vigorous campaign against it by the Women's Section.[14]

The regime used its welfare policies to intervene into private life in order to supervise the 'morals' of the population. Unmarried women between the ages of 17 and 35 were required to undertake six months' social service (*servicio social*), working in schools, orphanages, hospitals and kitchens. They provided both an *ad hoc* welfare system on the cheap, and also received indoctrination into Falangist values. The Women's Section also provided rural health visitors (*divulgadoras*) to combat the higher infant mortality rates amongst the agrarian poor. These overwhelmingly middle-class women – typical of the Section's permanent membership – checked in vain that couples were not using birth control, made sure that children were baptised and assessed their 'moral health'. The church also contributed through its charitable activities. It was a long-established pattern that recipients of charity were required to show evidence of religious practice and moral behaviour. In the post-war period the use of charity for the purposes of social control tightened. Not surprisingly, known supporters of the Republic and their families were often denied aid – or forced into religious and political conformity in order to survive. This played a major part in the apparent return to traditional patterns of behaviour across Spain, from attendance at church to following elaborate courtship rituals.[15]

In its attempt to create a Francoist mentality, and foster social conformity, the regime focused great attention on the formation of future generations. As a result, education policies reflected all the main themes of Francoist social discourse, as well as its repressive practices. The schools opened under the Republic's programme of secular education were either closed or handed over to the church and local authorities. Meanwhile, teachers became a particular object of repression, being seen as both politically and morally suspect. Thousands fell foul of the Law of Political Responsibilities and of the *comités de depuración* – often on grounds that they were not regular church attenders. School libraries were ransacked for 'unsuitable' books, which were often burned in public ceremonies.[16] A majority of church schools, subsidised from the public purse, were left alongside the rump of a state system. There was an acute shortage of school buildings and of trained teachers, and poor-quality recruits, chosen for their religious and political reliability were substituted. A budget was only established for school building in 1945. For many children in the countryside no schools were available, while the wealthy relied on private tutors. Schools served to reinforce class divisions, as the private church schools were the best equipped and staffed and were then consequently dominated by the middle classes.[17]

Whatever type of school children attended, the form of education was similar. Boys and girls were taught separately with different curricula emphasised according to gender. Religious instruction and attendance at classes in the 'formation of the national spirit' (i.e. political training) were compulsory for all throughout their school lives. In both there was a strong emphasis on the promotion of patriotic Spanish values. The basic curriculum also heavily emphasised the humanities – with the regime's version of past national greatness and the empire to the forefront. *Hispanidad*, the allegedly special cultural and racial characteristics of the Spanish world, was explained in classes of all kinds from history to literature. A strong antipathy to the 'Anglo-Saxon' world, meaning Britain and the United States, was inculcated.

Beyond this, the system sought to train pupils for their allotted role in the social and gender hierarchy. Girls were destined for the home, and received instruction in home economics and the demands of motherhood in special classes run by the Women's Section. Boys were fitted for the public world by being taught some maths and science (though this was often limited by scarce resources) and heavy doses of the humanities. Both the church and party took an elitist view of the mental capacities of Spaniards. Most were unfitted for leadership and needed to be directed throughout their lives: in this sense the regime thought of its people as essentially childlike at all ages. Therefore, the mass of pupils, particularly in the working classes, needed to be trained for everyday tasks and in docility – a quality that was considered signally lacking before the civil war. At the same time, a new elite that would run the regime and lead society into the future was needed. To this end Ibáñez Martín introduced a new qualification, the *bachillerato*, into the system that would serve as the basic path to university education for men. Those chosen for it – essentially children of the middle and upper classes – received separate special classes.[18]

The regime gave a special emphasis to the elite role of the universities. Subversion was rooted out. Academics were one of the groups most likely to be in exile after the civil war, having the material means and qualifications to make a life elsewhere. Mexico especially received many with open arms – inheriting one of the most talented generations of intellectuals produced in Spain. A majority of university professors had been enthusiastic Republicans – often very active politically as well – so purging those that remained was a priority. Although single women were allowed to remain as school teachers, in suitable areas of course, all female academics were ejected from the universities. The strong streak of anti-intellectualism in Francoism was also extended to libraries and archives which were 'purified' of offending volumes or simply shut. Appointments to teaching positions became dominated by Catholic Action and members of the ACNP in particular. To a certain extent there was competition for places with Opus Dei, which targeted the universities for the production of its own secular elite. The Consejo Superior de Investigaciones Científicas (CSIC) was dominated by Opus Dei members, and the organisation went on to create its own private universities in the 1950s. Students were dragooned into the residencies (*colegios mayores*) run by the church, and compulsory religious and political training continued. For most of the 'new elite' humanities and the law, traditional paths to professional careers in Spain, were the main subjects. But by the 1950s, economics, sociology and scientific and technical subjects were encouraged as well. The aim was to produce a new generation of leaders, thoroughly imbued with the religious and political ethos of the regime.[19]

Outside the formal education system, Spanish youth came wholly under the control of the FET. The university branch of the party, the Sindicato de Estudiantes Españoles (SEU) had existed as part of the pre-war Falange, providing a specifically male organisation that was a supporter of radical Falangism. Girls were directed into the junior branches of the Women's Section. During the war the party attempted to expand its hold over juveniles of both sexes with the creation of a whole variety of bodies, modelled partly on the scouts and partly on Nazi and fascist youth organisations, to cover children of all ages. These various *pelayos*, *balillas* and *flechas* (organisations for different youth groups according to age and gender) were eventually incorporated alongside the SEU into a general Youth Front formed in 1940. However, the church successfully ensured that membership remained optional for all 7–18 year olds. As a result, only a small proportion of children were ever enrolled and the juvenile branches had little impact. Those that did join – again mostly from the middle classes – found themselves engaged in political and military training. Meanwhile, membership of the SEU was compulsory for all university students and it remained a focus for the most radical wing of Falangist thinking.[20]

Another important aspect of regime attempts to influence behaviour and thinking was its extensive efforts to control access to information, cultural life and leisure. Once again repression was the starting point. The Republic had produced an open and experimental period in many aspects of cultural life, and most intellectuals, writers and artists had sided with the government in the civil war. Naturally, the Nationalists rejected all kinds of avant-gardism and vigorously opposed opinions different to their own. Journalists, writers and artists, musicians, and prominent sportsmen joined the list of those most under suspicion, and many thousands suffered execution, imprisonment and purging or were forced into exile. All aspects of regional identity were vigorously suppressed. Non-Castilian languages, symbols, songs, dances and rituals were forbidden.[21] Across Spain, streets were renamed in honour of Francoist alternatives and statues to unsuitable persons were removed. Even the names of regional dishes were changed and Russian salad became 'national salad'. Modern art, jazz music and popular dance were banned as immoral on religious or racial grounds. Many popular festivals and celebrations were suppressed. Rural carnivals were a particular target, as many involved the reversal of the social order for a day with processions in which disguised participants lampooned local dignitaries. Dress codes were enforced in public, with particular attention to women in short skirts or trousers.[22]

Organised censorship began during the war with the creation of a Press and Propaganda Office under Millán Astray, Franco's mentor from the army of Africa. It passed to the Delegation of Press and Propaganda of the newly formed FET in 1937, which was also given authority over film and radio. A press law introduced by Serrano Suñer in 1938 established rigid criteria for control and censorship, and laid down penalties for transgression. It was augmented in 1941 by a Law for the Defence of Language which banned the use of non-Castilian languages and of foreign loan words. After the war, censorship became the responsibility of the Vice Secretariat for Popular Education of the FET, and then passed to the Catholic-dominated Ministry of Education after 1945. Finally, in 1951, it was taken over by the new Ministry of Information and Tourism. Many other bodies had a say, including local priests and party authorities who were free to ban and censor in their municipalities. The army also had the right to suppress anything that 'offended military dignity'. Franco himself also intervened in particularly sensitive cases.

The result was a censorship that was all-pervasive but also highly arbitrary. Something passed by one body would fall foul of another. All printed matter was included: all books had to be submitted, and the editors of newspapers and magazines – all of whom had to be members of the FET or appointed by the church – were required to pre-censor their publications. There was a long and constantly changing list of topics mention of which was specifically banned. These ranged from the predictable – mention of the Republic, the existence of opposition, praise for the USSR – to the relatively trivial – reporting food shortages or fouls in football matches. Above all, the censorship itself could not be commented upon. The performing arts were also checked for their content. Plays and film scripts had to be submitted for scrutiny before licences were given for performance or filming. Censors not only banned and cut projects but also wrote in their own material. Politics and sex were the chief taboos. The ludicrous lengths to which the censors sometimes went were most graphically displayed in the case of foreign films, mostly American, which had to be dubbed into Spanish. Many were mutilated beyond recognition, with whole scenes considered unsuitable suddenly cut and with translated dialogue and plot lines changed to eliminate any hint of adultery, prostitution or pre-marital sex. Such prudery extended even to painting the limbs of women in short skirts or wearing bikinis. Stage shows were also checked for their possible sexual content, and for the suitability of any jokes or references to the state of Spain.[23]

As well as preventing 'perversion' creeping in from abroad the regime also tried to promote its own views. Its approach was very inward-looking, strongly *castizista* (equating Castilian with Spanish values), disparaging of foreign influences, imperialist and Catholic. Church and party control of the media allowed the dissemination of a wide range of straightforward propaganda and also more subtle messages. Propaganda was clearest in the case of the state news agency (EFE) which manipulated coverage in the press and on the radio. The same was true of the organisation for cinema newsreels and documentaries (Noticiarios y Documentales known by its acronym of NO-DO) created in 1942, whose upbeat and patriotic products were shown in every cinema. Entertainment was also carefully directed towards the creation of a so-called 'national culture'. Until the late 1950s when television appeared, the state radio monopoly was one of the main means used by the regime to this end. Almost every home had access to a receiver, even in the poorest parts of the country-side, and the radio was more popular than the print media. So as well as the news, a whole range of programmes was produced from music and dramas to children's stories. A similar role was played by a state film company, Compañía Industrial Film Española (CIFESA), and the range of cheap novels, magazines and comics sold at newspaper kiosks.[24]

Carefully sanitised historical epics, attempts to match Hollywood swash-bucklers and romances (made suitable for Catholic sensibilities), and spy stories were all disseminated through these means. More soberly, there were proper moral tales for both children and adults. Even Franco himself made a contribu-tion. In 1942 a film, *Raza* (Race), appeared with a screenplay written by the dictator. A thinly disguised allegory of his own family history, its main focus was the conflict between two brothers: one representing upright, patriotic values and the other dangerous liberalism (Ramón Franco, the dictator's brother). Not surprisingly, in the film everything ends happily and good triumphs over evil. Clearly, then, there was more concern with controlling 'popular' rather than 'high' culture. The regime did try to sponser novelists and poets sympathetic to its viewpoint through competitions and prizes. Official art was also encouraged, mostly concentrating on portraits of Franco, studies of soldiers and religious imagery. Similarly, more leeway was given to persons and organisations seen as supporters of the regime rather than outsiders. But by and large the dictatorship failed to produce a distinctive culture of its own, relying on the manipulation of existing forms and the suppression of alternatives.[25]

The regime was less assiduous in trying to organise other forms of leisure activity than its fascist and Nazi counterparts in Europe, if for no other reason than that resources were simply lacking. For instance no equivalent of the Italian *Dopolavoro* (Afterwork) organisation for workers was created. The exception was sport which was recognised as important as part of military training, moral education and a means of fostering national pride. After the civil war it came under the direction of the FET Delegación Nacional de Deportes headed by the Nationalist war hero, General Moscardó. The Women's Section also took a role in organising suitable activities. Contact sports and those seen to require physical strength were reserved for men, while women were confined to gymnastics and swimming. Participation at all levels came under Falangist control, with sports facilities, competitions and displays all controlled by party officials. Until the mid 1940s any sporting event began with the singing of the party anthem and fascist salutes.

Professional football was a particular focus, after some adjustments were made. The names and symbols of clubs in Catalonia and the Basque Country were changed to eliminate regional associations, foreign words were purged from the game's terminology, and the shirts of the national team were changed from red to blue. International competitions became a substitute for the regime's lack of imperial success, reaching a highpoint in 1950 with the defeat of the English team in the World Cup. Yet it proved impossible, even in the 1940s, to prevent regional teams from becoming symbols of identity. In this sense clashes between the regime's favourite side, Real Madrid, and Basque and Catalan teams became a continuation of the civil war by other means. Sport was also a double-edged sword in other ways. In athletics, for instance, Spain had a miserable record in the Olympic Games, hardly adding to an image of national greatness. Not surprisingly, Spanish defeats were played down as the product of foreign bias against the country.[26]

The attempt to dominate public space was also at the heart of attempts to create an iconography for the regime in the post-war years. In part this consisted of placing the symbols of the regime everywhere. Portraits of Franco and José Antonio adorned billboards and their names were inscribed on the walls of churches. The yoke and arrows emblem of the FET was attached to every possible building. New buildings, much-needed after the destruction of the civil war, consciously rejected modernist styles and tried to recreate an 'imperial' aesthetic based, in particular, on the architecture of Juan de Herrera, creator of the Escorial palace and monastery in the sixteenth century. Old public buildings, such as the Prado museum, were given Renaissance additions, and new ones – particularly government and party offices – aped older styles. There was also a series of monumental constructions celebrating the Nationalist victory in the civil war and commemorating their war dead. Perhaps the most important and grotesque was the so-called Valley of the Fallen carved into the mountains just outside Madrid. Built by thousands of Republican prisoners, it was a mix of monastery and mausoleum with a huge concrete cross that could be seen for miles around. Finally completed in 1959, it housed the remains of José Antonio – reburied in great ceremony – and was destined to be the final resting place of Franco himself. The creation of these triumphalist monuments was often closely tied to attempts to create public rituals. Religious and secular celebrations were used to impress the population with the permanence of the dictatorship. A whole series of special dates were commemorated by military displays and processions – the Day of Victory, Race Day, Franco's birthday, José Antonio's death. Failure to attend these numerous events, as well as Easter processions and saints' days, was dangerous in the immediate postwar period. Not surprisingly, the crowds were large and the fascist salutes apparently enthusiastic. They were a constant reminder of the presence of the regime, and served to perpetuate the memory of the civil war.[27]

THE LIMITS OF FRANCOIST CULTURAL AND SOCIAL POLICY

Undoubtedly the overall effect of Francoist cultural and social policies in the post-war period was to deepen divisions in Spanish society rather than create national unity or foster a general Francoist mentality. In many respects, however, this served the regime just as well. By suppressing alternatives and enforcing public conformity, Francoists were given a sense of security and comfort. From feeling that their social and cultural values were under threat, regime supporters felt assured of their permanence. That this only occurred imperfectly was not important either. Cultivating the image of a return to the past, albeit an idealised one, presented a static notion of society that was well suited to the essentially agrarian social bases of the regime in the 1940s and early 1950s. For the conservative peasantry, in particular, the defence of a Catholic identity and notions of community were very important. They provided compensation for the fact that they were not the main beneficiaries of the regime's economic policies. If the reality of Spain under Franco was not all that they wished, socially it was still better than the threat represented by the Republic. Clearly, the regime did not create a 'culture of consent', as one historian has described the social policies of fascist Italy.[28] Nevertheless, it did use cultural and social means to marginalise and neutralise opposition. Interventionist measures placed the population under the scrutiny of the regime. For urban and rural workers it was especially difficult to avoid the prying eyes of the servants of the church and the National Movement. In the harsh material and political circumstances of the 1940s, adopting an attitude of deference and submissiveness could be the difference between life and death. For rural dwellers, the proximity of the priest and the landed elites made outward conformity particularly vital. It was also difficult to avoid contact with the regime in many aspects of everyday life. Many ordinary ambitions and pleasures – playing or watching sport, having children, listening to the radio – involved the dictatorship.

The result was the atomisation of society at large as people sought to escape the attentions of the regime and retreated deep into private life throughout the 1940s and 1950s. Social solidarity was destroyed and the expectations of workers were systematically lowered. For opponents it became dangerous to express personal feelings or opinions in public, as it was impossible to tell who was listening or how they might be interpreted. Only in the home among family and with the doors shut was it safe. All forms of public information were suspect, to be ignored or carefully interpreted. The population became adept at reading between the lines of regime propaganda. Getting by dominated existence in the face of political repression and economic deprivation. Individual resistance was reduced to a petty scale: families speaking a regional language behind closed doors, furtive jokes at the expense of the regime. There was a great deal of despair. The level of suicides rose in the 1940s. In public people took the opportunities they were given for diversion, though the popularity of melancholy ballads suggests the oppressive mood. It was bread and circuses, without the bread. And American films of the 1940s, even after the cuts made to them, offered an entry into a very different world to the Spain of the hunger years. While the regime did not win the hearts and minds of the populace at large, it did marginalise the possibility of any popular cultural and social mobilisation.[29]

Only from within the ranks of the regime was dissent a possibility, and then there were limits. Mostly, it was a question of refusing to accept the boundaries laid down. Motives varied from the complaints of disillusioned Falangists to a simple desire to deal in reality rather than present the rosy picture. Some newspaper editors, for instance, attempted to circumvent the censorship to offer a more critical viewpoint than the regime preferred. The most prominent came from the magazine, *La Codorniz* 'The Quail' founded in 1942, which offered a satirical view that the censors often found uncomfortable. However, going too far led to fines, seizure of papers and dismissal.[30] Writers could also find themselves in difficulties for trying to publish views that failed to chime with the censorship. Camilo José Cela, a future Nobel laureate and, ironically, a censor himself until 1945, was a good example. His novel *La Familia de Pascual Duarte*, a sordid recounting of a murderer's confession of his crimes in the poverty-stricken countryside of Extremadura, was published in 1942 after much trouble with the authorities. However, his next book, *La Colmena* 'The Beehive' about the horrors of everyday life in Madrid was returned six times by the censors and eventually appeared in Argentina in 1951. Others, such as Miguel Delibes, a veteran of the Nationalist army, and Sánchez Ferlosio came in for much the same treatment.[31] Film-makers also faced great difficulty in presenting a more accurate picture of the reality of life for the majority. Those such as Carlos Saura, Juan Bardem and Luis Berlanga, on the margins of the regime, were constantly frustrated by the censors. Even a committed Falangist like Nieves Conde had difficulty in getting a showing of his portrait of rural life,

Surcos 'Furrows', made in 1951. It received no general release but was shown in a special session authorised by the director general of film, García Escudero, who was himself promptly sacked shortly afterwards for this and for allowing the showing of Italian social-realist films in an exhibition.[32]

Much the same pattern of limited toleration for critical voices that came from within the regime, leading to suppression if they went too far, was true for intellectual dissenters. Mostly, they came from the ranks of radical Falangism but some also claimed Catholic credentials. The most prominent were the small group who had provided the regime with many of its early symbols and 'revolutionary' edge. They included the poet, Dionisio Ridruejo, and the academics, Pedro Laín Entralgo, Antonio Tovar and Juan Antonio Maravall. In the 1940s they found the failure of national syndicalism and the stifling conformity of the regime hard to bear. After returning from fighting with the Blue Division on the Russian front in 1942, Ridruejo expressed these feelings in print and in a letter to Franco. Internal exile for a decade was his reward.[33] In the early 1950s Laín Entralgo and Tovar were appointed as rectors of Madrid and Salamanca universities respectively. Here they provided a sympathetic forum for the growth of discontent amongst Falangist students, which focused on demands for a more radical response to social problems from the regime, essentially a call for the rhetoric of the FET to be carried out in reality, and agitation for more open debate within the SEU.

Cultural events such as poetry readings, writers' conferences and film festivals at the universities became occasions for debate. This spread beyond Falangism to some degree. The Communist Party's policy of trying to attract student support played a part in this, though the numbers involved were small. However, it was important in the growing calls from within the student body for the abolition of the SEU. Even more important was the spread of cultural regionalism among the Basque and Catalan universities in the late 1950s. Students became the first real focus for a revival of regionalism, calling for teaching in the non-Castilian languages and the abolition of SEU. Within the student body this debate and agitation led to a great deal of internal conflict as well as clashes with the Francoist authorities. In 1956 this led to the student disturbances in the Castilian universities which, although members of the Communist Party were involved, were overwhelmingly within the ideological framework of Falangism. Meanwhile, in the Basque country and Catalonia, confrontation with the authorities was more direct, with student strikes and demonstration against the regime. The crackdown that followed was actually quite lenient in comparison to the treatment meted out to strikers. After all, those involved were the middle- and upper-class offspring of the regime's most prominent supporters. Heads did roll at the top, however, and both Laín and Tovar, as well as the Minister of Education, Ruiz Giménez, were sacked.[34]

This kind of criticism presented little real threat to the regime and worked in some ways to its advantage. Because it came from within the dictatorship, it was expressed in the language of Falangism, and/or took the form of 'high' culture such as art films or novels. Its wider impact was therefore strictly limited. Most people did not listen to the agonising of intellectual Falangists or read books like *Pascual Duarte*. Semi-toleration was easy for the regime, particularly after 1945 when a more liberal face was needed for the outside world. Some criticism and the appearance of cultural debate diverted attention from the more totalitarian aspects of policies. It also provided something of a safety valve. Although the frustrations of censorship, banning and fines did lead many – like Ridruejo, Cela and many students of the fifties generation – eventually to abandon the regime, this did not really matter while cultural and social control in general remained tight.

It became increasingly difficult to maintain these policies in the form in which they had been introduced in the 1940s. In particular, the regime's control of society was undermined by the consequences of the social changes unleashed by rapid economic development from the late 1950s onwards. In this sense the development strategy adopted by the technocrats of Opus Dei when they came into government in 1956 – fulfilling a major part of their educational aims – was more than just a turning point in economic performance; it also marked a shift in the whole cultural and social reality of Spain. It was this that Franco had grasped when he tried to resist the stabilisation measures of 1959. He sensed that the values for which the civil war had been fought would be diluted. He was right, and the technocrats wrong when they suggested that economic change and cultural, social and political continuity could be combined. The regime's whole approach to society throughout the 1940s and 1950s relied upon autarky and immobilism as its basis. A fixed vision of society and of social control, whether national syndicalist or national Catholic in nature, worked best in an equally fixed and unchanging society.

Population movement and social mobility in the 1960s made such control very difficult, and challenged the social hierarchies and forms of behaviour that the regime's policies were designed to reinforce. People were literally taken outside the established order through the processes of industrialisation and migration. This was especially so in the countryside, which was drained of a large part of the economically active population in around a decade. It is hard to overestimate the consequences of the collapse of traditional rural life that followed. Depopulated villages, with ageing populations, became common in central and northern Spain. The old social relationships based on the land, which had provided so many of the categories and assumptions written into the Francoist social vision, collapsed. For those who left for the cities the experience was hugely dislocating in many ways. The burgeoning concrete suburbs were often alienating, though a sense of communal solidarity was sometimes preserved when whole villages moved to the same apartment block in one of the new *urbanizaciones* of Madrid. Southerners moving to Catalonia or the Basque country also faced problems of cultural assimilation.[35]

Accompanying changes in the class structure – particularly the creation of a new working class and a professional middle class – also had their effect. Social mobility led to rising expectations that broke the fatalism of the 1940s and 1950s. Expanding incomes and full employment brought a greater sense of security and confidence to everyone in the industrial economy. There were also changes to the family and social life which could not be resisted. In one respect there was a much belated success for the regime in that Spain experienced a baby boom in the 1960s. However, this was clearly due to the more favourable economic climate than to the exhortations of the dictatorship. People had children because they could afford them. By the 1970s Spain had one of the youngest and fastest growing populations in Europe. This was another important aspect of change: a new generation that had no personal experience of the civil war and little memory of the harsh conditions of the 1940s came to maturity. Gender relations were also affected by economic change, as the need for female labour to work in the new industries and the service sector challenged the confinement of women to the private sphere.[36]

The social policies of the regime were further undermined by foreign influences, which had been so vigorously excluded until the end of the 1950s. Trade liberalisation and the end of autarky opened up the country not only to goods from northern Europe and the United States but also to new cultural and social experiences. This was a two-way street as Spanish workers migrated to northern Europe in search of work. They found in France, Germany and Switzerland a different culture from the one they had left behind. Spanish guest workers tended to be ghettoised, subject to racism and lower paid than local labour; nevertheless they found an affluence and freedom lacking in their own country. Not surprisingly, along with their remittances, they sent home news of conditions in other countries. The openness of European societies in cultural and social matters contrasted starkly with the attempts at stifling conformity under the Franco regime. Mass tourism in the 1960s further reinforced this sense that Spain was 'different', as the tourist advertisements had it. Although the regime was comforted by the fact that the millions of foreigners who came to Spain were largely physically contained on the coasts, it was impossible to shield the local population from them completely. Nor was it possible to control tourist behaviour or opinions in the same way as those of Spaniards. The days of the late 1940s when foreign women could be arrested on the beach for wearing a bikini were long gone by the 1960s, but topless bathing and a more uninhibited attitude to sex were jarring for young Spaniards. Tourists also brought foreign newspapers, magazines and books with them that presented a very different picture of the world from the censored press in Spain.[37]

The other main social development that came in part through outside contact was the so-called 'Americanisation' of life, meaning the development of consumerism and mass culture for most people. Relative affluence came with bewildering speed in Spain, banishing deprivation and the world of 'getting by' in a decade. Its most visible signs were the acquisition of consumer durables, which were luxuries for the elite in the late 1950s but affordable to a wide range of the population by the 1970s. So from a few people possessing a refrigerator or washing machine in 1960, the vast majority did by 1973. In 1960 only 4 per cent of the population had access to a car, but by 1973 more than a third of households possessed one. Shopping habits also began to change, with supermarkets appearing in the 1960s and department stores in the 1970s. Foreign goods flooded into the shops, often to be preferred to domestic products simply because they came from abroad. In cultural terms this included the arrival of rock and roll, youth culture and modern advertising. But perhaps the biggest change was the arrival of television. Ownership of television sets mushroomed after the beginning of regular broadcasting by the state-owned system in 1959. By the end of the 1960s it had become the main source of entertainment and news in most homes. The ability to buy and the need to sell, in both material and cultural terms, gave rise to a climate in which people ceased to simply accept what they were given – just as they no longer had to accept their fixed role in life – but had wider horizons.[38]

How to meet rising expectations, and deal with the problems that arose from change, presented major challenges to the regime. Having unleashed the social transformation of the country, the dictatorship was ill-prepared to adapt itself to retain its control over society. The cultural and social institutions of the regime had been constructed largely to meet the need to control a rural population. Suddenly, the established party structures, youth groups, the Women's Section, the clergy, Catholic organisations and churches themselves, lost their clientele. Local patterns of supervision and control that were built into village life disappeared with the population or simply became irrelevant.[39] At the same time, the new shanty towns and housing blocks in the cities sprang up so quickly that they simply lacked these inbuilt mechanisms of social control. Keeping a close eye on a mobile, urban population was not so easy. Social change also gave rise to new demands for education and welfare on a scale that could not be met from private means and required state action. From the end of the 1950s, far from shaping society, the regime increasingly responded to social change.

THE DILEMMAS OF THE DEVELOPMENT YEARS, 1958–1975

It was not the case that the regime straightforwardly became obsolete, an anachronism overtaken by social changes beyond its control. This suggests a relationship between industrial capitalist society and political structures of a very mechanistic kind. Modernity and dictatorship are not necessarily contradictory. However, it was clearly the case that the social circumstances in which the Franco regime had been created were changing. What was needed was an approach that was as consistent as the post-war policies had been and which addressed the problems of change in a way that kept the regime at the centre of cultural and social affairs. That no clear direction emerged was due to internal divisions within the regime about how best to proceed. The debate about cultural and social policies initiated from the late 1950s fractured the authoritarian coalition more than any other set of issues.[40]

The most dramatic and serious developments took place within the church. In the course of a decade it went from being one of the main pillars of the regime, to almost complete institutional disengagement. The process whereby the automatic identification of the interests of the church with the dictatorship was reversed began as a drifting away of individuals and groups, and ended with the defection of a major portion of the hierarchy as well. Many factors contributed to this re-evaluation. One was the gradual re-emergence of more liberal theological traditions that challenged integrist National Catholicism. These were strongest amongst the laity and priests who were active in the workers' organisations, Hermandades Obreras de Acción Católica and Juventud Obreras Católica, created as part of Catholic Action in the late 1940s. Their approach drew upon ideas in the Belgian church for the need for active engagement with society, that led down the road to greater awareness of the need for independent rights for workers, and eventually to Christian Democrat thinking about church–state relations. At the same time, and for similar reasons, priests in the Basque Country and Catalonia emerged as important voices for regionalism. In 1960 and 1964, respectively, groups of religious in the two regions presented petitions to the regime calling for linguistic and other 'national' rights to be respected. A powerful filip was given to this movement – largely suppressed by a traditionalist hierarchy in the early 1960s – by the conclusions of the Second Vatican Council in 1962 called by Pope John XXIII. Its more tolerant and liberal approach to social and political questions presented a serious problem both to the Spanish bishops and to the ideological underpinnings of the Franco regime.

How to respond to Vatican II divided the church and Catholics. Throughout the 1960s a younger generation of priests came to oppose the dictatorship actively. They engaged in clandestine dialogues with the underground political opposition and trades unions, including the communists. The regime tried to shift its position through a new law of religion in 1967, but it could not go far enough to meet the positions adopted by the Vatican without abolishing itself. Meanwhile, Catholic Francoists and the older bishops were appalled at developments and were determined to resist. Within the church, however, the newly appointed members of the hierarchy – who came to make up a majority by the 1970s – led by the liberal Cardinal Tarancón, began to move in the same direction as much of the priesthood. After much debate, in 1973 the bishops issued a joint statement, *The Church and the Political Community*, which declared the political neutrality of the church and its respect for social and religious pluralism. This reversal of the position of the church from unqualified support for the Nationalist cause in the civil war was a major body-blow to the regime. It made it very difficult to use the language and teaching of Catholicism as the exclusive property of the regime. Religion became disputed terrain and an arena in which independent cultural, social and political activity could take place. Furthermore, the institutions of the church which had been so important in the creation and delivery of policies were lost to the regime and, in some cases, became havens for opposition. This was especially the case in the Basque Country, where some priests shielded the activities of ETA.[41]

The debate within the church fed into, and was reflected by, divisions within the regime. These were never clear-cut, but essentially two camps emerged in the early 1960s. On one side stood the Catholic hard-liners, traditionally minded Falangists and the technocrats of Opus Dei. Not all favoured economic liberalisation, but they had common ground on cultural and social policies where they supported continuation with the 1940s. Most strongly represented by Carrero Blanco, they argued that it was vital for the regime to retain tight control over society and to maintain a distinctive social project. This did not mean, however, that the traditionalists were completely immobilist, but the reforms they favoured were those that they saw as strengthening the efficiency of the state rather than fundamental shifts in policy. Opposing them was an equally loose coalition of reformists that included more liberal Catholics (including Carlists) and Falangists, although in this case 'liberal' meant that they favoured the continuation of the regime but thought that some restructuring of policy was needed. They rejected the relative inflexibility of the hard-liners and favoured an *apertura* (opening up) in order to revitalise Francoism's relationship with society. Unless the real needs and demands of the population were met, they suggested, the regime risked becoming sidelined. This idea of reacting to people rather than simply telling them what to do reflected a growing interest in some quarters of the regime in public opinion, and the results of anthropological and sociological enquiries undertaken in the universities. The most prominent champion of this approach was Manuel Fraga Irribarne, a youthful university professor.[42]

The cabinet reshuffle of 1962 institutionalised the debate about reform. Fraga came in as Minister of Tourism and Communications and immediately became the chief advocate of change. During his period in office he ranged well beyond his defined area of competence, drawing together a coalition of *aperturistas*. A number of bodies within the regime had also become converted to the need for change. The least surprising was the Institute for Political Studies, the think-tank of the National Movement, which produced radical plans to abandon censorship and grant extensive regional rights. More unusual was the amount of rethinking within the Women's Section, where a younger generation of Falangist women argued for a greater public role and rights. All such talk was strongly dismissed by the hard-liners. Constant tension over policies ensued and no clear position ever emerged from the cabinet. The result was that a limited liberalisation raised expectations which were then frustrated at every turn by the rearguard actions of the traditionalists.[43]

Policies towards women and the family were a typical example of the half-hearted nature of the reforms that were produced. Women were given a greater range of rights. In 1958 the laws on adultery were repealed and the official position of head of the family was abolished. During the early 1960s laws were passed giving equal pay (although this was not implemented at the time), full rights to property and an end to the ban on married women working. However, these measures could be portrayed as necessary for the functioning of the economy – women were needed in the workplace and it was not always possible for them to be under the direct control of a husband or father. All other possible changes were blocked. Abortion and contraception remained illegal, but both were widely available virtually openly in the larger cities by the 1970s. It was still assumed that women would continue to take full responsibility for domestic duties, so no measures were taken to improve child care or increase allowances.[44]

Failure to meet changing and growing needs was evident in education as well. More resources were put into buildings and the recruitment and training of new teachers, but demand always outstripped supply. One big change did result from this. Because the private religious sector was completely unable to keep up, the public school system was recreated and improved. Some measures were also taken to gear the education system to the needs of an industrial society. Programmes for literacy – which did become almost universal in the 1960s – and greater emphasis on technical and scientific training were gradually introduced, and girls received a broader education. However, the system both produced poor results by general European standards and it remained very elitist despite some tinkering with the *bachillerato*. Much the same held true for the universities as well. Higher education did expand to accommodate a growing middle class – including women – though working-class recruitment was small. The number of universities doubled in the 15 years from 1960. However, ever larger classes, an almost complete absence of libraries and much poor teaching from underqualified Francoist professors devalued these positive developments for students.[45]

The most controversial inititative was a new press law introduced by Fraga as the centrepiece of liberalisation in 1966. Amongst other measures this ended pre-censorship and removed the need for newspaper editors and the heads of publishing houses to be approved by the regime. However, retrospective censorship remained, along with a range of punishments for transgressors. The result was confusion and contradiction. A much wider range of printed material – newspapers, magazines and books – became available by the end of the 1960s, including translations of the works of Marx and editions of previously banned novels by Spanish authors. The press had greater freedom to report on the inner workings of the regime, including on the MATESA scandals, and on the state of Spain in general. Likewise, it became easier to publish in Catalan and Basque, helping to fuel the revival of regional cultures and identities. Cinema and theatre productions also benefited from the lifting of control. Yet in reality there was no free press or freedom of expression. Intervention became completely arbitrary, with sudden swoops on newspaper offices or theatres when it was decided that an invisible line had been crossed. Stories that were allowed one week were considered unacceptable the next week. In one graphic example, Luis Buñuel's film *Viridiana* was accepted as the official Spanish entry to the Cannes Film Festival and then promptly banned in Spain itself.[46]

At the same time as the regime relaxed its hold through censorship, it effectively abandoned serious attempts to promote its own cultural and social vision. This was symptomatic of its inability to define its role and policies in the 1960s and 1970s. Control of television, which was a state monopoly financed by advertising, was the most important outlet. Other forms of entertainment, such as cinema, radio and live performance, were in steep decline as the audience for television rose. By the end of the 1960s television had become the chief form of leisure for most Spaniards. News programmes tended to contain dull domestic reports, including ever more infrequent glimpses of a clearly aged and increasingly infirm Franco, and exaggerated reports of disasters abroad. Entertainment was cheap and cheerful, continuing the regime's attempt to pacify the masses through mindless diversion and signalling the end of all attempts to influence 'high' culture. Sport was a mainstay, including a revival of the declining art of bullfighting through regular Sunday broadcasts of *corridas*. Gambling also featured, with the football pools and national lottery getting much attention. Soap operas and game shows made up most of the rest of the output.[47]

Wavering between toleration and crack-downs confused regime supporters and provided the space for growing cultural and social protest. During the 1960s the representatives of 'high' culture had virtually all been driven into the opposition camp. In art cinema, novels, poetry and prose, the condition of Spain was dissected. Student protest against conditions in the universities became endemic and scored a notable success in 1965 with the disbanding of the SEU, the only institution of the dictatorship to be effectively overthrown in the regime's lifetime. Though most professors remained wedded to the status quo, by the 1970s students were joined in their attacks on the regime by the non-tenured staff, often veterans of earlier protest themselves. Falangism ceased to be of any relevance as a vehicle of student revolt and various versions of Marxism took over. At a more popular level, as well, the regime came under attack, particularly in the regions. The so-called 'new song' of Catalonia was a prominent example of mobilisation around culture, with singers such as Lluís Llach giving voice to a variety of forms of discontent at well-attended concerts. Football matches between Catalan or Basque teams and Castilian ones became occasions for regional sentiments to be openly expressed, with crowds singing the banned anthems of their respective 'nations'.[48]

In the face of growing protest, the internal tensions of the regime were resolved by a return to the hard-line approach. Fraga and the reformists were dismissed in the cabinet reshuffle of October 1969. Having failed, as they saw it, to breath new life into the regime they took the path into opposition themselves. The 'monocolour' government of 1969 then tried to put the genie back into the bottle through the use of greater force. With reforms suspended under a series of states of emergency, censorship was tightened, newspaper editors were arrested, and the universities were under virtual occupation by the police. Repression – as in the economic and political spheres – was counter-productive, and protest only redoubled. More seriously still, the regime showed itself to be irrelevant to the cultural and social lives of the majority. The continued messages about the civil war and the need to counter communism seemed totally unreal, from a past that most Spaniards either never experienced or only dimly remembered. Well before the regime actually disappeared, a post-Francoist culture and society that was pluralist and independent of the state already existed in embryonic form. The rebirth of regional identities, a more tolerant Catholicism, acceptance of cultural and social experimentation and diversity, consumerism, and, above all, a desire for 'modernity' rather than an idealised past, were all in place. It was really only a matter of waiting for the chief symbol of the old order to pass away.

CONCLUSION

The last major symbolic act of the Franco regime was the burial of the dictator himself. With great ceremony he was interred alongside José Antonio beneath the great cross in the Valley of the Fallen. A week of public mourning was declared. Then, more or less, everyone got on with their lives and put the dictatorship behind them. Nowadays, curious tourists and handfuls of the ageing Francoist faithful are the only visitors to this grotesque monument to the 1940s. Yet even before his death, the Spain that Franco had sought to create after the civil war had almost passed away. The cultural and social enterprise initiated by the regime played a key part in both sustaining the dictatorship and eventually contributing to its demise. During the 1940s and 1950s the attempt to ingrain Francoist values into the fabric of society, although it did not succeed in its own terms, helped integrate the disparate Francoist social coalition and marginalised opposition. As this project unravelled during the 1960s in the face of changes which the regime was unable to deal with, the coin was reversed. Cultural and social mobilisation outside the control of the dictatorship helped establish an independent space for protest and underpinned political opposition. By the 1970s the regime had ceased to be the subject of private jokes and had itself become a public one – unable to cope with the modernity it had itself unleashed. After its demise, Spain experienced an explosion of cultural and social experimentation and renewal that underpinned the transition to democracy.

NOTES

1 For the development of the church and attitudes to it, see Frances Lannon, *Privilege, Persecution and Prophecy. The Catholic Church in Spain, 1875–1975* (Oxford, 1987) and Stanley Payne, *Spanish Catholicism: An Historical Overview* (Madison, 1984).

2 See Lannon, *Privilege, Persecution and Prophecy*, especially Chapter 7 and 'The Church's Crusade against the Republic', in P. Preston, ed., *Revolution and War in Spain, 1931–1939* (London, 1984), pp. 35–58; J. M. Sánchez, *The Spanish Civil War as a Religious Tragedy* (Notre Dame, 1987).

3 See Lannon, *Privilege, Persecution and Prophecy*, Chapters 2 and 6; J. Andrés Gallego, *Pensamiento y acción social de la Iglesia en España* (Madrid, 1984); D. Benavides Gómez, *El fracaso social del catolicismo español* (Barcelona, 1973). On Catholic unions and rural syndicates see Juan José Castillo, *El sindicalismo amarillo en España* (Madrid, 1977) and *Propietarios muy pobres. Sobre la subordinación política del pequeño campesino* (Madrid, 1979); J. Cuesta, *Sindicalismo católico agrario en España (1917–1919)* (Madrid, 1978). On the development of Opus Dei, see Jesús Ynfante, *La prodigiosa aventura del Opus Dei* (Paris, 1970).

4 For the views of the parties see José R. Montero, *La CEDA. El catolicismo social y político en la II República*, 2 vols. (Madrid, 1977); Martin Blinkhorn, *Carlism and Crisis in Spain, 1931–1939* (Cambridge, 1975); Julio Gil Pecharromán, *Conservadores subversivos: la derecha autoritaria alfonsina (1913–1936)* (Madrid, 1994); Raul Morodo, *Los origenes ideológicos del franquismo: Acción Española* (Madrid, 1985).

5 Quoted in Lannon, *Privilege, Persecution and Prophecy*, p. 200.

6 For Falangist thinking, see Sheelagh Ellwood, *Prietas las filas. Historia de Falange Española, 1933–1983* (Barcelona, 1984); Javier Jiménez Campo, *El fascismo en la crisis de la II República* (Madrid, 1979); Ricardo Chueca, *El fascismo en los comienzos del régimen de Franco* (Madrid, 1983).

7 See José Ramón Montero, 'Los católicos y el Nuevo Estado. Los perfiles ideológicos de la ACNP durante la primera etapa del franquismo', in Josep Fontana, ed., *España bajo el franquismo* (Barcelona, 1986), pp. 100–22; G. Cámara Villar, *Nacional-catolicismo y escuela. La socialización política del franquismo (1936–1951)* (Madrid, 1984), pp. 118–38; A. Cenarro Lagunas, 'El control de la sociedad arogonesa, campo de batalla de la pugna entre la Iglesis y FET y de las JONS (1939–1945)', in J. Tusell *et al.*, *El régimen de Franco (1936–1975)*, vol. 1 (Madrid, 1993), pp. 41–54.

8 Lannon, *Privilege, Persecution and Prophecy*, Chapter 8; A. Botti, *Cielo y dinero: el nacionalcatolicismo en España (1881–1975)* (Madrid, 1992); A. Alvarez Bolado, *El experimento del nacional-catolicismo, 1939–1975* (Madrid, 1976).

9 In general see Ellwood, *Prietas las filas* and Ricardo Chueca, *El fascismo en los comienzos del régimen de Franco*.

10 On the background to this thinking, see M. Nash, 'Control social y trayectoria histórica de la mujer en España', in R. Bergalli and E. M. Mari, eds., *Historia ideológica del control social* (Barcelona, 1989).

11 L. Falcón, *Mujer y sociedad* (Barcelona, 1984); Ian Gibson, *The Assassination of Federico García Lorca* (London, 1979).

12 M. T. Gallego Méndez, *Mujer, falange y franquismo* (Madrid, 1983) and R. Sánchez López, *Mujer española: una sombra de destino en lo universal (trayectoria histórica de Sección Femenina de Falange, 1934–1977)* (Murcia, 1990) are scholarly accounts. Luis Suárez Fernández, *Crónica de la Sección Femenina y su tiempo* (Madrid, 1992) and Pilar Primo de Rivera, *Recuerdos de una vida* (Madrid, 1983) are the offical history and autobiography respectively. On carefully sanitised role-models for women, see G. di Febo, *La santa de la raza: un culto barroco en la España franquista* (Barcelona, 1988) and Alison Weber, *Teresa of Avila and the Rhetoric of Femininity* (Princeton, 1990).

13 Mary Nash, 'Pronatalism and Motherhood in Franco's Spain', in G. Bock and P. Thane, eds., *Maternity and Gender Policies: Women and the Rise of the European Welfare States, 1880–1950s* (London, 1991), pp. 160–77.

14 On women's work and its history in Spain, see A. Espina, 'La participación femenina en la actividad económica: el caso español', in R. Conde, ed., *Familia y cambio social* (Madrid, 1982); R. M. Capel Martínez, *El trabajo y la educación de la mujer en España, 1900–1930* (Madrid, 1982); M. G. Nuñez Pérez, *Trabajadoras en la segunda República: un estudio de la actividad extradoméstica (1931–1936)* (Madrid, 1989); Tim Rees, 'Women on the Land: Household and Work in the Southern Countryside, 1875–1939', in V. Enders and P. Radcliff, eds., *Contested Identities: Women in Modern Spain* (New York, forthcoming); R. Behar, *The Presence of the Past in a Spanish Village. Santa María del Monte* (Princeton, 1986). During the civil war, in response to calls for the prohibition of prostitution, the Nationalist general Queipo de Llano replied that without it the morale of his troops would be undermined.

15 Gallego Méndez, *Mujer, falange y franquismo*, pp. 91–8, 124–5; Sánchez López, *Mujer española*; Carmen Martín Gaite, *Usos amorosos de la postguerra española* (Barcelona, 1987).

16 J. Crespo, *Purga de maestros en la guerra civil* (Valladolid, 1987).

17 On the general development of education, see A. Mayordomo, ed., *Historia de la educación en España*, 2 vols. (Madrid, 1990), part 5. On class divisions, see C. Lerena, *Escuela, ideología y clases sociales en España* (Barcelona, 1986).

18 On the nature of education, see G. Cámara Villar, *Nacional-catolicismo y escuela: la socialización política del franquismo (1936–1951)* (Madrid, 1984); Andrés Sopeña Monsalve, *El florido pensil: memoria de la escuela nacionalcatólica* (Barcelona, 1994); Rafael Vals, 'Ideología franquista y enseñanza de la historia en España, 1938–1953', in Fontana, *España bajo el franquismo*, pp. 230–45 and *La enseñanza de la literatura en el franquismo (1936–1951)* (Barcelona, 1983); Ramón Navarro Sandalinas, *La enseñanza primaria durante el franquismo (1936–1975)* (Barcelona, 1990). On *hispanidad* see L. D. Gómez-Escalonilla, *Imperio de papel: acción cultural y política exterior durante el primer franquismo* (Madrid, 1992). The *bachillerato* was divided into two grades in the late 1950s, giving different forms of higher education – technical training or a more academic education for high fliers.

19 J. Carreras and M. Ruiz Carnicer, eds., *La universidad española bajo el régimen de Franco (1939–1975)* (Zaragoza, 1991); Miguel Ruiz Carnicer, 'La formación política en la universidad franquista. Falange ante profesores y estudiantes', and M. Montero Díaz, 'La ACN de P y la reconquista intelectual de la universidad (1940–1945)', both in J. Tusell *et al.*, eds., *El régimen de Franco*, pp. 377–90, 391–404; Ynfante, *Prodigiosa aventura del Opus Dei*, pp. 37– 82; Salvador Giner, 'Power, Freedom and Social Change in the Spanish University, 1939–75', in P. Preston, ed., *Spain in Crisis: The Evolution and Decline of the Franco Regime* (Hassocks, 1976), pp. 183–211.

20 See Juan Sáez Marín, *El Frente de Juventudes. Política de juventud en la España de la postguerra (1937–1960)* (Madrid, 1988); Gallego Méndez, *Mujer, falange y franquismo*, pp. 99–104.

21 On the suppression of regionalism, see Edwards Hansen, *Rural Catalonia under the Franco Regime: The Fate of Regional Culture since the Civil War* (Cambridge, 1977); Hank Johnstone, *Tales of Nationalism: Catalonia, 1939–1979* (New Bruswick, 1991); Robert Clark, *The Basques: The Franco Years and Beyond* (Reno, 1979); Stanley Payne, *Basque Nationalism* (Reno, 1975).

22 Rafael Abella, *Por el imperio hacia Dios: crónica de una posguerra (1939–1955)* (Barcelona, 1978); Martín Gaite, *Usos amorosos de la postguerra*.

23 On the organisation and nature of the censorship see Román Gubern, *La censura: función política y ordenamiento jurídico bajo el franquismo (1936–1975)* (Barcelona, 1981); Justino Sinova, *La censura de prensa durante el franquismo (1936–1951)* 2nd edn. (Madrid, 1989).

24 On NO-DO see Sheelagh Ellwood, 'Spanish Newsreels 1943–1975', *Historical Journal of Film, Radio and Television*, 7/3 (1987), pp. 225–38.

25 Many of the films of the time actually offered very strong roles for women like Concha Piquer and Aurora Bautista, contravening the accepted codes on their place in society. See P. Besas, *Behind the Spanish Lens: Spanish Cinema under Franco* (London, 1986); Sopeña Monsalve, *El florido pensil* which is marvellous on children's comics and radio programmes; Manuel Vasquez Montalbán, *Crónica sentimental de España: une mirada irreverente a tres décadas de mitos y de sueños* (Barcelona, 1980).

26 C. Fernández Santander, *El fútbol durante la guerra civil y el franquismo* (Madrid, 1990); Duncan Shaw, *Fútbol y franquismo* (Madrid, 1987); J. MacClancy, 'The Basques of Vizcaya and Athlétic Club de Bilbao', in J. MacClancy, ed., *Sport, Identity and Ethnicity* (Oxford, 1995).

27 A. Bonet Correa, ed., *Arte del franquismo* (Madrid, 1981); G. Ureña, *Arquitectura y urbanismo civil y militar en el período de la autarquía* (Madrid, 1979); D. Méndez, *El Valle de los Caidos: idea, proyecto, construcción* (Madrid, 1982); P. Fernández Aguilar, 'Los lugares de la memoria de la guerra civil. El Valle de los Caidos: la ambigüedad calculada', and G. M. Hernández y Marti, 'Nacional-catolicismo y calendario festivo en Valencia', both in J. Tusell *et al.*, eds., *El régimen de Franco*, pp. 485–500, 531–42; María Angeles Civera, 'Origen y desarrollo de la Fiesta de la Hispanidad', *Historia y Vida*, 25 (1992), pp. 92–101; Javier Jiménez Campo, 'Integración simbólica en el primer franquismo (1939–1945)', *Revista de Estudios Políticos (1980)*, pp. 125–43.

28 The phrase is from Victoria de Grazia, *The Culture of Consent: Mass Organisation of Leisure in Fascist Italy* (Cambridge, 1981).

29 On life in the 1940s and 1950s, see Rafael Abella, *Por el imperio hacia Dios* and *La vida cotidiana en España bajo el régimen de Franco* (Barcelona, 1985). On popular song, see M. Román, *Memoira de la copla: la canción española de Conchita Piquer a Isabel Pantoja* (Madrid, 1993).

30 See Iván Tubau, *El humor gráfico en la prensa del franquismo* (Barcelona, 1987) and J. Terrón Montero, *La prensa en España durante el régimen de Franco* (Madrid, 1981).

31 See Barry Jordan, *Writing and Politics in Franco's Spain* (London, 1990) and Manuel Abellán, *Censura y creación literaria en España (1939–1976)* (Barcelona, 1980).

32 See Besas, *Behind the Spanish Lens* and Barry Jordan, 'Culture and Opposition in Franco's Spain: The Reception of Italian Neo-Realist Cinema in the 1950s', *European History Quarterly* (1991), pp. 209–38.

33 For their views see D. Ridruejo, *Escrito en España* (Buenos Aires, 1962) and P. Laín Entralgo, *España como problema*, 2 vols. (Madrid, 1949). See also E. Diaz, *Pensamiento español en la era de Franco (1939–1975)* (Madrid, 1983).

34 P. Lizcano, *La generación del 56: la universidad contra Franco* (Barcelona, 1981); Giner, 'Power, Freedom and Social Change'; José Maravall, *Dictatorship and Political Dissent: Workers and Students in Franco's Spain* (London, 1978).

35 Adrian Shubert, *A Social History of Modern Spain* (London, 1990), pp. 217–32 offers a summary of changes. See also J. Aceves and W. Douglass, eds., *The Changing Face of Rural Spain* (New York, 1976); Susan Tax Freeman, *Neighbours* (Chicago, 1970).

36 Joaquín Arango, 'La modernización demográfica de la sociedad española', in J. Nadal *et al. La economía española en el siglo XX* (Barcelona, 1987), pp. 201–36; J. Casas, *La participación laboral de la mujer en España* (Madrid, 1987).

37 Vasquez Montalbán, *Crónica sentimental de España*, is good on many aspects of this influx of foreign ideas.

38 The successive surveys by FOESSA, *Informe sociológico sobre la situación de España* (Madrid, 1966, 1970, 1975) are a good source of information on all aspects of change. See also M. Vasquez Montalbán, *La penetración americana en España* (Madrid, 1974).

39 On the decline in membership of the Youth Front, see Sáez Marín, *El Frente de Juventudes*, pp. 419–65.

40 For discussion of these issues, see Félix Ortega, 'Las contradicciones entre sociedad y política: el caso de la transición democrática española', *Revista de Occidente* 107 (1990), pp. 93–111 and Julián Casanova, 'Modernization and Democratization: Reflections on Spain's Transition to Democracy, *Social Research* 50, 4 (1983), pp. 929–73.

41 For the movement away from the regime, and its attempts to react, see Lannon, *Privilege, Persecution and Prophecy*, Chapter 9; J. Ruiz Rico, *El papel político de la Iglesia católica en la España de Franco* (Madrid, 1977); Norman Cooper, 'The Church: From Crusade to Christianity', in P. Preston, ed., *Spain in Crisis*, pp. 48–81; Botti, *Cielo y dinero*.

42 For an account of these tensions and their consequences for policy, see Stanley Payne, *The Franco Regime, 1936–1975* (Madison, 1987), Chapter 20.

43 In July the institute sponsored a conference, lasting a number of days with Fraga present, on means to adjust to changes. The papers are in Archivo General de la Administración Central (AGAC), Sección Presidencia, Cajas 9835–42.

44 Sánchez López, *Mujer española*; Geraldine Scanlon, *La polémica feminista en la España contemporánea* (Madrid, 1976).

45 Ruiz Carnicer and Carerras, *La universidad española*; Lerena, *Escuela, ideología y clases sociales*; Navarro Sandalinas, *La enseñanza primaria*.

46 See Kenneth Maxwell, ed., *The Press and the Rebirth of Iberian Democracy* (Westport, 1983). On the revival of regional languages, see Clark, *The Basques: The Franco Years and Beyond*, Chapter 6 and Alberto Balcells, *Catalan Nationalism* (London, 1996), Chapter 14.

47 See Jesús García Jiménez, *Radiotelevisión y política cultural en el franquismo* (Madrid, 1980).

48 See Shirley Magani, *Rojos y rebeldes: la cultura de la disidencia durante el franquismo* (Barcelona, 1987); R. Fiddian and P. Evans, *Challenge to Authority: Fiction and Film in Contemporary Spain* (London, 1988); Maravall, *Dictatorship and Political Dissent*, Chapters 5–7; Giner, 'Power, Freedom and Social Change'; Victor Pérez Diaz, *The Return to Civil Society: The Emergence of Democratic Spain* (Cambridge, MA, 1993).

7

The International Relations of Francoism

This chapter analyses Spain's place in the world and the role of external relations during the dictatorship. It is important to consider key aspects of the international relations of Francoism for a number of reasons. First, the external dimension is vital to understanding both its ideology and its survival in the post-war world. Second, the Franco regime took shape at a time of dramatic global changes – the rise of fascism and subsequently the outbreak of the Second World War, followed by the Cold War and decolonisation. These global events shaped the ways in which the regime was understood at the time. They also acted as structural constraints and shaped the environment in which the Nationalist regime could make policy. Spain constituted a relatively backward country inside Europe at the time of the dictatorship; internal politics were therefore particularly susceptible to the influence of events and of powerful actors from outside national frontiers. Third, an analysis of the foreign policy of the dictatorship is important because it had pretensions to empire. The imperial idea was central to the world vision of Francoist elites, especially those from the Falange and the army.[1] This made foreign policy a prominent concern of the dictatorship, especially in the early period. Fourth, foreign policy became an instrument of survival for the Franco regime in the turbulent world which emerged after 1945. The dictatorship came through these difficult years and the considerable external hostility which they entailed not simply by stealth, cunning or luck, though they were important, but by turning Spain into an important strategic ally of the US. And finally, foreign policy served to mobilise important supporters behind the government. Until the 1960s, foreign policy was a glue binding them into the dictatorship.

The most controversial aspect of Spain's international relations in the early part of the regime was the close relationship with Germany and Italy which the Nationalists developed in the 1930s. Both Germany and Italy assisted the Nationalist war effort. The role Spain later played in the Axis struggle for European domination between 1939 and 1945 is a matter of controversy and polemic. After 1945, the dictatorship embarked on a desperate search, first for survival and then for respectability in western eyes. Policy became a complex and contradictory mix of ideology, nationalism and pragmatism. The contradictions arose especially from the fact that many of the policies after 1945 were the result of the dictatorship's forced adjustment to unforeseen changes in the international system; they did not signify any real transformation of the ideological bases of the regime. They therefore sat very uncomfortably along-side many of the internal policies. But the regime's foreign policy consisted of more than simply reactions to outside events and there were areas of nationalist foreign policy even in the 1960s. In general, however, the regime was forced to come to terms with an international order for which it had little sympathy and in which it was increasingly regarded as an anachronism.

This chapter identifies how international events shaped the regime's foreign policy. It does so through an account of the main stages of foreign policy which draws attention to the major policy shifts which took place over time. Inter-estingly, the 'stages' of foreign policy which we identify correspond with Tusell's view of the regime as a whole which suggests that the major phases of Francoism were to a large extent imposed by external constraints.[2] This enables us to focus in detail on certain key issues: policy-making during the Second World War; the vital relationship with the US; policies towards the rest of Europe, especially the EEC; and Spain's attempt at developing 'special rela-tionships' in North Africa and Latin America. The chapter takes note of the attempts at innovation and the modernisation of the tools of policy-making. But it also emphasises how the success of these initiatives was circumscribed by a variety of factors, including the international rejection of dictatorship in western Europe, the problems facing Spain as a medium-sized country with an uneven industrial base and few natural resources, and the impossibility of empire-building in an international order committed to decolonisation.

UNDERSTANDING FRANCOIST FOREIGN POLICY

In the most general sense, Francoist foreign policy was determined by the ideological orientation of the regime, the reality of economic backwardness in comparison with its European neighbours, and the geographical location of the country on the periphery of Europe with security and imperial concerns in the western Mediterranean and North Africa. Of significance also was the Nation-alist perspective on Spain's past and on the role the country had played historically in shaping the modern world in the sixteenth, seventeenth and eighteenth centuries. The model for the Crusade, which was so important in justifying the uprising against the Republic, was the empire which had been established following national unification in the fifteenth and sixteenth cen-turies. The ties with Latin America and the Caribbean, the most important area under imperial control, acquired a particular symbolic resonance. They were used to postulate the existence of a hispanic world, an alternative world vision and a set of values opposed to Anglo-Saxon capitalism. The Francoist dream was that these ties could be revived in the form of a new bloc of countries for which Spain would be the leading member and guide. North Africa, which was to present a series of foreign policy challenges to Francoism, was especially important for the military, who dreamt of expanding territories under Spanish control beyond the Morocco Protectorate.[3]

The foreign policy of the dictatorship was, moreover, partly determined by the need to legitimise both the uprising of 1936 and the subsequent dictatorship which resulted from the civil war, though this became less pressing the longer the regime was in power. This strengthened the determination to make 'nationalist' foreign policy, that is policy which interpreted the world from a 'hispanic' perspective, in contrast to the dominant visions of the world which Francoists perceived as overwhelmingly Atlantic and Anglo-Saxon. Again, this was especially characteristic of the early years, though the theme resurfaced in different guises throughout the regime, from the *hispanidad* of the 1940s and early 1950s to the promotion of the country as a tourist centre with the slogan 'Spain is different' in the 1960s and 1970s.[4] Policy under Franco can therefore legitimately be criticized on the grounds that it reflects a 'hispanocentric insularity'.[5]

But foreign policy under the dictatorship was about more than what Spain's role in the world should be. It was an important tool for internal control and propaganda and it reflected how elites viewed themselves and the world. Cultural and ideological control during the dictatorship meant that, certainly until the 1960s, for most Spaniards the images of Spain and of the external world were constructed by the Francoist state. This was intensified by the fact that transnational contacts for ordinary citizens through travel, increased consumption and the media – which today form an essential part of Spanish political and cultural consciousness – were at a minimum until this time. The Spanish nation state under Franco was projected as a cultural leader and as a responsible player in an international system, willing to fulfil the obligations and duties which went with a post-imperial state.[6] By the 1960s, a further image of Spain as a rapidly developing country, pursuing policies aimed at modernising the economy, was superimposed on the idea of the country as a cultural giant, adding yet another layer of contradictions to foreign policy discourses.

Domestic factors, and in particular the relationship between the Francoist families, also affected foreign policy. Most cabinets were a delicate balancing act between the various factions of the Nationalist camp; Falangists, technocrats, reformers, the armed forces and Catholics, all of whom had to be accommodated. Each brought with them into government their own vision of the world and Spain's place in it. This problem was acute in the years up to 1957, though it would be wrong to dismiss it completely after that date. Foreign policy was also influenced by the new institutions of Francoism and the institutions of government. The Minister of Foreign Affairs could exercise some influence over policy, though he would never be able to determine it completely. But, more importantly, policy also had to be made within structural constraints outside the control of the government. The changing international conditions of the twentieth century affected the nature of foreign policy even more than it shaped the political economy of the regime.[7] In sum, therefore, shifts in foreign policy occurred as a result of domestic and/or international realignments of forces, though in practice, in view of Spain's dependence on the international system after 1945, it is difficult methodologically to separate out domestic political trajectories from the broader changes taking place in the international order.

What was seen to constitute foreign policy, and its function and purpose, also altered significantly during the long years of the Francoist regime. Between the end of the civil war and the rejection of autarky towards the end of the 1950s, the demands of the economy remained subordinate to politics. This applied to the construction of external relations as well as to other policy areas. But international changes affected policies significantly and slowly moved foreign-policy-making into a more economistic mode. The creation of the EEC in 1958 was to change the way economic elites perceived Europe. More generally, the new power of multinational corporations *vis-à-vis* states and the global triumph of the idea that development translates straightforwardly into capitalist growth and modernisation were transforming international relations by the end of the 1950s. As a result, the relationship between states and international markets came under review globally. Development strategies increasingly focused on the importance of the international market and global trade instead of the promotion of national self-reliance. Spain was no exception to this trend. As a result, policy-makers within the Spanish state gradually came to realise the importance of maintaining good relations with foreign investors. This process effectively meant an end to the belief, dominant at the beginning of the dictatorship, that the state could shape policy as it wished.

These changes prompted a realignment of the Francoist state, both internally and externally. First of all Franco himself, who had exercised substantial personal control over policy decisions in the early period of the dictatorship, was gradually removed from the centre of decision-making. Policy-making became more bureaucratic and institutions became more important. These changes inevitably affected the balance of power between the groups which together made up the authoritarian coalition. At the same time, the position of Spain within Europe and within the capitalist world altered significantly after 1957. This too had considerable implications for the design and implementation of foreign policy. By the 1960s, for example, foreign policy was increasingly perceived in policy-making circles as a means to expand Spain's economic presence in the world, in contrast to the earlier period when foreign policy was an integral part of an ideological crusade against the forces of communism, freemasonry and Protestant capitalism. We can contrast the foreign policy goals of López Bravo (Minister of Foreign Affairs 1969–73) and

López Rodó (Minister of Foreign Affairs 1973–74), for whom foreign policy was essentially about expanding markets and promoting economic development, with those of Serrano Suñer (Minister of Foreign Affairs 1940–2) and Gómez Jordana (Minister of Foreign Affairs 1938–9; 1942–5), and even Fernando María Castiella (Minister of Foreign Affairs 1957–69), who were motivated overwhelmingly by ideological visions of Spain's role in the world. The idea of Spain as a world leader, though never completely absent from policy declarations, became less important as foreign policy became a 'technical' area for making public policy almost like any other.

FROM AXIS SUPPORTER TO COLD WAR WARRIOR

During the civil war, the Nationalists had benefited from aid supplied by the Axis powers.[8] The importance of Axis aid to the Nationalist side was recognised at the time by the Burgos government and considerable efforts were deployed to retain good relations with Nazi Germany and with fascist Italy. The Nationalists received troops, armaments and even financial assistance from the Axis powers. Their assistance was sufficiently important for them to refuse to comply with the demands of the Committee for Non-Intervention during the civil war, despite the hostility this incurred for them from the British and French governments.[9] The Munich crisis of 1938, during which it seemed likely that a Europe-wide conflict would break out as a result of German annexation of territory in Czechoslovakia, provoked moments of panic, since the Nationalists feared that they would be drawn into a wider war which they had no guarantees of winning and which might, in the first instance, bring intervention in Spain from France in aid of the Republic. They declared their intention of remaining neutral early on in the crisis, risking Axis displeasure and indicating that they would be uncertain allies in the event of a major war. In the end – and fortunately for the Nationalists – the Munich crisis was resolved and the outbreak of the Second World War delayed until the end of the civil war.[10]

From then until the end of the Second World War, foreign policy is generally regarded as overwhelmingly 'ideological', in contrast to a more pragmatic approach later. Pollack and Hunter date the ideological period of foreign policy from the elevation of Ramón Serrano Suñer, the leading pro-Nazi in the circle closest to Franco, to Foreign Minister in October 1940, and attribute it to external influences.[11] In fact, however, it can be traced back to the first days of the Nationalist government under Gómez Jordana. The ideological foreign policy of the Franco regime during the Second World War was not merely a function of Nationalist pro-Axis sympathies, but those sympathies were a consequence of prior convictions about the world and a belief in an inevitable conflict between the forces of religion and order on the one hand and communism and godlessness on the other.

So as the civil war ended and the Second World War got underway, Spanish foreign policy was essentially determined by two contradictory forces: firstly, the Nationalists' extreme ideological hostility towards democracy and communism and their sympathy for the Axis, which was especially evident in the FET; and secondly, Franco's unwillingness to join the war. In the event, Spain edged nearer to conflict, although always stopping short of a full commitment, until the turning point in the war was reached and an Axis victory became less and less likely. Franco then switched track and began to untangle himself from the relationship with the Axis and to move again towards neutrality. The regime later made much of Franco's supposed prescience in keeping Spain out of the World War, but in fact analysis shows it to be less the result of planning and more a consequence of a number of unforeseen contingent events. The Nationalist government was aware that Spanish troops were too poorly equipped to enter the war and the economy too ruined to be able to sustain a war effort without substantial external assistance. The new government therefore requested the Axis to grant further aid in 1940 in order to make entry into the war possible, in the event of Franco deciding to do so. Spain asked for supplies of oil, wheat, coal, kerosene, cotton and fertiliser in quantities that the Nazi government found impossibly high and which they were unwilling to supply, indicating they they saw no urgent necessity to force Spain to enter the war. Internal debates about Spain's policy and negotiations with the Axis continued in this vein until they were overtaken by events and the time passed when joining the war would have brought benefits.

Franco himself was the major arbiter of policy and chief decision-maker in this period, though it was also important that policy satisfy important constituents of the Nationalist alliance, namely the Falangists, the army and even the more moderate, generally pro-Allied monarchical elements. The Falangists exercised a particular influence over policy in the early years of the war. They were eager to participate in a worldwide conflict in which two alternative systems – democracy/communism together and fascism – were competing. This, combined with the fact that the Axis looked like winning the war in 1940, weighed significantly on government decision-making. As a result, Spain moved towards participation on the Axis side by declaring non-belligerency – effectively a declaration of support for the Axis – in June 1940. This was coupled with the decision to send a division of volunteers to fight in the war. The notorious Blue Division joined the Nazi army in fighting on the Russian front in 1941.[12] Serrano Suñer, Minister of Foreign Affairs, blamed the outbreak of the war on Russia, thereby justifying Spain's participation on the Russian front as part of a global struggle against communism, without committing the dictatorship to coming into the war against the Allied democracies.

The Franco regime did not wish to be left out if the Axis looked likely to win, and particularly wanted to use the war to secure territory in order to reconstruct the lost empire which, it was hoped, would be the source of greatness again.

Therefore Franco held out to the Nazis the possibility of Spanish participation and asked in return for assurances and guarantees that Spain would be able to extend her control over North Africa. That Franco never lost sight of national concerns in his negotiations with the Axis is evidenced by his insistence that payment for entering the war would be greater Spanish power in North Africa. In pursuit of this end, Spanish forces in North Africa moved to occupy the international city of Tangier in June 1940.

Nonetheless, perhaps as a prelude to what was to come later, policy was always tempered with caution. Spain passed from neutrality in 1939, to the declaration of non-belligerency in 1940, and then back to neutrality in 1943, as it became clear that the Axis would be defeated. This caution also meant that Spain never broke off economic relations with the Allies, even during the pro-Axis phase of policy. In fact, Franco was able to use the threat of collaboration with the Axis to good effect in his negotiations with Britain and the US and gained much-needed credits and supplies. Franco's policy *vis-à-vis* the World War, even at this ideological stage in policy-making, was pragmatic in the end, therefore, despite the rhetorical gestures from the government.

Spain initiated a series of cultural and political overtures to Latin America during the war which were designed to turn the region into an echo of Spanish power once again. With the defeat of the Axis, the Nationalists were forced to concede that the possibility of reconstructing a Spanish empire in North Africa had ended, at least temporarily, and the dream of creating a 'special relationship' with Latin America took precedence in foreign policy for a time. The immediate post-war period constitutes the only time of the entire authoritarian regime when there was a serious attempt to fill the concept of *hispanidad* with some concrete meaning beyond the purely symbolic. The *Consejo de Hispanidad*, the skeleton of which was to survive in different guises throughout the dictatorship, had been created in 1940. It retained its importance after 1945 and, as a result, *hispanidad* was formulated more clearly. Spain came under suspicion from Washington at this time for spreading a doctrine that was seen as an apology for Nazism and fascism in the Americas. It was not hostility from Washington which curbed *hispanidad*, however, but a lack of enthusiasm on the part of Latin American states. In fact, there was clear evidence from the very beginning of the dictatorship, if the Francoists had chosen to look for it, that the policy would be poorly received inside Latin America.[13]

The international climate changed dramatically after 1945, posing problems for the regime and prompting important international realignments. In the aftermath of the World War, the regime found itself facing deep international hostility. Not only was Spain not admitted into the newly created United Nations (UN) but it was made clear that the country would not be accepted at all while Franco was head of state. In 1946, a blockade of Spain was discussed in the UN with the intention of bringing the regime down, and most member states of the UN withdrew their ambassadors.[14] A period of isolation ensued as a result of the diplomatic boycott. This had contradictory effects on policy inside Spain. On the one hand, it paralysed foreign policy initiatives and closed the Foreign Affairs Ministry off from international influences, deepening the conviction inside the Francoist camp that Spain was the victim of an international conspiracy. In the absence of regular and sustained international contacts, extensive use was made of the Diplomatic School (*Escuela Diplomática*) which had been created in 1942, and its nationalist orientation was consolidated.[15] Isolation also created economic problems for the country. But it united the Nationalists and offered an opportunity to bind the disparate elements of Francoism together in one enterprise. Skilful use was therefore made of the boycott by Franco himself in order to unify the regime coalition.

The short-term tactic for survival was to turn to Latin America. Overtures were made to the Latin American countries, a policy enthusiastically supported by the Falangists in particular, who imagined, mistakenly, that Latin America inhabited a similar cultural universe to Spain and shared some common geostrategic and geopolitical interests in resisting the establishment of an international order based on Anglo-Saxon cultural and economic dominance.[16] Unfortunately, at least for Spain, *hispanidad* was understood in Latin America as a right-wing, Catholic ideology, based on upholding Spanish interests and subsuming Latin America within them. It was rejected by Latin American nationalists, most of whom could be located on the left, and was acceptable only to rightist, generally racist, anti-democrats in the region. Given that Spain could offer no economic benefits to Latin America, there was little incentive for Latin American states to enter into an alliance.

The relationship with Argentina was the exception to this trend, however. Franco concluded an important agreement with the Argentine president, General Perón, in 1946 which created hope amongst Francoists that Spain had at last found a powerful ally, and one which would contribute to the creation of an international bloc that would operate as an alternative to the post-war order based on US hegemony. At this time Argentina enjoyed an enviable economic position and had emerged from the war years with a strong economy. But the deal was founded less on shared ideological commitments than the Francoists realised.[17] Instead, Argentina was acting from a perception of its own economic and geostrategic interests. In particular, the relationship with Spain offered the possibility of finding new markets for its beef and wheat products. The protocols signed by Franco and Perón included substantial credits extended by Argentina to Spain. The agreements were nevertheless suspended in 1949 because Spain found it impossible to pay for the imports, despite the credits and a renegotiation of the bilateral debt. Argentina, itself now going through economic problems, was unable to continue to extend credit. The suspension came after a much-publicised visit to Spain by Eva Duarte Perón in 1947, which was important inside Spain in its own right as evidence that the international repudiation of Franco was not total and indeed that some of the more interesting international figures chose to visit the country.

Turning to Latin America was always only a partial and unsatisfactory solution to Spain's problems and it was the onset of the Cold War that rescued the regime from international isolation. The regime was now able to manipulate its long-standing hostility to communism and to the Soviet Union to good effect. Franco's staunch anti-communism brought overtures, if not of friendship, at least of acceptance from the US government in 1947, which went as far as trying to include Spain in the Marshall Plan for the recovery of Europe, a move blocked by the European Allies. The regime sought to mend fences with the US by insisting on its anti-Communist credentials. Its much vaunted theory, dating from 1940, of two wars, one between the Axis powers and the Allies in which Spain remained neutral, and the second against the Soviet Union and communism in which Franco actively participated through the Blue Division – a theory which had seemed specious at the time, now came in rather useful.

NORMALISATION OF FOREIGN RELATIONS

More than any other single event, it was a deal in 1953 to lease Spanish territory to the US to be used as military bases which guaranteed the survival and the partial international rehabilitation of the authoritarian regime.[18] The deal, therefore, marks the early 1950s out as a transition period for Francoism. On the one hand, the regime clung to its rigid hostility to all things foreign, especially at the level of discourse. On the other hand, economic necessity pushed Franco into a deal with the US, the details of which were secret and the impact of which was minimised by the Francoist press.

It was to the US that Franco owed his survival. The deal was sufficiently important to American national interests to force the US government to agree to support Spain's incorporation into the international system once again, even though no political changes had taken place internally. From the US perspective, the new arrangements with the Franco regime were part of a move to strengthen western defences in the Mediterranean and ensured that Spain, strategically located to control access to the area, would remain anti-Soviet. The US government was therefore pushed by the Pentagon towards accepting that its long-term interests dictated that it come to an understanding with Franco. However, pressure from the Pentagon notwithstanding, the authoritarian regime also had to work long and hard to persuade President Truman that it was internationally acceptable. A Spanish lobby was created in Washington after 1945 at considerable expense, composed mainly of Catholics and rightists with access to Congress and the press, with José Félix Lequerica, briefly Foreign Minister in 1940, as head of the operation.

The good offices of Lequerica, combined with the international tension characteristic of the period from 1947 to 1950 which galvanised the Pentagon into action, brought President Truman very reluctantly round to offering Franco a deal. As a result, only a few years after pressing for a UN boycott, the US was championing Spain as a potential candidate for entry into the UN and even considered supporting Spanish membership of the North Atlantic Treaty Organisation (NATO), a move which was blocked by European members. In 1950, as a sign that international opinions were changing, the UN General Assembly voted to revoke the condemnation of Spain issued in 1946, making it possible for embassies to operate fully again in Madrid. In 1951, Spain was allowed to join some of the UN bodies and opened discussions with the US. By 1955, Spain was admitted to full UN membership and to the Bretton Woods system.

Franco was in control of the negotiations for the bases deal, receiving the US negotiators for discussions personally.[19] It was to be the last grand policy which the Caudillo himself supervised in detail. It was pushed through in the teeth of opposition from hard-line Falangists who were unable to come to terms with an international system which was now predicated on the US global reach and which left no space for building a 'third way' between communism and capitalism, the project dear to Falangism. The signing of the pacts also signified, therefore, a recognition on the part of the state of the need to tame the Falange. Henceforth its voice in policy-making circles was to decline. Nonetheless, the full implications of the deal and the emptying of meaning of the Falangist-inspired idea of *hispanidad* were slower to permeate through public policy. Autarky was also doomed politically as soon as the bases deal was signed, since Spain was now in fact opening up to external interests and was in receipt of foreign credit, both of which were inevitably to undermine plans for nationalist economic development.

The Pacts of Madrid of 1953, then, as the bases deal was formally known, constituted the corner-stone of Spanish–US relations under Franco, and were to last into the 1980s, beyond Franco's own lifetime, with some minor modifications.[20] Under the agreement, Spain ceded to the US a number of military bases of which the four most important were the air bases of Torrejón, Morón de la Frontera and Zaragoza and the naval base of Rota on the Mediterranean. The deal shifted the terms of Spain's international relations completely, making it impossible for the dictatorship to continue to argue that it represented a 'third way' or indeed that policy was overwhelmingly national-ist. As a result, foreign policy discussion essentially revolved thereafter around the consequences, direct and otherwise, of this deal.

In return for the bases, the dictatorship received much-needed economic assistance. US credits to Spain in conjunction with the pacts were initially in the region of $125 million, of which 50 million were for military equipment and 75 million for economic assistance. Because there was considerable hostility to

Franco in the US Congress because of his earlier identification with the Axis, the pacts were an executive agreement and were not open to congressional discussion. Under a separate agreement, Congress approved credits to Spain of $91 million for further military equipment and 10 million under the general heading of defence spending credits. Additionally, the US backed loans from the World Bank and signed the first of a series of educational and cultural agreements. Furthermore, the Spanish economy received a much-need injection of dollars through the construction of the bases and the spending power of the US citizens who arrived with the deal. Finally, the bases deal gave the go-ahead to US companies who wanted to invest in Spain. The direct economic value, that is even without the stimulus provided to the economy by US citizens spending dollars inside Spain, of the pacts between 1953 and 1963 has been estimated at over $1.5 billion.[21] This was approximately the equivalent of four years' worth of exports to the Spanish economy.

In spite of the economic assistance, however, the cost to the regime, in terms of loss of face internally and damaged sovereignty, was high. Criticism of the deal came primarily from civilian quarters; the army on the whole was happy about the increase in defence spending and equipment that the deal implied. In fact, it may be that the pacts calmed the armed forces in a moment of tension with the dictatorship because of the state's inability to maintain defence spending.[22] But the price which was paid elsewhere was great. Washington strategists had argued that the bases were important as potential launch pads for strikes against the Soviet Union.[23] To this end, the air bases had the potential to service B-47s, planes with nuclear-bomb-carrying capability, and submarines with nuclear weapons were allowed to use the facilities at Rota. There was, therefore, the possibility of counter-strikes from the Soviet Union on US bases located on Spanish territory. Nonetheless, a provision allowing planes to carry nuclear warheads was a secret part of the agreement. Yet Spain was not part of a defensive pact which guaranteed Allied assistance in cases of attack in the way that NATO did. Nor did the pacts formally commit the US to come to Spain's assistance on a bilateral basis. So Spain was, in theory, exposed to attack but without allies if such attacks ever took place. Furthermore, the bases were located close to population centres, putting at risk a large number of Spanish citizens. The bilateral relationship established by the bases deal was asymmetrical, then, in the extreme. Not surprisingly, the deal generated resentment within the Francoist elite. It did not end the anti-Americanism which characterised Franco-ist ideology, especially among Falangists, though it tied the government's hands and created a situation whereby the regime was committed rhetorically to resisting US hegemony but was in practice highly dependent on US aid.

The 1953 agreements did have a positive effect, though, by beginning the process of opening up the economy to the outside world. However, they also gave US companies a head start in Spain. The deal opened the economy to US investors, initially through contracts to build and supply the bases. The presence of US multinational corporations continued to increase throughout the 1950s and really took off after liberalisation of the economy in 1959. In the 1960s, multinationals from the US were the most important of the foreign companies which invested in Spain. It would be plausible to argue that they came to dominate the Spanish economy in the 1960s, partly because they arrived first in the 1950s when the economy remained closed to investment from elsewhere.

It is significant that the discussion of Spanish–US relations so far has focused overwhelmingly on security and economic aspects. In fact, there was little else. It was not a typical relationship between the US and a major European country in any sense. Although it is certainly the case that the US's bilateral relationship with all European countries was unbalanced in the 1950s and 1960s in that US economic production, its military capacity and its diplomatic influence tilted the balance in its own favour, Spain was reduced to the status of a mere satellite in its relationship with the US in a way that did not occur with any other major European country.[24] It was not even formally consulted on international questions by Washington because it was not a member of the diplomatic, military or economic alliances which took shape in the post-war world. All of this generated a peculiar attitude towards the US in policy-making circles. It was recognised that the economic recovery in the 1960s, perhaps even the survival of the regime, had depended on US assistance. Nevertheless, the basic inequality of the relationship was the source of substantial resentment, feeding the already established prejudices of the governing elite of Franco's own generation in particular, which had come to maturity remembering the humiliation of the Spanish empire in the Americas, with the defeat by the US in 1898 and the subsequent 'loss' of Cuba, Puerto Rico and the Virgin Islands which followed.

RESIDUES OF NATIONALISM AND THE SEARCH FOR INTERNATIONAL INTEGRATION

The economic problems which had haunted the regime from its establishment led to the formation of a new government in 1957, dominated by the technocrats of Opus Dei. They were determined to push through the internationalisation of the Spanish economy, in the first instance through agreements with the IMF, the World Bank and the OECD. The new climate of relations with the US made this possible for the first time. This was then followed by the decision to open up the economy to foreign capital, thereby ending the protectionist stance which had earlier been thought of as the way to promote industrialisation. Henceforth, development was associated with the deepening of linkages with the international economy. The culmination of the first stage of internationalisation was the Stabilisation Plan of 1959, the turning point for the regime in terms of the design and implementation of its international and domestic political economy.

The goal of the plan was vast. As a government memorandum of 1959 states, it was meant to 'align the Spanish economy with the countries of the western world'.[25] A long process of economic catching up ensued. Not only did policies after 1959 reflect a changed bias in the state's development ideology, but policy also became more straightforwardly western and conservative. Nevertheless, the new policies were not agreed without internal resistance. The Ministry of Foreign Affairs did not fully agree with the policy of internationalisation and the way in which it was being carried out. Two contradictory policy tendencies, therefore, struggled for dominance at the end of the 1950s: the first, led by the new technocrats from the economic ministries, promoted close relations with western capital and sought good relations with western states; the second set of policies, which were rhetorically powerful, emerged from the Ministry of Foreign Affairs and attempted to defend a particular vision of Spanish sovereignty. The key issues for the foreign-policy nationalists were the need to renegotiate the bases deal and the insistence on recovering Gibraltar for Spain. Consequently, foreign policy was to some extent out of line with the overall trend of policy-making in the 1960s in that some of it was based on asserting national rights even if this meant upsetting powerful international actors.

Fernando María Castiella was Minister of Foreign Affairs throughout most of this period of change and international reorientation. His period in office lasted from 1957 until 1969 and he pushed for nationalist policies in a number of areas. He was also responsible for the first real attempt to modernise the implementation of foreign policy since the creation of the new authoritarian state. Pollack and Hunter see the appointment of Castiella as almost as significant for policy-making in Spain as the end of Francoism and the transition to democracy itself.[26] While this is certainly an exaggerated view, Castiella's time in office constituted the first period of real continuity in policy design and the first serious attempt to modernise the bureaucracy inside the Palacio de Santa Cruz. These changes made possible many of the foreign policy initiatives of the regime in the 1960s.

Recovering the Rock of Gibraltar from the control of the British was particularly important to Castiella. He argued that Spain should accept the consequences of pursuing the issue even if it damaged commercial relations with the UK, which in fact it did. In 1964, the British government cancelled an important shipbuilding order that had been placed with Spanish shipyards. Castiella made pointed contrasts in speeches to the UN between Spain's acceptance of decolonisation in Guinea and North Africa and the UK's refusal to do so in Gibraltar.[27] Although he was successful in getting the UN to deal with Gibraltar within the framework of decolonisation in 1965, he was unable to persuade the British government to enter into negotiations over sovereignty. Castiella offered the British the right to retain a military base on the Rock in return for sovereignty over the territory in 1966. The British government, however, refused to discuss sovereignty and offered instead to allow a Spanish representative to take up office in Gibraltar in order to oversee Spanish interests and fulfil consular functions. The discussions stalemated at this point.[28] Castiella went on to close the frontier between Gibraltar and Spain, but in private it seems that his aggressive stance was curbed by the rest of the government and by Franco himself. Franco preferred to deal cautiously and counselled Castiella to adopt an attitude of moderation towards the British.[29] Even though the details of policy had moved out of the hands of the Caudillo by this time, no new initiatives could be undertaken without his consent, and it would seem that he kept the issue from coming to the boil. Gibraltar was nonetheless useful inside Spain as a way to keep the flames of nationalism burning and it gave the regime some credibility which it was in danger of losing in the eyes of ultra-nationalists.

Gibraltar not withstanding, nationalism was only really pursued in foreign affairs up to a point. It was principally confined to rhetoric. Furthermore, when nationalist policies did emerge from the Ministry of Foreign Affairs, they were unsuccessful because Spain's leverage in international negotiations was poor. Powell argues convincingly that policy stances in the early 1960s on renegotiation of the bases deal and Gibraltar were a substitute for Spain's lack of influence on the 'big' issues of global politics at the time.[30] They were also sops to the nationalist lobby inside Francoism. North Africa, for example, where Spain might have tried to exercise some independent policy, continued in practice to be neglected.[31] Ultimately, therefore, the conservative pro-US lobby inside Francoism won out on almost all issues.

Meanwhile the new development strategy of internationalisation inevitably raised the question of relations with Spain's European neighbours and with the EEC. In 1962, it was decided that Spain could not afford to be outside such an important organisation. The decision to court the EEC was a reversal of much of what Francoism had stood for in the early period of the dictatorship. Unlike the deal with the US, however, overtures to the EEC met with only limited success. The European countries could afford to take a more principled line on Francoism than the US, and Spain was rejected on the basis that it did not fulfil the minimum criterion for membership – that states have democratic forms of government. This was a considerable slap in the face for the regime. In fact, there had been considerable opposition to the application among sectors of the dictatorship, since it could have been expected that the regime would be exposed to an international humiliation.

Despite being rejected for membership, however, Spain managed to pursue ever closer links with the EEC through the 1960s. European economic integration and growth meant expanding markets inside the EEC, mainly for agricultural products. Spain was able to supply some of these goods. Also, increasing industrial production inside the EEC meant that new markets were actively sought. Again Spain proved useful. So, although barred from full membership because of the dictatorship, the country was able to establish significant trading links as the decade progressed. At the same time, Spanish emigrants were working in EEC countries and tourists from EEC countries were visiting Spain in huge numbers. Imports from the EEC rose from 25.2 per cent to 49.3 per cent of total imports between 1960 and 1970, although exports to the EEC declined in the same period. In 1970, Spain was eventually rewarded with some preferential access to EEC markets as part of the EEC's policy of Mediterranean preferences. It was granted this without having to dismantle the Spanish barriers to industrial goods coming into the country from outside. The deal was not compatible with the international rules of trade as determined by the General Agreement on Tariffs and Trade (GATT), which raised some problems. More importantly, it was criticised because some of the positive effects for Spanish trade were undone just three years later by the expansion of the EEC to include the UK, Denmark and Ireland. Additionally, the deal did little to address the growing trade deficit between Spain and the EEC.[32] Still, it was a success of sorts – though not one the hard-line nationalists particularly relished. Relations with Europe had always been more important to the technocrats, and it was perhaps appropriate that the incorporation of Spain inside the Mediterranean preferences policy was achieved in 1970, under the auspices of the new Foreign Minister, the technocratic Gregorio López Bravo, not Castiella.[33]

Perhaps one of the most unexpected aspects of the new policies of the 1960s was the radical change in attitude towards the Soviet Union and the eastern bloc countries. The position the Soviet Union had occupied in Francoist discourse had always been clear: it constituted the world centre of a godless revolution and the conspirator-in-chief of international communism, aiming to undermine Christian Spain and bring communists to power. But, instead of becoming more anti-Soviet, Spain opened itself up to new relationships with the Soviet Union and eastern Europe in the 1960s. Consular relations were established with all the Warsaw Pact countries except the Soviet Union, partly in a search for new markets. This strategy was commercially successful and by 1967 Spain was selling goods to eastern Europe worth around 4.6 billion pesetas, rising to 8.2 billion in 1972.[34] Commercial relations were also established with China, followed by an exchange of ambassadors. It even seemed possible that diplomatic relations would be established with the Soviet Union for a brief time in 1964. The decision to promote relations with eastern Europe had more than commercial aspects to it. It was also part of a strategy to lessen dependence on the US and to reduce the likelihood of a Soviet strike on a US base inside Spain, the logic being that the Soviet Union was less likely to attack one of the bases if the countries were on amicable terms. Last but not least, the Soviets proved strong supporters of Spain in the UN on the issue of Gibraltar.

The relationship with the US was under constant review throughout the 1960s, especially during the negotiations to renew the 1953 agreements.

Castiella led attempts to renegotiate the deal, with the aim of winning some concessions from the US in return for the bases. A second agreement was signed in 1963 with relatively little friction. But the negotiations for the third agreement were long drawn out and the background was increasingly tense. In 1966 a US B-52 plane had accidentally dropped four atomic bombs over Spanish territory, adding further to the climate of urgency in the talks. Not only did Spain try to win more economic aid in return for conceding the bases, but they also sounded out the US on Gibraltar, pressed for a formal defence pact to be signed and requested an increase in military aid. Spain did win some concessions, notably the establishment of joint sovereignty over the bases. But the US steered clear of supporting Spain on Gibraltar. The US also refused to support Spain in disputes with Morocco over territory in North Africa. Additionally, the Spanish claimed that US military aid had declined by 52 per cent between 1962 and 1968 in comparison with the period 1953 to 1962. Castiella pushed claims for military aid of around $1 billion which he failed to secure.[35]

The inescapable conclusion is that the renegotiations were unsuccessful in safeguarding Spanish national interests. The basic problem was not simply Francoism, but the fact that Spain had few resources in the 1960s with which to bargain. Additionally, although Castiella attempted to drive a hard bargain, his position was undermined because government policy was to avoid antagonising the US due to the country's dependence on foreign capital. As a result, the renegotiations were the nails in the coffin both of Spanish nationalism and of Castiella's own career. He was removed from office in 1969 in order to unblock the third round of bilateral agreements which were signed a year later. It is worthy of note, however, that the general dissatisfaction which the deal with the US provoked, and which had become a national issue by the 1970s, led to the decision to press for full integration into NATO as soon as it became an option on Franco's death.

THE REMNANTS OF EMPIRE: THE 'SPECIAL RELATIONSHIPS' OF LATIN AMERICA AND NORTH AFRICA

Part of the Nationalist justification for the 1936 uprising was to restore Spain to a position of imperial greatness. The new authoritarian regime intended to extend its power in North Africa and to establish a 'special relationship' with the Latin American countries as part of its drive to extend Spain's influence beyond national frontiers. The Francoist concept of these relationships was predicated upon Spanish leadership. Tusell, indeed, goes as far as describing them straightforwardly as 'the vestiges of imperialism'.[36] However, Spain was unable to function as an imperial metropolis for either Latin America or North Africa during the Franco regime because of its complete lack of material or ideological power. This was to prove one of the major weaknesses in the strategy. By the end of the dictatorship, therefore, not only had the years of isolation followed by dependence on the US weakened Spain's international presence, but the policy of encouraging 'special relationships' had also failed.[37]

This did not prevent the regime from making at times extravagant claims about its foreign policy and from attempting sporadic overtures to Latin America and occasional empire-building strategies in North Africa. Latin America contined to play an important role within foreign policy discourse. The Francoist government saw the continent as the ideal territory for the spread of hispanic ideals immediately after winning the war. In the first phase of the dictatorship, when the regime thought itself to be fulfilling a God-given mission, Latin America appeared to the Francoists as the next area of the globe to be liberated from the dangers of communism and freemasonry. But Spain's first attempt in 1939, when the Spanish government launched a campaign against the Chilean Popular Front, had failed to win friends in Latin America and had been acknowledged internally as a complete failure.[38] After this, policy towards Latin America gradually became less overtly ideological, and was predicated upon a common cultural heritage rather than on any shared political commitments. Instead of attempting to influence the internal politics of Latin American countries, the dictatorship tried to use the region to bolster its own uncertain international presence. Latin America continued to occupy an important position within Francoist discourse and was useful in articulating a structured set of national interests, at least at the level of rhetoric, in what was otherwise a defensive foreign policy. A strong pro-Latin policy was especially favoured by Falangist groups who tended to dominate in the bureaucracy of the *Consejo de Hispanidad*. It became, in fact, one of their last fiefdoms with the technocratic domination of the public sector throughout the 1960s.

The most interesting relationship between Spain and a Latin American country during the dictatorship was that between Spain and revolutionary Cuba. Castiella was Foreign Minister at the time the policy was formulated, in the early 1960s. He seized the chance to make a grand gesture of hispanic solidarity at little cost. Spain refused to break off relations with the island after the revolution and ran the small risk of incurring US hostility for signing a series of trade deals with Cuba. Important orders were placed in Spanish shipyards for a fishing fleet by the new Cuban government. A series of cultural exchanges were also arranged between the two countries which allowed the Cubans their only foothold in Europe in the 1960s when the anti-Cuban boycott was observed by the rest of Europe. But, like the deal with Argentina in 1946, the Cuban policy was made to stand for policy towards Latin America as a whole, although by the 1960s there was in reality no general policy towards the region left at all. Solidarity with Cuba therefore acquired significant symbolic importance inside Spain. But in fact it hardly challenged US hegemony in the region and only marginally affected Spain's relations with the US. The policy won credibility with the foreign-policy nationalists and provoked very little annoyance in Washington, for whom military bases and good terms for US-based companies investing in Spain continued to be assured.[39]

Relations with North Africa were predicated on rather different ideological bases. Also, in contrast to Latin America which was of interest to the Falangists, North Africa was of most interest to the army which saw there an opportunity to recover the national glory lost with the end of the empire in the Americas. There were other important differences. North Africa had never been the object of sustained colonisation, unlike Latin America. Instead, the Spanish-African empire was restricted to small coastal settlements.[40] Even the Moroccan Protectorate, which was established in 1912 and which was central to Spanish claims to empire, was sparsely populated and scarcely incorporated into the economy. But Francoist diplomacy was able to cover these deficiencies by making claims about the existence of a special relationship with the Mediterranean Arab world as a result of long historical associations stretching back to the period before the reconquest. Franco had also distinguished himself in campaigns in North Africa, which added to government interest in the region. It was therefore to be expected that the authoritarian regime would accord the area considerable importance.

But dreams for the recovery of past glory were impossible to fulfil. Spain was simply unable, given the international climate in favour of decolonisation, its own very limited military and economic resources and its absence of international allies, to make real the dreams of empire embodied in the Francoist project. While the interest that the army took in the region prevented full-scale decolonisation, Spain was forced to give up the Protectorate in Morocco in 1956 after the French withdrew from the region. As a result, Spain found itself embroiled in what was to prove the first round of struggles for the independence of the Spanish Sahara in 1957.[41] Franco was to be forced into ceding the zone known as Cape Juby, occupied by the Spanish and bordering on the newly independent Morocco, early in the following year. A final retreat from the western Sahara came in 1975.

The reluctant withdrawal from most of the colonial possessions in North Africa did not hinder a more general *rapprochement* with the Arab states in North Africa and the Middle East. Spain had sent Spanish Moroccan representatives to the Arab League in 1946, with the aim of winning support in the face of the diplomatic boycott. Franco did not recognise the state of Israel when it was created in 1948 and was rewarded with Arab support when the UN voted on Spanish questions before 1955.[42] Economic and cultural agreements were signed with a series of states in the region, including Egypt and Jordan in 1952, and were important economically and symbolically for Spain. But despite the importance accorded to these agreements, especially before 1955, the policy was a poor substitute in the eyes of nationalists for territory under Spanish control.

INTERNATIONAL RELATIONS AT THE END OF THE DICTATORSHIP

Francoist foreign policy had revealed some dynamism and innovation in terms of policy design in the 1960s. But policy was also affected by the disputes between those Francoists who sought to promote a nationalist foreign policy and those who wished to create a new foreign policy which was pro-western and which had US approval. Therefore the impact of nationalist policies, many of which were rhetorically important for the dictatorship, was limited because of the characteristics and contradictions inherent in Francoism. Nationalist policies could not be carried through from design to implementation. In order to be successful, new policies had to count on the support of political coalitions with access or control over key areas of the state. The nationalist foreign policies introduced after 1957 lacked firm institutional back-up from within the authoritarian state and instead the drive for good relations with the US prevailed.

Ultimately, all policy-makers in the 1960s still had to have the support of Franco in order to implement their policies. So, although Franco's interest in foreign affairs declined after 1957, matters still had to be referred to the dictator himself. This increasingly meant that decisions rested with an individual who was tired, fearful of taking risks and whose world vision was out of touch with reality. There were no institutional alternatives to winning Franco over to a particular policy and no recourse to appeal after his final decision. All of this affected the way in which policies were put into effect and how far they could be implemented. There was no bureaucratic independence within the Ministry of Foreign Affairs that could be built on. At the same time, Franco's personal ties with the technocrats were on the increase.

Foreign policy was thus caught in the struggle within the authoritarian coalition which underwrote state authority and which slowly fractured in the 1960s, by which time it was beginning to break up into opposing camps. This led to severe ministerial in-fighting after 1957 and sometimes to policy blockage. The divisions in government were partly motivated by personal ambition, but they were also ideological. This aspect should not be discounted despite the new 'pragmatic' approach which characterised the dictatorship by the mid 1960s. Divisions over foreign policy reflected to some degree fundamental disputes about Spain's place in the world and nationalist policies clashed with the pro-western views of the technocrats. The technocrats sought closer relations with western capital and therefore good relations with western states. They argued that there would be little room for manoeuvre in determining external policies until Spain was more economically developed. The nationalists, by contrast, suggested that independent policies could be pursued in some areas in spite of the fact that levels of economic development were behind those of the US and most of western Europe. These debates were played out in cabinet discussions but the balance of the government favoured the technocrats, reflecting the fact that these groups had greater access to the final decision-making mechanisms of the state, as far as high politics was concerned: that is to Franco himself. Overall, by the 1960s, cabinets were dominated by technocrats concerned with implementing policies of economic modernisation through liberalisation and foreign investment, a process which they saw as endangered by a foreign policy that was too nationalist.

The end of the dictatorship was characterised overwhelmingly by ever more rapid shifts towards technocratic, neo-liberal policy options. Deeper links with the external world were established, not just in monetary and economic policies, but were a feature of policy-making generally. Hence foreign policy became a concern for ministries outside Foreign Affairs and there was severe competition between ministers for control of contacts with the external world. Story and Pollack capture this perfectly:

> Ministers in regular touch with the outside world were able ... to supplement their alliances within the regime with external relations. Yet the economic policy ministers, the foreign minister, the armed forces minister or the more domestically oriented bureaucracies, such as housing or social security, were beholden to Franco. As external dimensions came to bear on an ever wider range of policies, internecine struggles developed for supremacy in the conduct of external affairs.[43]

What this meant was that Castiella, as the last nationalist Foreign Minister, had to fight a rear-guard action inside the cabinet to retain control over the direction of foreign policy: a battle that he finally lost.

In democratic polities, politicians facing difficulties in getting their policies carried out from inside the government have the option of appealing to groups outside, and to civil society more generally, in an attempt to build new political coalitions for specific policies. This is rarely the case with authoritarian regimes and was certainly not the case in Spain under Franco. This meant that nationalists were unable to court the support of those groups in the opposition who may have intellectually or academically approved of the new foreign policy, weakening the likelihood of their success still further. It is hard to avoid the conclusion, ironical though it may seem given the essentially nationalist rhetoric of the Francoist regime, that the possibilities for implementing nationalist policies were fundamentally damaged by their association with the Francoist state.

In sum, the defence pact with the US constrained the degree to which Castiella could plausibly present foreign policy as independent. During the Cold War, diplomatic and commercial partnerships were of secondary importance compared to security alliances and could not be presented as the basis for an alternative foreign policy. The relationship with the US set the parameters in which all other foreign policy initiatives had to operate. This meant that the nationalist policies of the 1960s were difficult to implement and contradicted security policy. Relations with the Soviet Union and the eastern bloc were inherently limited, as was Spain's relationship with Latin America, by the defence pact with the US.

These failures made Spaniards look even more towards their neighbours in Europe. By the 1970s, the success of the EEC was in no doubt. As a result, by the end of the dictatorship, Spaniards of all political persuasions were implicitly comparing themselves to their European neighbours. Europe had come to be the standard against which the regime was judged. The economic opening up of Spain in the 1960s meant that the state could no longer pretend to be the sole nexus for meetings between Spanish interest groups and external ones. The state had lost its sole right to represent the country in all international arenas. The impact of this was incalculable, as Spaniards challenged the images the Francoist state imposed of life in Spain and elsewhere in the rest of Europe. At the same time, the areas of policy which were beyond the exclusive control of the state proliferated. In this respect, Spain was no different from any other society entering the 1960s when mass consumption and new forms of production increased popular expectations at the same time as they diminished state capacities for social control. At the level of discourse, the Francoist state continued to insist that its policies shaped economic, social and cultural progress in the country. But this was challenged on all levels – by business people who sought new markets and less state control for their economic activities; by people from the theatre, film-makers, writers and intellectuals, who wished to participate freely in Europe's dynamic cultural movements; and by ordinary people, who wished to have access to travel, education, films and the social rights of other Europeans, such as civil marriage, contraception and divorce.

But relations with the European countries were marred by the continued rejection of the dictatorship. Unlike the US, the democracies of western Europe were never prepared to forget Franco's ambiguous policies during the Second World War in the name of the *realpolitik* of the Cold War and they were quick to respond, especially symbolically, to manifestations of exceptional brutality by the regime and any severe abuses of human rights. European countries protested vigorously during the trial of Julián Grimau, the Communist Party member executed in 1963. Requests were made, unsuccessfully, for clemency. The Burgos trials in 1970 focused European attention on the human rights situation in Spain. This was renewed in 1975, when five members of ETA and the left-wing organisation FRAP were executed, despite calls in the European Parliament for the state to reprieve them. The executions led to the temporary withdrawal of EEC ambassadors from Madrid.

Nevertheless, the marked distaste for dictatorship notwithstanding, the European governments ignored the closer ties which were being forged between Spain and the EEC at the economic level particularly by non-state actors throughout the 1960s and 1970s. Indeed, by the 1970s, European investment was for the first time surpassing US investment and the EEC had become Spain's main trading partner, with the US accounting for only 15 per cent of Spain's total exports by 1970. This forced EEC member states to recognise that Spain would have to be considered for membership after Franco's eventual demise. It was also the basis through which Francoists claimed that their policies had in fact been a success and that Spain was undeniably part of Europe. Francoists claimed to be responsible for modernising the country through the policy of tying the economy irrevocably to Europe and securing trade deals with the EEC. As Foreign Minister, Gregorio López Bravo declared that Spain had decided 'to place its roots in Europe: our destiny is decided'.[44]

The opposition to the dictatorship insisted, by contrast, that economic growth in the 1960s, for which the technocrats claimed credit, was a feature of all European economies at the time and had little to do with Francoist policies. They suggested further that the persistence of the dictatorship put Spain out of kilter with the rest of Europe and that Franco, far from tying the country into Europe, had condemned it to remain on the political periphery of the continent. So, while the regime stressed that it had deepened economic links with Europe, turning the country into a major recipient of European investment and a supplier of Mediterranean-based primary products to the EEC, the opposition stressed that Spain had been forced to abrogate its right to participate in the creation of a new Europe. The need to enter Europe as a member of the EEC became a rallying cry of the architects of the transition as Europe was turned into a symbol not just of economic prosperity but of dignity and freedom within opposition discourse. It was Franco's inability to integrate Spain into Europe which was perceived as his ultimate failure. By the end of the dictatorship, therefore, foreign policy was as much a matter of deep ideological division as it had been at the beginning.

CONCLUSION

Foreign policy constituted an important area of policy-making for the dictatorship. On the one hand, it was perceived as an instrument for making Spain great again and for the construction of a new empire. On the other, it was a discourse through which the disparate groups within the authoritarian coalition could be brought together. But, by the end of the regime, foreign policy had been put to a use completely unexpected in 1939: it had served to bring the country into an alliance with the US which was to be its salvation. The Pacts of Madrid in 1953 effectively sealed the position of the regime, guaranteeing that international hostility would not bring it down, though condemning the regime to a highly unsatisfactory bilateral deal with the US which satisfied few Spaniards, even in the Francoist camp. Indeed, by the end of the regime, the foreign and security policies of the dictatorship were repudiated almost in their entirety by the opposition. It is not surprising that new bases for foreign policy were sought in almost all important areas during the transition to democracy.

NOTES

1 The key statement of Francoist imperial pretensións was made in J. M. Areilza and F. M. Castiella, *Reinvindicaciones de España* (Madrid, 1941).
2 J. Tusell, *La dictadura de Franco* (Madrid, 1988).
3 R. Criado, *Sahara: Pasión y muerte de un sueño colonial* (Paris, 1975).
4 For a discussion of *hispanidad*, see L. Delgado Gómez-Escalonilla, *Imperio de papel. Acción cultural y política cultural durante el primer franquismo* (Madrid, 1992).
5 S. Ellwood, *Franco* (London, 1994), p. 125.
6 J. L. García Delgado, *El primer franquismo. España durante la segunda guerra mundial* (Madrid, 1989).
7 On Francoist foreign policy generally, see J. M. Armero, *La política exterior de Franco* (Barcelona, 1978); M. Espada Burgos, *Franquismo y política exterior* (Madrid, 1988); and J. W. Cortada, ed., *Spain in the Twentieth Century World: Essays on Spanish Diplomacy 1898–1978* (London, 1980).
8 For details on this period, see W. Bernecker, ed., *España y Alemania en la Edad Contemporánea* (Frankfurt am Main, 1992); K. J. Ruhl, *Franco, Falange y el Tercer Reich. España en la Segunda Guerra Mundial* (Madrid, 1986); and J. Tusell and G. Quiepo de Llano, *Franco y Mussolini. La política española durante la segunda guerra mundial* (Barcelona, 1985).
9 H. Thomas, *The Spanish Civil War* (New York, 1963). See also D. Smyth, *Diplomacy and the Strategy of Survival. British Policy and Franco's Spain, 1940–1941* (Cambridge, 1986).
10 J. A. Durango, 'La España nacionalista ante la crisis de Munich: Nuevas evidencias empiricas', in J. Tusell, S. Sueiro, J. M. Marin and M. Casanova, *El Régimen de Franco (1936–1975)*, vol. 2 (Madrid, 1993).
11 B. Pollack and G. Hunter, *The Paradox of Spanish Foreign Policy (London,* 1987), pp. 8–10.
12 R. Serrano Suñer, *Entre Hendaya y Gibraltar* (Madrid, 1973), first published in 1943.
13 See M. Huget Santos, P. Pérez Herrero and A. Nino, *La formación de la imagen de America Latina en España, 1898–1989* (Madrid, 1992); C. del Arenal and A. Najera, *España e Iberoamerica. De la hispanidad a la communidad iberoamericana de Naciones* (Madrid, 1989); and J. C. Periera, *Las relaciones diplomaticas entre España y America* (Madrid, 1992). For a discussion of the errors and failings of the policy of *hispanidad*, see J. Grugel and M. Quijada, 'Chile, Spain and Latin America: The Right to Asylum at the Onset of the Second World War', *Journal of Latin American Studies*, 22, 2 (1990), pp. 353–74.
14 F. Portero, *Franco Aislado* (Madrid, 1989). For a detailed discussion of the UN resolutions against Spain, see A. J. Lleonart, *España y la ONU* (Madrid, 1978–85).
15 J. L. Neila Hernández, 'Escuela Diplomática: La articulación de un instrumento para la acción exterior del estado (1942–1958)', in J. Tusell *et al.*, *El Régimen de Franco*.
16 L. Delgado Gómez-Escalonilla, *Imperio de papel*.
17 M. González de Oleaga, 'La alianza Franco-Perón: una aproximación crítica desde la perspectiva de la dependencia, 1946–1951', *Hispania*, 169 (1988), pp. 14–21; R. Rein, 'El Pacto Franco-Perón: justificación ideológica y nacionalismo en Argentina', *Estudios Interdisciplinarios de América Latina y el Caribé*, 1, 1 (1990), pp. 1–18.

18 A. Viñas, *Los Pactos Secretos de Franco con los Estados Unidos* (Barcelona, 1981).

19 P. Preston, *Franco: A Biography* (London, 1993).

20 A Marquina, *España en la política de seguridad occidental, 1939–1986* (Madrid, 1986).

21 A. Viñas, *Política comercial exterior de España (1931–1975)* (Madrid, 1979).

22 M. González García, 'The Armed Forces: The Poor Relations of the Franco Regime', in P. Preston, ed., *Spain in Crisis* (Hassocks, 1976).

23 B. George and M. Stenhouse, 'Western Perspectives of Spain', in K. Maxwell, ed., *Spanish Foreign and Defense Policy* (Boulder, 1991).

24 On the idea of Spain as US satellite, see J. M. Armero, *Política exterior de España en democracia* (Madrid, 1989); and F. Moran, 'La política exterior española', *Leviatán*, 16 (1984).

25 C. T. Powell, 'Spain's External Relations 1898–1975', in R. Gillespie, F. Rodrigo and J. Story, *Democratic Spain Reshaping External Relations in a Changing World* (London, 1995).

26 B. Pollack and G. Hunter, *The Paradox of Spanish Foreign Policy*. Their argument reflects fundamentally the vision of Fernando Morán, Foreign Minister in the first Socialist government after 1982. See F. Morán, *Una política exterior para España* (Barcelona, 1980).

27 Espada Burgos, *Franquismo y política exterior*, p. 229.

28 D. S. Morris and R. H. Haigh, *Britain, Spain and Gibraltar 1945–1990* (London, 1992).

29 Preston, *Franco*.

30 Powell, 'Spain's External Relations'.

31 S. Fleming, 'North Africa and the Middle East', in J. W. Cortada, *Spain in the Twentieth Century World*.

32 A. Tovias, *Foreign Economic Relations of the European Community: The Impact of Spain and Portugal* (Boulder, 1990).

33 E. Baklanoff, *La transformación económica de España y Portugal* (Madrid, 1980).

34 J. L. Schneidman, 'Eastern Europe and the Soviet Union', in Cortada, ed., *Spain in the Twentieth Century World*, p. 168.

35 M. Vasquez Montalbán, *La penetración americana en España* (Madrid, 1974).

36 J. Tusell, *La dictadura de Franco* (Madrid, 1988).

37 Emphasising 'special relationships' is a strategy of medium-sized states. It is important in Spanish foreign policy discussions to the present day. See J. Grugel, 'Spain and Latin America' and R. Gillespie, 'Spain and the Maghreb: Towards a Regional Policy?' both in Gillespie, Rodrigo and Story, eds., *Democratic Spain*.

38 Grugel and Quijada, 'Chile, Spain and Latin America'.

39 See J. Roy, 'España y Cuba: una relación *muy* especial?' in J. Roy and J. A. March, eds., *El espacio iberoamericano* (Barcelona, 1996).

40 J. N. Hilgarth, *The Spanish Kingdoms 1250–1516* (Oxford, 1976).

41 Criado, *Sahara: pasión y muerte*.

42 R. Rein, 'Outpaced by the West: Israel's Spanish policy, 1953–1956', *Mediterranean Historical Review*, 8, 2 (1993), pp. 74–104.

43 J. Story and B. Pollack, 'Spain's Transition: Domestic and External Linkages', in G. Pridham, ed., *Encouraging Democracy. The International Context of Regime Transition in Southern Europe* (London, 1991).

44 Quoted in Pollack and Hunter, *The Paradox of Spanish Foreign Policy*, p. 134.

After Franco: The Transition to Democracy and the Legacy of Francoism

Franco died in 1975 and the first general elections were held in 1977. Today, the casual visitor to Spain would find few obvious reminders of the dictatorship. This is partly due to the success of the transition to democracy which means that the politics and culture of Spain are pluralist and tolerant and that few Spaniards now have less than a total commitment to the democratic political system. But it is also due to what might be termed a 'pact of oblivion' established during the transition and solidified in place alongside democracy itself. Spaniards do not on the whole wish to probe into the crimes committed by the dictatorship and they have chosen to remember Francoism as little as possible in their daily lives. They are unwilling to take part in open discussions which might prove painful and divisive and they prefer to consign the authoritarian regime firmly to the past. Symbols of the dictatorship have been quietly removed and streets named after prominent regime figures such as José Antonio Primo de Rivera, the founder of the Falange or General Mola, the Nationalist officer, have been changed. The king is a much-revered symbol of national unity and democracy and it would be regarded as bad taste to question too deeply his early relationship with Franco. Far more important in the view of the population at large was his decided stance in favour of the new democracy in 1981 during an attempted coup staged in the Cortes, when he threatened to go into exile if the military took control of the country.

Yet despite its obvious success now, the transition to democracy was by no means assured as soon as Franco died. He had left behind a set of institutions which were aimed at guaranteeing the continuation of authoritarianism, or 'Franco's peace', under a monarchy. The Francoist institutions had to be dismantled and new ones erected in their place. Two years passed before these institutions were replaced by a constitutional monarchy and executive power was placed in the hands of a democratically elected parliament. More important even than this, all political groups had to commit themselves to operating within a democratic culture. Democratic outcomes always contain a degree of uncertainty for all actors. This meant that the political right, the army, the church and the economically powerful had to accept that they would have to make compromises politically and socially, and even have to accept defeat in some policy areas. This process of change in political behaviour took time. As a result, democracy was by no means a secure outcome in Spain until at least 1982.

For these reasons, it would be wrong to see democracy as simply a natural outcome of the way Spanish society and the economy had developed in the 1960s and 1970s. To do so would mean conceptualising democracy almost as a delayed political liberalisation, following the economic liberalisation which began in the 1950s and continued throughout the 1960s. This is an ahistorical model of social and political change and of capitalism. It is deterministic in that economic prosperity is seen as leading lineally to a more developed civil society, and in particular to a more dynamic and independent middle class. It can also be termed a functionalist approach, in that it sees the Francoist institutions as functionally inadequate for the complex capitalist society which Spain had become by the 1970s and therefore condemned to disappear. It is dangerous too, in that it oversimplifies our understanding of the transition. For the success of the transition was by no means pre-ordained. It was due to the important changes which had taken place within Spanish political culture, to the responsible behaviour of political actors, and to the rapid changes which were taking place in the balance of power between civilians and the military. Nevertheless there remained a number of obstacles standing in the way of democracy after Franco's death. There were serious problems – some of the long-standing conflicts of modern Spain, in fact: the challenge of regionalism; the electoral weakness of the right; social and class tensions; and the role of the army in politics. The 'story' of the transition is one in which Spaniards, both the political elites and ordinary citizens, learned to value compromise and democracy more than they emphasised the issues which separated them.

The origins of democratisation in Spain lie in the crisis of the Francoist state. This crisis was the consequence of a complex process of social conflict, involving the eruption on to the political scene of new social and political actors, the proliferation of opposition and the inability of the regime to find a path of continuity after Franco. The crisis of the authoritarian state led to a series of bureaucratic and political changes inside Francoism, some of which were eventually to bring sectors of the right into cooperation with the political groups demanding democratic reform. Although changes inside the dictatorship were evident from the beginning of the 1960s as a result of industrialisation, the growth of social conflict and the rebirth of the opposition, the regime began to suffer rapid bureaucratic disintegration after the assassination of Admiral Luis Carrero Blanco in December 1973. The dictatorship had lost the political initiative and it was never to recover it.

Demands for change intensified during the two years left to the regime before Franco's own death in November 1975. Following the ineffectual government headed by Arias Navarro, Adolfo Suárez was appointed Prime Minister by the king in 1976. This move was greeted with scepticism at first by those in favour of democratic change, but Suárez went on to prove his determination to introduce democratic reform and as a result was the victor in the first democratic elections of June 1977 with his hastily formed party, the Unión de Centro Democrático (UCD).[1] Elections are not sufficient to make a democracy, however, and Spain lacked that most elementary of democratic structures – a constitution. To write the constitution was therefore the most important task of the new parliament.

During the transition, politics were largely caught between, and determined by, the negotiations and bargains which were struck between political elites – both Francoist and democratic – and the pressures and demands for change and for the establishment of a new democracy from below.[2] Maravall suggests that after the 1977 elections 'the process of consolidating democracy became largely a task for the "political class"'.[3] By this, he means that the new democratic political elite was still in fact in the process of formation. For the first time since before the civil war, political elites of all ideological persuasions looked for ways to compromise and to agree on the framework of politics. This move towards 'consensual unity' was important because it meant that all important politicians and parties accepted the institutional rules of the democratic game.[4] But popular support for democratisation was also important. In Catalonia and the Basque Country some of this popular pressure was channelled into demands for the resolution of the regionalist question. To some extent, the politicians, now operating in the framework of an emerging but fluid competitive party system, were pushed by popular demands for political change.

Drafting the new constitution was the work of a seven-party team appointed from a Cortes sub-committee of 36, itself responsible to parliament for the text. The parties responsible for drafting the constitution were the governing UCD, with three representatives, plus the Socialists, the Communists, the Catalan centrist and nationalist party, Convergencia Democrática de Catalunya, and the newly formed right-wing party, Alianza Popular (AP), which each had one representative on the team.[5] The negotiations were often tense and agreement difficult to reach, especially on the question of the Catholic church and its role in democratic Spain and on regionalism. Discussions sometimes lasted through the night. The problem was that the new right-wing party, AP, led by ex-Francoist Manuel Fraga who was also the party's delegate in the negotiations, was often out of sympathy with changes other members of the constitutional team were prepared to accept.

A draft was finally reached in July 1978. Significantly, UCD had moved towards relying on negotiations with the left, marginalising AP. Fraga tried to seize the initiative towards the end of the negotiations, by agreeing to most of the articles but blocking the reform of such matters as divorce, abortion and church–state relations. His aim was to win over the UCD which contained many conservative Catholics to the right of Suárez himself.[6] But Fraga's initiative was undermined from within his own party, which was generally even further to the right than he was on constitutional reform. This made it impossible for UCD to work in anything more than an *ad hoc* fashion with AP, since the governing party was irrevocably committed to producing a democratic constitution. This image of AP, unable to block reform and unable to dominate the discussions, was a symbol of the deterioration of the right during the transition and of the fact that it had yet to find a way of operating in the new political system. Because it had been protected by the state under Franco, it was unable to assert authority during the transition negotiations.[7] Amendments to the draft delayed final parliamentary approval until October 1978. It was passed overwhelmingly by the Cortes, although the Basque Nationalist Party (PNV), which had been excluded from the negotiations, abstained in the vote. AP split, with 8 of its 16 deputies (including Fraga) voting in favour, 5 voting against and 3 abstaining.

The most controversial sections of the new constitution, and those to which the right objected, dealt with the church, education and autonomy for the regions. These were, as we have noted, long-running cleavages in Spanish society and were among the conflicts which had led to the civil war and sustained the dictatorship in power. These divisions did not disappear with the start of democracy. But there was a new-found spirit of compromise. The left accepted that the church would retain some power, that the political 'author-ities . . . maintain relations with the Catholic church', and that the state would continue to offer some funding to private religious schools.[8] The right, meanwhile, had to accept a degree of regional autonomy. The constitution therefore recognized the different 'nationalities' of Spain. It did not use the stronger term, the 'peoples' of Spain, however, as the Catalan and Basque nationalists had wanted. As a result, the constitution was not accepted in the Basque Country when it was put to a referendum in 1978.[9]

While these negotiations for the constitution were going on, the economic situation confronting the country was deteriorating. The catalyst to the eco-nomic crisis which hit Spain in the mid 1970s was the oilprice rises of 1973–4 and 1978. The country was completely dependent on oil imports for industry and the oil-price rises therefore increased the costs of energy and production and of most imports. The situation was made worse by the inequitable and chaotic tax system, by the inefficient and overprotected state which had developed under Franco and by poor export performance, a result of the increasing uncompetitiveness of Spanish industry. At the same time, social hardship during the recession was intensified by a welfare system which offered little protection to the poorest in society. Meanwhile inflation reached 27.4 per cent in October 1977. Suárez opened negotiations on economic policy with the political parties in the opposition and the trade unions so that these problems did not undermine the transition itself. These tripartite negotiations led to the Moncloa Pacts of autumn 1977, which were an attempt to stabilise the social and economic environment so that political reform could continue. Without the formal deal sealed by the pacts, the government feared that the ultra-right and the army would undermine the transition through subversion and violence.[10]

Suárez offered the left and the trade unions a deal which in effect kept wage increases below the rate of inflation in return for a promise to introduce a comprehensive package of economic reforms, including reforms of tax and welfare. In fact the reforms promised by the government did not materialise. But the deal did contribute to more stable socio-economic conditions, with strikes falling significantly in number. The trade unions accepted that the chances of the right approving the democratic reforms would increase if they took a 'responsible' attitude of not pushing for sectoral gains at this time. As a result, the Moncloa Pacts prevented the kind of polarisation which could have undermined the transition. At the same time, this reflected the left's strategy of prioritising political change over economic gains.

The background to the Moncloa Pacts and the constitutional negotiations was a rising tide of violence from the right and increasing demobilisation on the part of the left. The negotiations, much of which took place behind closed doors, increased the sense that political leaders were becoming distanced from society at large. An unwillingness to trust politicians was, in part, a reflection of the years of Francoist culture which equated party politics with self-aggrandisement and anti-national behaviour, but it was also a consequence of the style of politics the new democracy was assuming. Organised demonstrations in favour of democratisation declined after 1978 because the left and the trade unions, now signatories guaranteeing social stabilisation, had undertaken to slow down popular demands and social protest. More importantly, the social cohesion which had been built up in the workers' organisations in favour of democratisation began to fragment. As violence, both from the right and from ETA, came to assume a more important role in politics, displacing the popular struggle for democracy, it pushed the parties towards trying to close the democratisation process as quickly and as uncontroversially as possible. All of this meant that the transition was extremely fragile, a fragility which was to increase during the UCD governments of 1979–82. Ultimately, it made possible the attempted revenge in 1981 by the ultras in the army.

Following the approval by referendum of the constitution, fresh elections were called for the spring of 1979. Although Suárez and the UCD won the elections and he was able to form a minority government, problems continued to bedevil the new democracy. These included: the ultra-right's rejection of the left and of regionalism, leading to attempts to subvert the political system; and the radical Basque separatists' decision to use terrorism in order to force Madrid into concessions. In short, Spanish democracy faced a crisis of governance, the roots of which lay in the Francoist period during which the army had come to believe itself the guarantor of national unity. Political debate and conflict had been forced to the margins of the political system by the state. As a result, it mushroomed inchoately now.

The most pressing and immediate problem Suárez had to confront was regionalism. The constitution had provided for autonomy, but the devolution of power to the regions became enormously complicated in practice, not least because the constitution recognised the right of all the regions of the country to a measure of self-government, not just the Basque Country, Catalonia and Galicia, regions with a long-standing history of separatism. The politics of each region was different, with regional identity strong and well organised in the Basque Country and in Catalonia, weak in some regions, such as Castile-La Mancha (New Castile) and Castile-León (Old Castile), and suddenly springing up in unlikely areas where there had been no tradition of independence from Madrid, as in Andalusia. All of this meant that separate negotiations with Madrid had to be held.

The cases of Catalonia and the Basque Country were recognised as urgent, however. There was a clear sense that, after years of harsh repression of any manifestation of regionalist sentiment by the Francoist state, democratisation could not be achieved without recognising the particular patterns of historical development in these regions which were marked out by a long tradition of independence from Castile. The importance of resolving the issue was increased by the economic importance to Spain of both regions and, in Catalonia, by the fact that economic elites favoured rapid decentralisation. In the Basque Country, meanwhile, ETA's willingness to force the pace through violence, and the other Basque nationalists' ambiguous loyalty to the constitution kept regionalism prominent on Suárez's agenda.

A Catalan Statute of Autonomy was passed in October 1979, but resolving the Basque problem proved more complex. It was, however, the *quid* of the transition and was central to its success. The problem was all the more intractable because important sectors of Basque finance and banking capital had supported the dictatorship, giving Basque nationalism a sectarian and class component that was absent in Catalan nationalism. Whereas for the Catalans nationalism had 'a multi-class dimension, independent of political confrontations between competing class interest', in the Basque Country it was riven with class divisions.[11] The absence of factors of convergence within the Basque Country only made the politics of devolution more complicated. These problems were made worse by the violence that accompanied the transition in the Basque provinces. Some of the violence came from ETA, the Basque separatist movement, but some also came from the state and from right-wing terrorists.[12] The transition elsewhere in Spain was bringing Spaniards together and encouraging positions of consensus and compromise, but this was slow to happen in the Basque Country. Levels of political mobilisation and class consciousness remained higher than elsewhere in the Country and ultra-left parties mushroomed. Indeed, the extent to which the experiences of the transition years in the Basque provinces are comparable to those in the rest of the country has been questioned.[13]

The first draft for a statute of autonomy reflected Basque insistence on the region's right to secede from Spain. Clearly doomed to defeat in the national Cortes, the PNV leader, Carlos Garaicoexea, negotiated an agreement with the UCD in July 1979. The result was the Statute of Guernica. This set up a regional parliament, accepted Spanish and Euskera (the Basque language) as official languages in the region, provided for the creation of a regional police force alongside though not instead of the national police, established a television channel in Euskera and gave the region powers over certain social policies such as education. The statute was rejected by the militarist hard-liners of ETA and the political party close to ETA, Herri Batasuna, who described it as 'embracing the Moncloa',[14] but it was accepted with reluctance by the mainstream nationalist party, the PNV. It was approved by referendum, amidst a climate of increasing violence, although by only 53.2 per cent of the Basque electorate.

In the long-term, the Statute of Guernica proved to be the most important factor in the consolidation of the new democracy. It was Suárez's greatest achievement. As a result, the largest of the nationalist parties, the PNV, was brought into mainstream politics. It represented an important compromise between centralists and separatists and most Basques came to accept the new constitutional order which they had first either rejected or refused to endorse. But, even now, at the end of the twentieth century nationalism has far from disappeared as a political problem. ETA has remained a potent force and regionalism still dominates the political agenda.

With the passing of the Basque and Catalan statutes of autonomy, the immediate problem appeared to be resolved. But more problems were to follow. The new constitution had set out two different paths to regional autonomy. In the most important regions, autonomy was through 'fast-track' negotiations, first approved by the Cortes and then submitted to a referendum within the region involved. Elsewhere, a referendum had to be organised first, in order to see if autonomy was desired. Providing that all provinces in the region voted in favour, an autonomy statute could be negotiated, presented to parliament and then, subject to popular approval by referendum, become law. This proved an enormously complicated process and more time-consuming and conflictual than had been anticipated. The debate on autonomy dragged on, drawing the government, the political parties and Spanish public opinion into hostile discussions which contributed to unrest in sectors of the army. The process was speeded up in the early 1980s, but not before an attempted coup in 1981 revealed just how disturbed the army had been by the devolution negotiations.

The year 1979 marked the high point of the UCD's success in government. But it was soon undermined by the ever-present political violence, with 123 people killed in acts of terrorism in 1979 alone, as well as by the regionalist debate and by economic problems. Perhaps more than anything else, the image of the government deteriorated with the collapse of the Moncloa Pacts, the symbol of cross-class social and economic consensus. The pacts ended in December 1978, leading to the introduction of a set of economic measures aimed at reducing public expenditure and introducing wage ceilings below the level of inflation. Strikes increased once again in 1979 and the UCD incurred fierce opposition from the left, demonstrating that on economic matters it was conservative, however progressive the party might be on political issues.

Part of the problem lay in the fact that the UCD was not a political party in the normal democratic sense. It did not have a powerful social base, a membership structure or internal decision-making procedures typical of democratic political parties. It had arisen out of the collapse of Francoism and it was not sensitive to the moods of the electorate.[15] UCD was essentially a party of local rightist notables or 'barons', who had emerged from the Francoist state. Without any overarching ideology, it was basically a 'syndicate of interests'.[16] Consequently, it was extremely fragmented and the factions worked almost as separate parties within the party, rather like the Francoist families within the Francoist state. All of this made it difficult for Suárez to govern once the early transitional phase was over. The UCD's electoral performance in local and regional elections deteriorated after 1979 as the internal tensions within the party increased. This provoked an internal crisis which ultimately culminated in Suárez's resignation in 1981.

The slow disintegration of the governing party inevitably affected the transition itself. The greatest threat to democracy came from the rising assertiveness of the military, which reached a peak with the coup attempt on 23 February 1981.[17] A unit of the civil guard forcibly seized control of the Cortes while parliament was debating the formation of a new government following Suárez's departure, Calvo Sotelo of the UCD having failed to win enough votes on a previous occasion. The parliament had effectively been taken hostage. Meanwhile, army units from Brunete, just outside Madrid, and Valencia mobilised in support of the coup. The parliament was occupied at 6.30 p.m.; the king went on state television in the early hours of 24 February, publically disassociating himself from the coup attempt and calling on the military to respect the constitutional order which had been 'approved by the Spanish people'.[18] Before speaking on television, he had made clear in telephone conversations to army officers that he would not assist, support or accept military intervention in politics. His swift actions, coupled with the complete repudiation of the attempt by the entire political class, including Manuel Fraga and the AP, and massive popular demonstrations in Madrid and other large cities, effectively brought the coup attempt to a close.

But the coup had revealed a number of important weaknesses in Spanish democracy. First, the problem of military–civilian relations had not been resolved and reforming the military would in fact constitute a major task undertaken by Socialist governments in the 1980s. Second, it appeared that democracy was still fragile and the intense and bitter debates between and within the democratic parties – such as those which were taking place early in 1981 in the Cortes and which were effectively preventing the formation of a new government – were damaging the new system. The coup of '23-F', as it became known in Spain, taught the leaders of the political parties that they needed to preserve democracy at all costs and that they must work together to do so, rather than fighting for small victories for their own parties, particularly at moments of political tension. And third, the coup attempt revealed the importance of all citizens participating in the construction of democracy – not just the political elites. The demonstrations against the coup were important indications of the popular demand for unity across the political spectrum in defence of democracy.

To a large extent, the political elites did respond to these demands. Leopoldo Calvo Sotelo was quickly installed as Prime Minister of a new government and opposition in parliament was far more muted. Meanwhile, the Socialists moved towards positions of consensus and moderation, a route the Communists had trodden earlier.[19] But while it brought the Communists no great electoral successes, it helped reassure the right, the army and the Catholic church that their anxiety about a Socialist victory, which now seemed inevitable in the following general elections, was largely groundless.[20] The Socialist Party, led by the charismatic figure of Felipe González, did indeed win the general elections of 28 October 1982, opening a new phase in the democratisation of Spain.

Since the elections of 1982, the political system has moved towards consolidation. Elections have been held regularly, openly and freely. The military has, on the whole, accepted that civilians run the political system. Spain's membership of the EEC and entry into NATO in 1986 acted as external supports for democratisation and signalled to recalcitrant Francoists that no return to dictatorship would be permitted.[21] Indeed, by the end of the 1980s, the Spanish transition was regarded as a model and the collapse of authoritarian regimes in Latin America and eastern and central Europe provoked a flurry of academic and political interest in it.[22] In particular, the key to the success of the transition was seen as the convergence of all parties around the centre of politics, as the right abandoned authoritarianism and the left ceased to endorse Marxism.

However, the transition to democracy was not planned and there was no 'guiding hand' ensuring a successful outcome. Liberalisation was piecemeal and its consequences were often unforeseen. It is also important to remember that the Spanish transition to democracy is by no means perfect. Although the transition was successful, there remains an important legacy from the past and from Francoism in particular. The Francoist state created and reproduced an authoritarian culture, the consequences of which are still discernible. This was identified, in fact, as problematic for the transition as early as 1982 by Maravall, and in some aspects it continues to undermine the foundations of democracy in present-day Spain.[23] Consequently, in our final review of the dictatorship, it is also important to pay some attention to Franco's legacy.

Some of the problems facing Spain's young democracy, many of which owe their origins to the legacy of the dictatorship, need to be addressed urgently if democracy is to be consolidated.[24] For example, many of the institutions of the state still lack democratic accountability; ETA continues to pose a political and a security problem; the police and the security forces have employed unconstitutional means in their fight against terrorism; and there have been a number of documented examples of financial corruption involving the political parties and agencies of the state, yet the institutional response to corruption has been ambiguous. Partly as a result, there is an acknowledged crisis of representation within the political system, which led in the early 1990s to a growing disillusionment on the part of the electorate with political parties in general. Additionally, the success of the Socialist Party after 1982 and the weakness of other parties meant that it came to dominate the state in the 1980s to such a degree that some analysts spoke of a blurring between the party and the state.[25] These features should not be exaggerated but they do represent lacunae in democratic consolidation. The solutions to these problems are tasks which still lie ahead for the Spanish people, both leaders and society at large, in their struggle to overcome the remnants of 40 years of authoritarianism.

NOTES

1 On the role of the king and his relationship with the UCD, see J. Story, 'Spanish Political Parties: Before and After the Elections', *Government and Opposition* (Autumn 1977), pp. 36–52.

2 See José Maravall, *The Transition to Democracy in Spain* (London, 1982), p. 3 for an explanation of this analytical framework. He argues that the transition was determined by reformist politics 'from above', popular pressure 'from below', the political context of the country and the process of transition itself. For accounts of the transition, as well as Maravall, see P. Preston, *The Triumph of Democracy in Spain* (London, 1987); C. Abel and N. Torrents, eds., *Conditional Democracy* (London, 1984); R. Carr and J. P. Fusi, *Spain: Dictatorship to Democracy* (London, 1979); J. Coverdale, *The Political Transformation of Spain after Franco* (New York, 1979); D. Gilmour, *The Transformation of Spain: From Franco to the Constitutional Monarchy* (London, 1985); D. Share, *The Making of Spanish Democracy* (New York, 1986). For detailed aspects of the transition, though not a narrative account, see D. Bell, ed., *Democratic Politics in Spain* (London, 1983). For an excellent commentary on many major events as they occurred in Spain during the transition, see J. L. Cebrián, *Crónicas de mi país* (Madrid, 1985), which brings together some of the most important articles from the influential paper, *El País*. For a perceptive and entertaining introduction to the changes democracy has meant to Spain, see J. Hooper, *The Spaniards* (London, 1995). For a brief but analytical account of the transition which sets it in its international context, see J. Story, 'Spain's Transition to Democracy', in J. Story, ed., *The New Europe* (Oxford, 1993).

3 Maravall, *The Transition to Democracy in Spain*.

4 R. Gunther, 'Spain: The Very Model of the Modern Elite Settlement', in J. Higley and

R. Gunther, eds., *Elites and Democratic Consolidation in Latin American and Southern Europe* (Cambridge, 1992).

5 On the creation of the new constitution, see G. Peces-Barba *La elaboración de la constitución de 1978* (Madrid, 1988).

6 On AP, see M. Fraga, *Alianza Popular* (Bilbao, 1977); and R. López-Pintor, 'Francoist Reformists in Democratic Spain: The Popular Alliance and the Democratic Coalition', in H. Penniman and E. Mujal-León, *Spain at the Polls, 1977, 1979* and *1982* (Durham NC, 1985).

7 J. M. Maravall and J. Santa María, 'Political Change in Spain and the Prospects for Democracy', in G. O'Donnell, P. Schmitter and L. Whitehead, eds., *Transitions from Authoritarian Rule* (Baltimore, 1986).

8 See Gilmour, *The Transformation of Spain*, p. 198.

9 In the Basque provinces 55.3 per cent of the electorate abstained; 30.86 per cent voted 'yes'; and 10.51 per cent voted 'no'. In Spain as a whole, the constitution was approved by 89.7 per cent of the electorate.

10 S. Ellwood, 'The Extreme Right in Post-Francoist Spain', *Parliamentary Affairs* 45, 30 (1992), pp. 29–44.

11 F. Hernández, 'El nacionalismo catalan y la socialización nacionalista', *Sistema*, 43–4 (September 1981).

12 See the Amnesty International report, *Spain: A Question of Torture* (London, 1985).

13 Mario Onaindia, originally of the small Basque party, Euskadiko Esquerra, later a Socialist, claimed 'it is not as if the same transition is taking place in Euskadi [the Basque country] later or even more slowly . . . it is rather a different transition. And furthermore, there exists some doubt as to whether a transition is taking place at all'. M. Onaindia, 'Transición democrática en Euskadi', *Leviatán*, 21 (1985), pp. 12–27.

14 Manifesto of Herri Batasuna, June 1983.

15 C. Huneeus, *La Unión de Centro Democrático y la transición a la democracia en España*, (Madrid, 1985). See also J. Hopkin, *Factionalisation in the Spanish Transition to Democracy*, Muirhead Papers No 12, University of Birmingham, 1996.

16 Maravall and Santa María, 'Political Change in Spain', p. 95.

17 See Felipe Aguero, *Soldiers, Civilians and Democracy* (Baltimore, 1995) for an excellent account of the military during the transition and the coup attempt itself. For more journalistic accounts, see M. A. Aguilar and I. Puche, *El golpe: anatomia y claves del asalto al congreso* (Barcelona, 1981); and J. L. Martín Prieto, *Técnica de un golpe de estado: el juicio de 23-F* (Barcelona, 1982).

18 Diario 16, *Historia de la Transición* (Madrid, 1986), p. 661.

19 For details on the changes in the Socialist Party, see R. Gillespie, *The Spanish Socialist Party* (Oxford, 1989). See also D. Share, 'Two Transitions: Democratisation and the Evolution of the Spanish Socialist Left', *West European Politics*, 8, (1985), pp. 66–82; J. F. Tezanos, 'Continuidad y cambio en el socialismo español: el PSOE durante la transición democrática', *Sistema*, 68–9 (1985), pp. 31–42; and A. García Santemases, 'Evolución ideológica del socialismo en la España actual', *Sistema*, 68–9 (1985), pp. 43–54.

20 On the changes within the Communist Party, see P. Preston, 'The PCE's Long Road to Democracy, 1954–1979', in R. Kindersley, ed., *In Search of Eurocommunism* (Basingstoke, 1981) and P. Preston, 'The PCE in the Struggle for Democracy in Spain', in H. Machin, ed., *National Communism in Western Europe* (London, 1983).

21 Story, 'Spain's Transition to Democracy'.

22 F. Bayo, 'La democracia en la política latinoamerican de España: el caso del Cono Sur', *Síntesis*, 25 (1994), pp. 89–97; J. Grugel, 'Spain and Latin America', in R. Gillespie, F. Rodrigo and J. Story, eds., *Democratic Spain* (London, 1995).

23 Maravall, *The Transition to Democracy*.

24 For a good overview of the legacy of Francoism for the political system, see P. Heywood, *The Government and Politics of Spain* (Basingstoke, 1995).

25 P. Heywood, 'The Socialist Party in Power', *ACIS* 5, 2 (1992), pp. 4–15.

Select Bibliography

This bibliography is not intended to be an exhaustive list of publications; it is, rather, a guide to further reading. We have tried to list most of the works which we think are important in English, but where a Spanish text is particularly good we have included it. Although British historians have had a long-standing interest in contemporary Spain, it is always good to complement their work with historical interpretations from Spanish analysts whenever possible.

THE HISTORICAL BACKGROUND TO THE DICTATORSHIP

Raymond Carr has written two good overviews that put the Franco period into historical context: *Spain, 1808–1975* (Oxford, 1982) and *Modern Spain, 1875–1980* (Oxford, 1980). Two books cover the whole of the immediate origins of the dictatorship in the Republic and the civil war. Gabriel Jackson, *The Spanish Republic and the Civil War in Spain 1931–1939* (Princeton, 1965) is older but still worth reading, while George Esenwein and Adrian Shubert, *Spain at War. The Spanish Civil War in Context, 1931–1939* (London, 1995) is a recent synthesis. The Republic can be approached via Stanley Payne, *Spain's First Democracy. The Second Republic, 1931–1936* (Madison, 1993), and Paul Preston, *The Coming of the Spanish Civil War. Reform, Reaction and Revolution in the Second Republic*, 2nd edn (London, 1994). Amongst the enormous output on the civil war, good accounts are Paul Preston, *The Spanish Civil War*, 2nd edn (London, 1996) which has a very full bibliography, and Sheelagh Ellwood, *The Spanish Civil War* (Oxford, 1991).

FRANCOIST POLITICS

Not surprisingly, there are a number of detailed accounts of the Franco regime in English and they tend to concentrate on the whole on the politics of the period. The best is Stanley Payne, *The Franco Regime* (Madison, 1987). It is perhaps too long for an introduction to the period but it is invaluable for detail of policies and of political deals, and it ties together internal and external policies very well. Also of interest is Raymond Carr and Juan Pablo Fusi, *Spain:*

Dictatorship to Democracy, 2nd edn (London, 1981). The collection of articles edited by Paul Preston, *Spain in Crisis* (Hassocks, 1976), produced when the final denouement of the regime was not yet clear, is a good place to start too. His collection of articles on the military and the right, *The Politics of Revenge: Fascism and the Military in Twentieth Century Spain* (London, 1990) is also required reading. These should be complemented by Preston's monumental biography, *Franco* (London, 1993). Two shorter biographies are available: Juan Pablo Fusi, *Franco, a Biography* (London, 1985) and Sheelagh Ellwood, *Franco* (London, 1994). Charles Powell's biography of the king, *Juan Carlos: Self-Made Monarch* (London, 1996), contains interesting material relating to Franco's relationship with the royal family and the first third of the book is a good introduction to aspects of the 'high politics' of the regime.

There are a number of introductory accounts in Spanish worth consulting. Older versions include Sergio Vilar, *La naturaleza del franquismo* (Barcelona, 1977) and the two-volume study by Ricardo de la Cierva, *Historia del franquismo* (Madrid, 1975; 1978). More modern works include Javier Tusell, *La dictadura de Franco* (Madrid, 1988); J. A. Biescas and M. Tuñón de Lara, *España bajo la dictadura franquista* (Barcelona, 1980) and the excellent collection edited by Josep Fontana, *España bajo el franquismo* (Barcelona, 1986).

When thinking about the structures and politics of the regime it is impossible to escape the influence of Juan Linz's penetrating analysis. Perhaps his most influential article is 'An Authoritarian Regime: Spain', in E. Allardt and Y. Littunen, eds., *Cleavages, Ideologies and Party Systems* (Helsinki, 1964). He analysed political parties in 'The Party System: Past and Future', in S. M. Lipset and S. Rokkan, eds., *Party System and Voter Alignments* (New York, 1967) and 'The New Spanish Party System', in Richard Rose, ed., *Electoral Participation: A Comparative Analysis* (London, 1980). See also Juan Linz and J. R. Montero, *Crisis y cambio: electores y partidos en la España de los ochenta* (Madrid, 1986). Amando de Miguel, *Sociologia del franquismo* (Barcelona, 1975) is also a classic account.

There are some excellent studies of the different groups within the regime. For the party, see Stanley Payne, *Falange: A History of Spanish Fascism* (Stanford, 1961), Ricardo Chueca, *El fascismo en los comienzos del régimen de Franco. Un estudio sobre FET y de las JONS* (Madrid, 1983) and Sheelagh Ellwood, *Prietas las filas. Historia de Falange Española, 1933–1983* (Barcelona, 1984). There is also a shorter English translation of the book by Ellwood, published as *Spanish Fascism in the Franco Era* (London, 1987). Also worth consulting are the articles by Martin Blinkhorn and Paul Preston in Martin Blinkhorn, ed., *Fascists and Conservatives* (London, 1990). For the church the outstanding study is Frances Lannon, *Privilege, Persecution and Prophecy. The Catholic Church in Spain, 1875–1975* (Oxford, 1987). See also Stanley Payne, *Spanish Catholicism* (Madison, 1984) and Guy Hermet, *Los católicos en la España franquista* (Madrid, 1985). On the military, see Preston (above), Stanley

Payne, *Politics and the Military in Modern Spain* (Madison, 1967) and Felipe Aguero, *Soldiers, Civilians and Democracy* (London, 1995), although the latter deals in most detail with the end of the regime and the transition period.

On opposition to Franco, see Linz's article 'Opposition To and Under an Authoritarian Regime: The case of Spain', in Robert Dahl, ed., *Regimes and Opposition* (New Haven, 1973), which shaped later studies of the opposition to Franco. Other works on opposition include Javier Tusell, *La oposición democrática al franquismo* (Madrid, 1977), which is a detailed narrative account with a useful guide to further reading in Spanish; Hartmut Heine, *La oposición política al franquismo* (Barcelona, 1983); Sergio Vilar, *Protagonistas de la España democrática: la oposición a la dictadura* (Paris, 1968); and *Franquismo y anti-franquismo* (Barcelona, 1985). See also Fernando Jáuregui and Pilar Vega, *Crónica del antifranquismo* (Barcelona, 1980). Paul Preston's article 'The Anti-Franco Opposition: The Long March to Unity', in *Spain in Crisis* is a useful short account. Regional opposition in the Basque country is well covered: see Stanley Payne, *Basque Nationalism* (Reno, 1975); Robert Clark, *The Basques: The Franco Years and Beyond* (Reno, 1979); and *The Basque Insurgents. ETA 1952–1980* (Madison, 1984) and John Sullivan, *ETA and Basque Nationalism The Fight for Euskadi 1890–1986* (London, 1978), which also contains a good bibliography. The best book in Spanish is Gurutz Jáuregui, *Ideología y estrategia política de ETA*, 2nd edn (Madrid, 1985). Catalan nationalism is less well served, but a good beginning is the translation into English of Alberto Balcells, *Catalan Nationalism* (London, 1996). Edward Hansen, *Rural Catalonia under the Franco Regime: The fate of Regional Culture since the Civil War* (Cambridge, 1977) and Hank Johnstone, *Tales of Nationalism: Catalonia, 1939–1979* (New Brunswick, 1991) are good studies. Norman Jones's 'The Catalan Question since the Civil War', in Preston, *Spain in Crisis* is also still worth reading.

There are several good accounts of the transition, most of which have an overview of the authoritarian regime as well. Paul Preston, *The Triumph of Democracy in Spain* (London, 1987) and José María Maravall, *The Transition to Democracy in Spain* (London, 1982) are among the best. On the post-francoist political system, Paul Heywood, *The Government and Politics of Spain* (London, 1995) is a good starting point.

THE POLITICAL ECONOMY OF FRANCOISM

Good works in English on the economy are unfortunately in short supply. The best short introduction is by Joseph Harrison, *The Spanish Economy: From the Civil War to the European Community* (London, 1993) which also contains a good bibliography. Less satisfactory, but still worth consulting, are two books by Sima Lieberman, *The Contemporary Spanish Economy: A Historical Perspective* (London, 1982) and *Growth and Crisis in the Spanish Economy, 1940–1993* (London,

1995). An interesting reassessment of growth is provided by Leandro Prados de la Escosura and Jorge Sanz, 'Growth and Macroeconomic Performance in Spain, 1939–93', in Nicholas Crafts and Gianni Toniolo, eds., *Economic Growth in Europe since 1945* (Cambridge, 1996). The article by Joan Esteban, 'The Economic Policy of Francoism: An Interpretation', in Preston, *Spain in Crisis* still merits attention. The older works by Alison Wright, *The Spanish Economy, 1959–1976* (London, 1977), Charles Anderson, *The Political Economy of Modern Spain* (Madison, 1970) and Richard Gunther, *Public Policy in a No-Party State* (London, 1980), though superseded by works in Spanish, remain useful. For the longer term background, the translated collection of essays edited by Nicolás Sánchez-Albornoz, *The Economic Modernization of Spain, 1830–1930* (New York, 1987) and Joseph Harrison, *The Spanish Economy in the Twentieth Century* (London, 1985) are a good beginning.

The difficulty in recommending works in Spanish is where to begin: a revolution in economic history has taken place and the range and quality of work is impressive. Overviews that place the Francoist period in context are provided by Gabriel Tortella, *El desarrollo de la España contemporánea: historia económica de los siglos XIX y XX* (Madrid, 1994); José Luis García Delgado, ed., *Lecciones de economía española* (Madrid, 1996); Leandro Prados de la Escosura and Vera Zamagni, eds., *El desarrollo económico en la Europa del Sur: España e Italia en perspectiva histórica* (Madrid, 1992); and Jordi Nadal *et al.*, eds., *La economía española en el siglo XX* (Barcelona, 1987). On the first period of Francoism, see José Luis García Delgado, 'Estancamiento industrial e intervencionismo durante el primer franquismo', in Josep Fontana, ed., *España bajo el franquismo* (Barcelona, 1986) and J. Ros Hombravella *et al.*, *Capitalismo español: de la autarquía a la estabilización 1939–1959* (Madrid, 1973). For the whole period, Manuel Jesús González, *La economía política del franquismo (1940–1970)* (Madrid, 1979), remains useful.

On agriculture, the required reading is James Simpson, *Spanish Agriculture: The Long Siesta, 1765–1965* (Cambridge, 1995). An excellent overview in Spanish is provided by Ramón Garrabou *et al.*, eds., *Historia agraria de la España contemporánea. 3. El fin de la agricultura tradicional (1900⁸1960)* (Barcelona, 1986). For industry, the article by Juergen Donges, 'From an Autarkic towards a Cautious Outward-Looking Industrialisation Policy: The Case of Spain', *Weltwirtschaftliches Archiv* (1971) remains remarkably perceptive.

Broader economic relations are covered by Carlos Moya, *El poder económico en España (1939–1970)* (Madrid, 1975) and Ramón Tamames, *La República: La era de Franco* (Madrid, 1973). For the Syndical Organisation the best introduction remains Miguel Aparicio, *El sindicalismo vertical y la formación del estado franquista* (Barcelona, 1980). Sebastian Balfour deals perceptively with urbanisation, industrialisation and working-class consciousness in *Dictatorship, Workers and the City* (Oxford, 1989), drawing on interviews and documents relating to Barcelona. Joe Fowraker has also analysed the role of the rural and urban working class in the later years of the Franco regime: see 'The Role of Labour Organisations in the Transition to Democracy', in R. Clark and M. Haltzel, eds., *Spain in the 1980s* (Cambridge, 1987); and *Making Democracy in Spain: Grass-roots Struggle in the South, 1955–75* (Cambridge, 1989). Robert Fishman, *Working Class Organisation and the Return to Democracy in Spain* (Ithaca, 1990) focuses on the transition, but has a lot to say about the independent unions under Francoism as well.

CULTURE AND SOCIETY

For a good introduction to Spanish social history, see Adrian Shubert, *A Social History of Modern Spain* (London, 1990). Chapter 5 is an excellent account of social changes under Franco. There is no real overview of culture under Franco, but the collection of short articles edited by Helen Graham and Jo Labanyi, *Spanish Cultural Studies: An Introduction* (Oxford, 1985), has an enormous amount of good material. In Spanish, the wonderful book by the novelist Manuel Vasquez Montalbán, *Crónica sentimental de España: una mirada irreverente a tres décadas de mitos y ensueños* (Barcelona, 1980) is a good place to start. The works of Rafael Abella, *Por el imperio hacia Dios: crónica de una posguerra (1939–1955)* (Barcelona, 1978) and *La vida cotidiana en España bajo el régimen de Franco* (Barcelona, 1985) are also useful.

In addition to Frances Lannon's book on the church (above), the study of National Catholicism by A. Botti, *Cielo y dinero: el nacionalcatólicismo en España (1881–1975)* (Madrid, 1992) is a good overview. Work on women and the family in English remains scarce: Mary Nash, 'Pronatalism and Motherhood in Franco's Spain', in Gisela Bock and Pat Thane, eds., *Maternity and Gender Policies: Women and the Rise of the European Welfare State, 1880–1950s* (London, 1991) is excellent. In Spanish, see the books on the Women's Section of the FET by María Teresa Gallego Méndez, *Mujer, falange y franquismo* (Madrid, 1983) and R. Sánchez López, *Mujer española: una sombra de destino de lo universal* (Murcia, 1990). Education can be approached via C. Lerena, *Escuela, ideología y clases sociales en España* (Barcelona, 1986) and Gregorio Cámara Villar, *Nacional-catolicismo y escuela. La socialización política del franquismo (1936–1951)* (Madrid, 1984). A marvellously witty and revealing picture of school life and childhood in Franco's Spain is given in Andrés Sopeña Monsalve, *El florido pensil: memoria de la escuela nacionalcatólica* (Barcelona, 1994). On the universities and student opposition, see Salvador Giner, 'Power, Freedom and Social Change in the Spanish University, 1939–1975', in Preston, *Spain in Crisis* and José María Maravall, *Dictatorship and Political Dissent* (London, 1978).

Two good books in English on different aspects of cultural and social life under the dicatorship are P. Besas, *Behind the Spanish Lens: Spanish Cinema under Franco* (London, 1986), a good guide to the cinema, and Barry Jordan,

Writing and Politics in Franco's Spain (London, 1990) which focuses on literature. J. Terrón Montero, *La prensa en España durante el régimen de Franco* (Madrid, 1981) is a reasonable introduction to the press.

INTERNATIONAL RELATIONS

José María Armero, *La política exterior de Franco* (Barcelona, 1978) is a good introduction to the whole period, as is Juan Carlos Perieira, *Introducción al estudio de la política exterior de España* (Madrid, 1983). Benny Pollack and Graham Hunter, *The Paradox of Spanish Foreign Policy* (London, 1987) is really an account of foreign policy during the transition, but chapters one and two deal briefly with some of the main themes of the francoist period. Kenneth Maxwell, ed., *Spanish Foreign and Defense Policy* (Boulder, 1991) also deals with policy since democratization, but contains some useful insights into the past. Manuel Espada Burgos, *Franquismo y política exterior* (Madrid, 1988) and J. W. Cortada, ed., *Spain in the Twentieth Century: Essays on Spanish Diplomacy, 1898–1978* (London, 1980) contain some very interesting material.

Certain periods of Spain's international relations are dealt with very extensively and in detail; others, by contrast, have received very little attention. Unfortunately, most of the best work is published in Spanish. Angel Viñas's research is vital to any understanding, especially of the international political economy of Francoism. See *Política comercial exterior di España, 1931–1975* (Madrid, 1979). His most influential book, however, deals with the relationship with the US: *Los pactos secretos de Franco con los Estados Unidos* (Barcelona, 1979). This is, without a doubt, the best source on the bases deal. Antonio Marquina, *España en la seguridad occidental 1939–1986* (Madrid, 1986) is also good and takes a security perspective on foreign policy.

Franco's ambivalent policies during the Second World War are usefully covered by memoirs, especially Ramón Serrano Súñer, *Entre Hendaya y Gibraltar* (Madrid, 1973). Antonio Marquina et al., *El impacto de la Segunda Guerra Mundial en Europa y España* (Madrid, 1986) is helpful. Castiella's account is also illuminating: Fernando María Castiella, *España ante las Naciones Unidas* (Madrid, 1968). Federico Portero, *Franco Aislado* (Madrid, 1989) is a good account of the first period of foreign policy. D. S. Morris and R. H. Haigh, *Britain, Spain and Gibraltar, 1945– 1990* (London, 1992) is a detailed account of the disputes over the Rock, although it is rather biased in its approach.

INDEX